THE
ART OF MEN

(I Prefer Mine al Dente)

ALSO BY KIRSTIE ALLEY

How to Lose Your Ass and Regain Your Life

THE
ART OF MEN

(I Prefer Mine al Dente)

KIRSTIE ALLEY

ATRIA BOOKS

New York   London   Toronto   Sydney   New Delhi

ATRIA BOOKS
A Division of Simon & Schuster, Inc.
1230 Avenue of the Americas
New York, NY 10020

First Atria Books hardcover edition November 2012

ATRIA B O O K S and colophon are trademarks
of Simon & Schuster, Inc.

For information about special discounts for bulk purchases,
please contact Simon & Schuster Special Sales at
1-866-506-1949 or business@simonandschuster.com.

The Simon & Schuster Speakers Bureau can bring authors to your
live event. For more information or to book an event contact the
Simon & Schuster Speakers Bureau at 1-866-248-3049 or
visit our website at www.simonspeakers.com.

Designed by Kyoko Watanabe

Manufactured in the United States of America

10   9   8   7   6   5   4   3   2   1

Library of Congress Cataloging-in-Publication Data

Alley, Kirstie.
   The art of men (I prefer mine al dente) / by Kirstie Alley. —
1st Atria Books hardcover ed.
      p. cm.
   1. Alley, Kirstie.   2. Actors—United States—Biography.   I. Title.
   PN2287.A533A3 2012
   792.02'8'092—dc23
   [B]
   2012032844

ISBN 978-1-4516-7358-6
ISBN 978-1-4516-7360-9 (ebook)

This book is dedicated
to my father, who spoiled
me for all other men, thereby
wrecking my life. I love you . . .

Contents

Contents

Contents

THE
ART OF MEN

(I Prefer Mine al Dente)

I've given my memoirs far more thought than
any of my marriages. You can't divorce a book.

—GLORIA SWANSON

Introduction

ELEANOR ROOSEVELT, Golda Meir, Mother Teresa, Rosa Parks, Harriet Tubman, Helen Keller, Catherine the Great, the Virgin Mary: all of these women were powerhouses worthy of respect and admiration. Yet none of them influenced my life to any great degree. Let's take it down a notch: my mother, my sister, my female neighbors, cousins, schoolteachers, piano instructors, directors, producers, and acrobat coaches didn't influence my life in a major way.

My grandmother influenced my cooking, and the girl across the street from us wore cool, almost-white lipstick that I've copied over the years, but other than that, almost 99 percent of my life's influences have come from Men.

Not necessarily good influences, but influences nonetheless.

This is odd because I get along swimmingly with women. I'm probably considered a "woman's woman." The majority of my best friends are chicks. Women rarely cause conflicts in my life, probably because I don't have sex with them. If I were a lesbian this book might have been titled *The Art of Women* or *The Art of Vaginas*.

Women have rarely caused me heartbreak and have taken a backseat in my career. From a young age I was surrounded by women who were, well, bitches. My mother was mean, my sister hated my guts, and my piano teacher thought I was a boy.

At around age three, I just sort of wrote women off as troublemakers.

There was one exception: my aunt Mary, with her jet-black hair, smoldering blue eyes, and lips like Elvis. I copied everything she did, from her red nail polish to her genuflecting and black mantilla. (She was Catholic, so I became Catholic.) She had a pet raccoon, so I later raised six. She wore White Shoulders; so do I on occasion. She smoked cigarettes and left her lipstick imprint on each. I smoked, too, and made sure everyone could differentiate my cigarettes from the rest in the ashtray by the lipstick stain.

I adored Mary; she was extraordinary in every way. She had a tarantula in her swimming pool one summer. She was like Jane Russell, buxom, sexy, and all woman. She was the perfect role model.

She died of lung cancer when I was 13. She was the last woman who had any magnitude of influence over me.

This book is about the Men in my life and how they have influenced it. Men, Men, glorious Men! I actually get silly and dizzy just saying the word "Men." I hate and adore them. I need yet reject them. I was born boy crazy, and it turned to man crazy by the time I was 15. Men are these curious creatures who total a little over half of the earth's population. They are troublesome, complex, brutal, and gentle. My life would have been unlivable and drab without them, unbearable really. Men are not at all like women, and women who treat Men like they are women are doomed. Even supergay men cannot be treated like women; after all, they are Men, just Men who love Men.

I've come to realize that Men are actually an art form. There is definitely an art to Men: the loving of them, pleasing them, sexing them up, cheering them on, controlling them, making them feel important, giving them the right amount of attention without smothering them, taking care of them when they are sick, blowing smoke up their asses when they feel weak or vulnerable, and blowing them when you don't want to without them knowing you don't want to. These are just some of the tasks women must be able to perform in order to handle the Men in their lives artfully—skillfully, gracefully, but mostly covertly.

The stories in this book belong to me. They are mine. They denote how Men have influenced my life, not the other way around. They reflect my experiences of love, loss, evil, joy, revenge, and triumph. One interesting phenomenon was revealed as I began writing about the Men in my life: they are not just happenstances any more than the brush-strokes of Manet or John Singer Sargent are accidental. They are works of Art. Men are malleable. They aren't dissimilar to paintings. They can be colorful or dull, overworked or minimal, interesting or boring, lively or dead. They can emote light and happiness or darkness and loathing. Some you want to keep in the family, some you want to put on the auction block. People may be in awe of your painting. Others just can't see what you see in it. They come in all ages and sizes, some are erotic, some are classic, a few are magnificent, but many are landscapes.

Whatever form Men have taken in my life, they have culminated in a giant collage in my soul. They are my treasures, my heartaches, and my gifts. They are my Artwork. After 60 years of life, I continue to strive to perfect The Art of Men . . .

I like children. If they're properly cooked.

—W. C. FIELDS

The Art of "Retarded" Young Men

MIDWAY THROUGH filming *Look Who's Talking Too* with John Travolta, we were night shooting in an airport in Vancouver; it was about 2:00 a.m., and it was freezing. I couldn't wait to wrap and get back to my cozy hotel room. Turns out I was one month pregnant, and it was really hard to stay awake. I recall being so tired that if I'd fallen into the gutter and a Nazi put a Luger to my head and threatened to blow my brains out if I didn't rise—I would have told him to pull the trigger.

Just as we were filming the last shot of the evening, an airline captain approached me. He informed me that his 20-year-old "retarded" son had recently been in a horrible car accident that had almost taken his life. He had been badly burned and had broken both legs and an arm. He told me his son was my number one fan and that he'd brought him to the set to meet me. He inquired as to whether it was possible, right after we finished shooting, that I could come into the hangar and take just a minute to meet him. Suddenly me being pregnant and freezing my ass off didn't have much relevance. A retarded (it wasn't politically incorrect to say that word back then), badly burned, and broken lad had traveled all this way just to meet me. Of course I said yes!

When we completed the final shot of the night, the director yelled, "Cut, print, wrap." John escorted me to the hangar, and I set eyes on the poor, retarded, bandaged young man sitting in a wheelchair. I took a deep breath because he was covered in gauze and splints and was more damaged than I had imagined. When I approached him he began to laugh and gyrate in his wheelchair back and forth. He was ecstatic to meet me. These are the times being a celebrity really pays off—to bring that much joy to an individual is . . . joyous.

He put his bandaged hand out—I took it. He said in his retarded way, "I love you." I reciprocated, "I love you, too." He pulled me closer. He was really strong! "I love you," a little louder and more audible. "I love you, too," I said. He then took both my arms and pulled me much closer. "I love you, I love you, I love you," he said, and I proclaimed, "I looove you soooo much" in the sort of half-real, half-anxiety-ridden way you'd act if a retarded boy was mauling you. He was holding me so tightly it was actually hurting me, but he was retarded, so I persevered.

The next thing I remember is that he put both arms fully around me and was squeezing me so intensely that I feared I would stop breathing. Suddenly he flipped out of his wheelchair, pushing me down on the ground, and was lying on top of me. I began to get nervous—I was pregnant—and he'd just been in a hideous accident with broken bones and third-degree burns. As he was face-to-face atop me he began chanting, "I love you, I love you, I love you," and started slightly humping my legs. My fear turned to nervous, hysterical laughter, and then I noticed this odd thing happening around me. The crew members were watching us—so was John—and so was the retarded kid's dad. I began reaching out to them, mildly pleading for help, nervously saying

"OKAY, OKAY, I love you, too, but I don't want you to get hurt. Hey, you guys," I said, reaching for the director and cinematographer, "need a little help here."

But no one would help me. No one would reach back for me. I felt like I was in a bad episode of *The Twilight Zone*. John just kept smiling this bizarre smile; he looked like Chucky. Why wasn't anybody helping us?? Why wasn't anyone worried that either I would miscarry or the retarded boy would have to be taken to the emergency room . . . again??!! I really started to flip my shit, and I began tearing up. My eyes were welling and my mind was racing as I tried to pry the broken, retarded, burned, humping young man off me. My panic increased, "You guys! He's going to get hurt! John! I'm pregnant! Help us! Somebody PLEASE help us!!!" Like a bad dream of being stuck in the middle of a satanic coven, the ring of camera crew, directors, John, the retarded boy's father, and everyone else began laughing like jackals. I almost fainted.

Then . . .

The retarded boy leaped up and started ripping his bandages from his face! Was it a miracle?! Had this "retarded" young man's love for me healed him???

No! It was Woody Harrelson. Fucking Woody Harrelson!

I hadn't had a single clue. It was the perfect caper. He wasn't even filming in Vancouver!! No, he had traveled all the way from LA, JUST to trick me. The entire cast and crew were in on the prank.

To this day Woody and I remain excellent friends—I would do anything for Woody—and he would do anything for me . . . or to me.

Whenever you find a great man, you will find a
great mother or a great wife standing behind
him, or so they say. It would be interesting
to know how many great women have had
great fathers and husbands behind them.

—DOROTHY L. SAYERS

The Art of Hopelessly Honest Fathers

THE ONLY simple man I've met is my father—one of the last
men standing who believes honesty, virtue, monogamy, and integrity prevail.

My father slept with one woman exclusively until he was 60 years
old, until the day she died. He gives the word "monogamy" its original
meaning. For him, marriage is black and white—there is no gray. You
are in or out—you are faithful or you are gone.

I have tried to live up to his example, as I think my dad's philosophy
is sane and helps a marriage survive. Let's face it, much of the crazy shit
throughout history has been due to the complications between men

and women. Relationships can create unfathomable joy or insurmountable pain, confusion, and suffering. Wars have been waged because of love. My father was my role model in regard to marriage; he made it look effortless. I attempted to follow in his footsteps, but in hindsight, it seems I didn't get the entire memo.

While I was married to Parker, I was filming the miniseries *North and South*. I'd fallen madly in love with a fellow costar. I was married. He was married. I'd thoroughly justified this love affair, asserting, "We haven't had sex—we haven't done *anything* sexual. I just LOVE him; he's my soul mate." And it WAS true. We never did have sex . . . of any kind.

Girls *always* tell their friends about their love affairs. Perhaps men keep it on the down low; women never do. I had complete agreement from my friends that this love affair was correct. It was romantic. It was destiny. We were soul mates. "Soul mates": the term I've come to discover means *I need a reason to cheat on someone or get out of my current relationship, so I'm gonna go find a "soul mate" to keep this from seeming so sleazy.* At least six soul mates have drifted into my path over my lifetime, so that sort of shoots holes in the "ONE soul mate" theory.

So my girlfriends, the other actresses on *North and South*, had it all worked out that I should ditch my husband, my soul mate should ditch his wife, and we should run off into the wild blue yonder and set up house. Our conspiring was endless. Basically, my soul mate and I agreed this was an excellent plan that we would execute the moment shooting came to an end. It was sorta like running off to join the circus, only dumber.

My father came to visit me toward the end of filming. We were standing on a baseball field when I made the decision to pour my heart out to him regarding my soul mate. No doubt he would understand; no question that he would give us his blessing. I was Daddy's Little Girl, and he would never deny me the love of my life! I put on my best lovesick-actress face and began my Academy Award–caliber spiel . . .

"Daddy, although it isn't right," I began with uncanny eloquence,

"I've fallen deeply in love with someone, and we all know that people can't help who they fall in love with or where and when it happens. You just have to grab on to it, embrace it, and run with it, and although people will be hurt, it's really in the best interest of all of us that we end up with who we should be with because that's the way the stars align and that's how destiny is supposed to work, Daddy. In fact, Daddy, you're NEVER gonna believe who it is, I mean you met him at dinner last night, and I know it's just crazy and you must think I've gone mad or something, hahahaha, and are wondering if I need to be hauled off to the nuthouse, but I can assure you this is all well thought out, and my decision is already made and in fact, SEE, there he is right out there on third base." I pointed to my devastatingly handsome love-god, who gave us a big wave while flashing his gorgeous knock-me-dead smile. "Destiny has taken an unpredictable turn, Daddy, and although we 'haven't done *anything*'"—I wanted to make sure he remembered that even if I was married, I was still his little girl and pure as the driven snow—"although we haven't done *anything*," I continued, "I love him madly and I just can't imagine my life without him. He's my soul mate, Daddy, he's my future."

Daddy looked at me with those pale blue eyes that are reminiscent of old movie stars like Rory Calhoun and Robert Mitchum. He smiled and leaned in close, took a long pause, and said, "You're married. Knock it off."

This is the man who shaped my life, who told me things like "Telling the truth will make your life easier," and "Killing someone is more acceptable than adultery because killing someone can be a crime of passion, a knee-jerk reaction to something shocking. Adultery is premeditated, Kirstie. It is planned. It is the thing that will kill relationships and leave one or both forever devastated."

My father is not a lecturer, a pontificator, or a man of many words. But DAMN, when he does open his mouth, he lays out the purest, most simplistic truths ever uttered.

"Knock it off" pierced my love-stricken heart like an X-Acto knife ripping through a cardboard box. Predictably, he dropped those three words: KNOCK IT OFF, and then said, "You know what's right." God, I've hated those words my whole life! "You know what's right." It makes me feel like I have to be responsible for stuff!! It makes me feel like there's no room for FATE or SERENDIPITY.

YES!!!! I KNOW what's right . . . I'm not into RIGHT today, Daddio . . . I'm into LOVE . . . Oh lord, why did I tell you in the first place?? You're all, "I'm monogamous. I'm one life, one wife." UGH!!! WHY did I confide in someone who is so, so, so HONEST?!!

Now, of course I didn't "knock it off" upon demand. I strung the soul-mate adventure out, as usual, to the final millisecond so that I could make damn sure parting would be the kind of sorrow found only in *Casablanca*. I had to ride that sharp edge of destroying my marriage and his. And when my soul mate and I were in our final dramatic throes, we vowed that we would always be soul mates, and although we were "good people" and doing the "right thing here" by parting ways, we would eternally love each other . . . *the most.*

It makes me laugh now; stupidity is like that. Profound lovers' words always seem to echo of idiocy after the tryst is over.

But my father's words did not fall on deaf ears, just stupid, rebellious, unethical ears.

Unfortunately for my poor husband, this was not the last man I would fall madly in love with while I was married; I just had to give one more of them a whirl. That next man went on to become the husband of my now–best friend, Kelly Preston.

If you ask me what I came to do in this world, I, an artist, will answer you. I am here to live out loud.

—ÉMILE ZOLA

The Art of Monkeys

MY GRANDFATHER admired and encouraged my wild ideas. He embraced them and validated their existence. He allowed me to be an artist. He also contributed to my art by joining in and helping me achieve my wacky dreams. He went along with my eccentric idea of owning many monkeys by volunteering to buy my first one when I turned eight.

He helped me put salt on sparrows' tails until I actually caught one. He never smashed my dreams.

He applauded the little beautiful things I created. The bouquets of flowers I picked for him. The May baskets I cut from construction paper and filled with posies and candy. The way I combed his hair for hours sitting on his lap   all forward, swooped to the side, slicked back, swirled around his head, or waxed standing straight up into the air. He complimented each hairstyle.

Out of 26 grandchildren, I was his favorite.

He bought me the most beautiful dolls. My dad had to tell my grandfather, "Dad, she is not your only grandchild. I have two more of 'em at home. You can't buy her all these things and not buy them for the other kids. It makes them jealous."

My grandfather responded by saying, "By God! It's my money, and by God, I'll buy her whatever the hell I want to." Perhaps you see where I got my attitude. That was that, and, of course, the following Christmas I got a doll that was three feet tall and wore a bright red dress. The other grandchildren got tops.

Although I only knew him for seven years, he gave me enough inspiration to last a lifetime.

He taught me to turn darkness into light, and later in my life I turned drug money into flowers, to remind me of bad being changed to good and to remind me of him.

I now spend the same money that I used to spend weekly on drugs, approximately $400, to buy flowers for my home or to send to people I love. To this day, every time I see a sparrow I think of my grandfather and me, out in his yard, armed with tiny Morton saltshakers, attempting to put salt on the tails of sparrows, just for the opportunity of holding one in our hands.

When my grandfather left this world, I spoke to him every night. I felt his strong presence in my room for almost a year. When I could no longer perceive him, I tried writing him letters and burning them in the bathroom sink. Somehow I thought the smoke would carry my messages to him wherever he was.

I will never forget my grandfather and the magical way he reinforced who I really am. He helped me realize that dreams *are* reality, not the other way around.

He never had the opportunity to buy me a monkey, as he died when I was seven. I have a fleet of lemurs now, and not a day goes by that they don't remind me of my grandfather, Clifford William Alley. I named my son after him, William True Parker.

People always ask me how I maintain such a beautiful life, and I always answer, "Through my grandfather."

I shudder at the thought of men . . .
I'm due to fall in love again.

—DOROTHY PARKER

The Art of Sticks

I TOOK MY first lover when I was five. We had moved from a tiny house on Estelle Street in Wichita, Kansas, to a modest trilevel house on Bellaire Street. Although the "upstairs" of the cedar-and-brick house was only seven steps up, I would gaze for hours out the window as if I were positioned high above the magnolias at Tara. It was from this crow's nest that I spotted lover number one: Henry, a handsome chap who shared the date of my birth. He wasn't younger or older; he was of "neutral" age to me. Henry and I began our affair by leaping off the roof of Tara. We held tea towels above our heads, holding the four corners together to fashion parachutes. Although they did little to break our falls, they somehow ensured we broke nothing important.

Henry had green eyes like mine, and had a green tent in his backyard. It was the tent that beckoned us to take shelter during a rainstorm and gave us the refuge we needed to "get busy." Since we were both inexperienced lovers, we had to get creative with our sex tools . . . I chose a stick.

It was riveting to poke his wiener with my stick, and although I was only five, I was bright enough to know that flesh touching flesh was taboo. But stick-to-flesh? That was acceptable. Repeated stick touching proved effective for his arousal as I noticed he grew from tiny to sorta tiny. In fact, the gesture worked like clockwork: tiny . . . stick touch . . . sorta tiny . . . tiny . . . stick touch . . . sorta tiny.

In and out his wiener would go, and it was then it dawned on me: I was in full control of Henry's wiener! An enormous sense of well-being surged through my veins like some strange fever. The power of sexual domination flooded over me. Henry was under my stick's control. I had to refrain from throwing back my tiny head and laughing maniacally. Then he attempted to put a stick in my bottom, but I made it clear from the get-go that I would maintain a stickless bottom . . . I didn't like it then, and don't like it now. Sort of a standing policy of mine all these years: no objects allowed in my ass.

When my mother rang the dinner bell, it ended that day's work. It's amazing how even children know getting jiggy in a sexual fashion will be frowned upon by adults, but no one ever told me not to stick sticks on dudes' penises. As I grabbed my shorts and headed out of the tent, I told Henry that I would return the next day. I felt confident knowing I could holler at Henry any day at any time and he would come panting like a lovesick puppy.

Ahhh, this was the moment I realized I could manipulate men . . . with sticks.

Live a good life. If there are gods and they are just,
then they will not care how devout you have been
but will welcome you based on the virtues you have
lived by. If there are gods, but unjust, then you should
not want to worship them. If there are no gods, then
you will be gone but will have lived a noble life that
will live on in the memories of your loved ones.

—MARCUS AURELIUS

The Art of Wielding a Hammer

THERE ARE these men in Kansas. They are quiet, unsung, heroic men. They had a profound influence on me when I was a child and I've carried their influence with me into adulthood. These men are called Mennonites.

I have no idea or profess to know any details of what Mennonites believe in, and I could frankly care less. They dress similar to the Amish people, and travel sometimes in horse-and-buggies. The men seem to have beards and the women wear ankle-length dresses and they sort of stay to themselves. What I can say about them is that they are the most uniquely helpful and generous people I have observed.

Growing up in Kansas meant witnessing the aftermath of devastating damage and loss of life caused by tornadoes. When I was around eight, there was a catastrophic tornado in Udall, Kansas. My parents took us kids to see the damage the day after. The town was basically leveled, and people were staggering around in a daze like haunted zombies. The confusion is massive after a tornado hits, as people have lost everything. I saw the body of a dead woman wrapped around a claw-foot bathtub in the rubble. There was an eerie silence that prevailed, except for the sound of hammers hitting wood. A little in the distance were the Mennonites, about eight men total. They had begun rebuilding a barn. Not for themselves, but for a family who had lost theirs in the tornado. The family hadn't called them or hired them or invited them. They just showed up, which is their MO.

The Mennonite men were quietly, professionally raising a barn, right before our eyes. Their Mennonite wives were serving food to people, homemade, delicious food consisting of shepherd's pie and cherry pie. They were quiet people. They just went about their job of resurrecting a town one barn by one house by one meal. I asked my dad, "Who are those people?"

He said, "They are Mennonites. When bad things happen they just appear and help people out."

It was my "come to Jesus" moment, without Jesus. I started crying, I couldn't believe there were people like that who appear out of nowhere and just help. They didn't look haunted or frazzled, confused or dazed, like the rest of the people milling around the aftermath. They looked confident. They smiled sweetly and respectfully as they served people meals. They took care of the ones who had lost their homes, their family members, and their livestock.

I made a mental, age-eight note: Mennonites are good people. I like them. I hope if anything ever happens in Wichita, they come to help.

Throughout my adult life doing my own charity work with my own church group, the Scientology Volunteer Ministers, I have encountered the Mennonites. Two days after the devastating Greensburg, Kansas, tornado, which obliterated an entire town, I flew in with my group to offer help. As we provided ice, food, clothing, and basic amenities, I could see the Mennonites with their now heavy equipment off in the distance, clearing mangled trees and the shredded remains of houses and farm buildings. It gave me strength to comfort the people who had lost everything as they formed a line in front of me to tell me their own personal tragedies.

We stayed in Greensburg for a few days, doing whatever was needed. Sometimes I hear people degrade religions or the people in those religions. Okay, who am I fooling, it's rampant. But let me tell you this: if you've spent much time in disaster zones, you know all too well it is the religious groups who swoop in to help. In Greensburg, for example, it was the Baptists preparing and serving most of the food. It was Catholic Services trucking in clothes. You had us, the Scientologists, importing literally tons of ice to keep the National Guard and other relief workers from roasting to death. And of course the Mennonites working tirelessly to clear the land to make room for new growth. In Greensburg, as in all disaster zones, the goal is to restore hope and life to those areas. No one cared that the cup of ice I handed them or the new baby clothes we gave them came from Scientologists. They were just grateful to have them. And I never gave a thought to what religious group was feeding us or holding the hand of a mother who had just lost a child, other than *thank god that person showed up to hold her hand.*

The Mennonites lit the fuse for me. They taught me charity, humanity, and contribution. They proved to me that any help is better than none and that religion actually has nothing and everything to do with how you help your fellow man.

The Mennonite men in particular taught me that the quiet rebuilding of a human life can begin with something as simple as a hammer and a nail.

Creativity takes courage.

— HENRI MATISSE

The Art of Heroes

MY BROTHER, Craig, is four years younger than I am, or is it three? I'll opt for three because it makes me feel more youthful. Craig was a little guy growing up. He was smallish in stature and was easily intimidated by people, including our mother.

When we grew up in Wichita, we weren't allowed to go to kindergarten until we were five. Some weird equation was in place, like if you were turning five within that year, you could attend, so Craig started kindergarten at age four. My birthday is in January, so I was almost six when I started. I never quite understood the equation, and I still don't. There's a BIG difference between a four-year-old and a six-year-old, especially with boys. I've always felt Craig started school too young, and I think it had a profound effect on his development. You may already be able to see that I feel an overwhelming compulsion to always keep my little brother out of harm's way. Craig wasn't a wallflower or anything, he was just so innocent and naive, so easily frightened, and on occasion he did some strange things to keep people from finding that out.

One Friday night, when I was around 12, I got a phone call while staying overnight at my best friend Becky's house. It was Collette, my sister.

"Kirstie, did you leave the iron on before you left tonight?" she asked.

I panicked. I knew I turned the iron off right before I left for Becky's house . . . didn't I? But . . .

"Why?" I asked.

"Because the house almost burned down . . . we had a big blaze and the fire detectives are here!!" she blurted out.

Fire detectives???? What the hell are fire detectives?? My heart was pounding . . . DID I leave the iron on? HAD I been the cause of almost burning down the house?! HAD my sister told the fire detectives that I'd borrowed her pink Lady Van Heusen blouse without asking, ironed it, then intentionally left the iron on intending to burn down the house so that she would stop screaming at me for borrowing her stuff without asking??

"NO, COLLETTE!! I didn't LEAVE THE IRON ON!!!!!!" When in doubt of your guilt, YELL REALLY LOUD so that everyone will believe in your innocence!

Lucky for me, it turned out that Craig had been terrified to be left alone in the house but didn't want anyone to know, so he contrived a swell plan.

He took Mingo, my mom's Maltese, up to the attic and started a small fire. His reasoning was that he would quickly call a neighbor and tell them he smelled smoke. The neighbor would then rush over to find the source. After they found the "small" smolder in the attic, they would put it out and then say, "Craig, this fire must have been started by some electrical malfunction. You aren't safe here! You'd better come next door and stay with us until your folks get home . . . and Craig, great job spotting the fire, the whole house could have burned down. Your mom and dad will be so proud of you. You're a HERO!"

That's the way Craig saw the scene unfolding. That was his bright idea. He lit the match, but there was no smoldering. The flames began immediately. He freaked out, grabbed Mingo, and climbed down the ladder of the attic. He bolted next door to the neighbors claiming, "THE HOUSE IS ON FIRE!!!" Of course he pretended he had no idea how it started.

But the fire detectives did. It took them about five minutes after the fire was extinguished to find the exact point of the flash. They knew the fire began with a match, and they knew it was started intentionally. My sister, of course, didn't find it necessary to call me and tell me that I hadn't started the fire, so I spent the night in terror of going to jail for arson. When I found out the arsonist was my little brother, I had mixed emotions ranging from sympathy to fear that he might end up a serial killer. I knew from this point on that I had to do more to protect him . . . especially from himself.

One time my mother was going to spank him, so I came swooping in with a flourish. "NO!!!! Don't spank him! I did it, I DID it!!! Spank ME!! Spank me instead of Craig!"

This made my mother furious, so she spanked us both.

Another time my sister wrapped Craig and his friend Stewart in strips of white sheets, like mummies, and then pushed them down so they couldn't move. I had to intervene and throw a rubber knife at her back and hit her with an empty milk jug until she gave in and untied them.

I not only protected my little brother; I gave him all sorts of opportunities. In fact, I gave him his first business opportunity when he was around six. I charged girls in the neighborhood 15 cents to see his dick. I positioned him in my upstairs bedroom, brought the johns up to my room, closed the door, and commanded him to drop his pants. He did as I asked, and the girls glanced ever so quickly at his wiener. No touching, just witnessing it, and only for about 15 seconds. They paid the 15 cents, one dime and one nickel. I kept the dime and gave Craig the nickel because it was bigger than the dime, and he thought it was worth more . . . because I had told him it was.

Word spread, and we made more in that one day than we would have pulling weeds for a week. We would have continued the enterprise, but I figured it was only a matter of time before our operation got busted, and god knows what the punishment for pimping would have resulted in.

Our mother was a tough cookie. She was verbally crushing and prone to spanking with rulers, yardsticks, flyswatters, and belts. Tragically, my dad owned a lumber company, so we had plenty of Alley Lumber Company yardsticks in the house. She was the queen of the backhand. Her hands were skinny and bony. She was only five foot two but packed a mighty slap in the mouth. My brother was her favorite, which isn't saying much. It paid off later in his life, but she was as demeaning and relentless to him as she had been to my sister and me. My mother was witty, intelligent, and funny, but with no warning or provocation she could flip out and scream so viciously it rendered her prey paralyzed. I could see clearly what she was doing to my brother. She was introverting him, belittling him, making him into a victim. My sister, Collette, was defiant with the "I HATE YOUs!!" she would scream right in my mother's face. My mother would backhand her again, and Collette would get this deranged look in her eyes and yell, "I REALLY HATE YOU!!" WHACK!! Wow!! She would never back down!

I was the second child, usually the peacemaker. My way of keeping the peace was to duck. My lifelong friend Eric and I have a routine we've done since childhood. He plays my mother, and the second his backhanding hand rises above his waist, I duck! Ahhh, we never tire of this ridiculous impersonation of my mother.

Our lives went on like this with our mom. My brother was so cute when he was little that anyone with a heart would have eagerly volunteered to protect him. My dad never knew these things were going on, as my mom didn't let him see that side of her, and we were too afraid to rat her out because of what she might have done when he went to work the next day and we were left alone with her.

Protecting Craig became my self-appointed job. I always had an eye on my brother and would intervene between him and my mom when necessary.

As Craig got older, he began to gain confidence. One night after school when I was 16, my mother and I were having an argument in the kitchen. She was accusing me of being a whore, something she seemed obsessed with. I was indeed not slutty or a whore, and in fact I was a virgin. We were really going at it.

"I KNOW WHAT YOU WERE DOING LAST NIGHT!!!!!" she screamed. "You know what we call girls who do what you did?? We call them WHORES!!"

"Mother! I didn't do anything! I didn't have sex! I didn't do ANY-THING!!"

SMACK!!! The back of her veiny hand, the same veiny hand that I now possess, cracked across my face. Sometimes she would smack me, and it would sting, but this time it was hard enough that my head was thrown to the left of my shoulder. I whipped around and began to stare her down or cry or both, when out of nowhere I saw these hands and arms come flying into frame, like a close-up in a movie. Then I saw these hands grab her by her shoulders, lift her from the floor, and slam her into the refrigerator.

"THAT is the LAST time you will EVER hit her!!!! You under-stand??? THE LAST TIME!"

The hands belonged to my baby brother. My sweet, frightened, gentle brother. My mother's eyes were wider than a deer's in headlights. She was silenced. He hadn't hurt her . . . much.

She never hit me, or any of us, again.

My brother was my hero . . . still is.

I saw the angel in the marble and
carved until I set him free.

—MICHELANGELO BUONARROTI

The Art of Lost Loves

EARLY IN life I learned what it was to lose a man, and I was
blindsided by the way the breakup occurred.

I was 10 years old. This boy, Jim, fell in love with me the minute he
laid eyes on me. It was one of those obvious, immediate crushes that
you pray for after age 40. He followed me like a puppy from room to
room. He would call me nightly and have his mother say that I was *muy
linda* (very pretty).

He wasn't Latino, but he still chose Spanish as his language of love.
I guess Jim figured a foreign language would razzle-dazzle me, especially
there in the heartland of Kansas. He constantly told me how beautiful
I was—sweet for a boy of 10, which is how old Jim was when he came
into my life.

He loved me so deeply and so thoroughly that it left me no choice
but to . . . play impossibly hard to get and to be sporadically, completely uninterested. Like at the skating rink on Saturdays. It was my

pattern that the more gaga Jim was over me, the more I was forced to flirt with his older brother, Hale.

Don't get me wrong, I wanted to love Jim as passionately and openly as he loved me, but loyalty and devotion just weren't in my makeup at this early age. I was boy crazy as hell, but only with randoms like Steve U., Steve S., Larry C., Jamie K., and Bobby R. These were the ones I was drawn to; the guys who ignored me set my heart aflame.

Hell, I just didn't trust myself to come up to the mark that young Jim had set for me. A few years passed, but Jim's love for me didn't.

It was an "on" period for me and Jim; I was being kind to him and loving him back. We were 12 then, and he seemed much more interesting. Jim's family was extremely wealthy; they owned a huge construction company in Wichita, lived in a huge mansion, belonged to the country club, and had a "children's line."

In today's age, lots of kids have phones in their rooms, cell phones, or private lines, but in the old days kids beat the hell out of each other to talk on the one telephone in the house, and only really rich families had private lines for their children. They were listed just like that in the phone book:

Dr. E. L. Smartypants—316-433-7588
Children's line—316-433-7589

Jim called and asked me to meet him at "fun night" the coming Saturday at his swanky private school, Collegiate. Jim said he and Eddie would be there early, so could I be early, too. Eddie was Jim's best friend, from an even wealthier family. Eddie's family lived in a historic landmark Frank Lloyd Wright house, and Eddie had this extraordinarily beautiful mother. She was single and quite the catch.

My best friend, Becky, went to Collegiate, too. I think all the rich people, including Jim's and Becky's families, got together and built the private school so that their kids could be properly, privately educated so as not to end up dumbbells like the rest of us.

I'd already planned to spend the night with Becky and go to Collegiate's fun night with her and Jennifer, another really rich kid whose mother I later ended up being the maid for.

When we arrived, most of the boys were dicking around, acting aloof with the girls. Jim was with Eddie. He didn't care, he came right up to me and said, "You wanna go swing?"

"Swing" of course meant sit on the swings and kiss, which is what we ended up doing for about an hour. Be still my schoolgirl heart! That night I was as smitten with Jim as he was with me.

Jim was wearing a beautiful gold watch, and I was admiring it so that I could touch him more. I was holding his wrist, admiring his watch when suddenly the devil must have risen up from hallowed earth and inhabited me. My burning love for Jim turned into embarrassed, shy, evil intentions. "Oh yes, this watch is beautiful, Jimmy, it's a real beauty, is it a Twist-O-Flex?" I asked.

Twist-O-Flex was a newly invented watch of the 1960s, with a very limber, linked, highly flexible wristband. I knew that this watch was indeed *not* an inexpensive Twist-O-Flex, but with Lucifer lurking in my psyche, I had no will of my own.

"Jim, may I hold your watch?" I asked as slyly as a henhouse fox. He slipped it from his wrist. "It's so gorgeous, Jim," I said softly, coyly, like sugar butter soup. Jim cooed and looked doe-eyed as I admired his fetching gold watch, and then SNAP like a horse's neck at a rodeo. "Jim, is this a Twist-O-Flex?" I grabbed the band with both hands and maniacally twisted the watch into a mangled pretzel, crackle-twist, twist, torque, crackle, crackle. There! The princess of darkness had done her work.

As quickly as I'd snapped into the Antichrist, I snapped back. There was Jim, looking shocked. His beautiful, contorted gold watch lay in the palm of his hand where I'd quickly deposited it after my "fit."

No words were or could be spoken for several minutes.

"You nut!" he finally said. "Certifiable!" He began to laugh. "You're out of your mind and that's why . . . I love you."

Oh my lord, why can't I find a "Jim" these days? A Jim who thinks I'm gorgeous and extraordinary even when I'm in the middle of a demonic grand mal seizure?

We had so much fun that night. I vowed to love Jim forever and never again flirt with his brother, Hale . . . until the following Saturday at the skating rink.

This is how it went for the next two years. His love for me was too overwhelming, and the more I tried to love him back as strongly, the more it triggered the diabolical spirit within my soul, and I would do or say something ridiculous to spoil it and push him away.

Jim was a handsome boy, really handsome, with blue eyes and dark hair, beautiful teeth and a wonderful smile. That's why it's hard to believe that right in the middle of madly making out in a field behind the swim club pool months later, I took the opportunity to trip Jim and wrestle him to the ground, screaming and teasing that he was the only boy I'd ever kissed who insisted on wearing really pointy-toed Beatle boots! Wild with laughter, I yelled, "Beatle shoes, Beatle shoes, Jim Richie wears Beatle shoes!"

Hale later developed a crush on my sister, and that pretty much ruined the brother-flirt thing for me. Besides, I was starting to fall in love with Jim. I'd not made fun of him, broken any of his possessions, or tripped him in months. I hadn't laughed like a hyena at his shoes in weeks. My resistance was crumbling, my demon was quelling.

Jim said he was going camping with Eddie at his ranch on Friday and would call me when he returned on Monday. They were going on a survival weekend, which I thought was very macho, very male. But it was fine with me; I was supposed to babysit the kids across the street on Sunday night anyway, and their mom didn't like me tying up the phone line.

My friend Jennifer called me Saturday morning. She said, "You don't need to come and clean my mom's house today. Oh, and by the way, guess who's dead?"

"I don't know, who?" I asked.

"Jim and Eddie. Jim and Eddie are dead. They got asphyxiated last night at the ranch."

To this day I can't believe the casualness in Jennifer's voice when she relayed to me the death of Jim and Eddie.

"Gotta go now, are you okay?" asked Jennifer.

Oh yes, I'm fine, good-bye.

Children walk around like zombies just like adults after death, like someone has hit you with something hard, right between your eyes, stunning you into numbness and unreality. I stumbled around this way all day and into the night. On Sunday I was lying on the sofa across the street, babysitting, when the news came on. My charges were long since asleep, so I was alone when the story of Jim and Eddie came on the 10 o'clock news. As the reporter smirked and told the story of the two Wichita boys from prominent families who had been asphyxiated, the film footage began to show two bodies being carried from the little shack where Jim and Eddie had holed up that night and lit the gas stove for heat. The faulty gas stove with no safety in case the flame went out.

You couldn't identify which one was Jim and which was Eddie. Blankets were over their bodies. Then I saw something specific, and I knew. The very bad Beatle boots were peeking from one of the blankets. Very pointy Beatle shoes on a camping trip? How absurd.

Hey Jim? Why in the hell are you wearing Beatle boots on a camping trip? Who's gonna trip you now?

I thought I, myself, would die that night. Partly because of lost love and partly because of all the stupid, mean, evil, thoughtless dumb things I'd done to Jim during our four-year juvenile relationship.

I didn't stop crying until I arrived at the double funeral for Jim and

Eddie. Double caskets, double families, friends, and guests. Eddie's mother wore a black dress, black stockings, gloves, and handbag, and a dramatic black hat, draped with a gossamer veil. She nearly fainted several times as she walked down the long aisle of the Catholic church. Handsome men flanked her and caught her at each falter.

By contrast, Jim's mother was dressed in a cream-colored suit. Her hair was styled, yet simple. She had a lovely crocheted handbag, and she smiled a lovely, soft smile as she walked down the aisle to her family's place. She emanated something very powerful—hope and spirituality and knowledge. A certainty that life does not end when our fragile bodies do.

I'll never forget the contrast between Eddie's mother and Jim's. Jim's mama was radiant in her faith.

You are *muy linda*, I said telepathically to Mrs. Richie that day. You are truly the embodiment of your son's vast ability to love.

> But men are men; the best sometimes forget.

> —SHAKESPEARE

The Art of Queers

'VE NEVER gone for bisexual men. I just figure they can't make up their minds, and indecisive men don't interest me. I have, however, been heartbroken by one gay man whom I found myself hopelessly in love with when I was 14.

My gay love's name was Jeffrey, and our affair took place at Kansas University when I went to art school for the summer. I was 14. He was 18. I was in love with him. He didn't know I existed.

It was a fine arts school, featuring artists, musicians, and dancers. Although Jeffrey was a ballet dancer and ran about in tights, it was impossible to detect he was gay.

I knew nothing about people being gay. Literally. I didn't know it existed. It sounds impossible in this day when even five-year-olds know the definition. Other than hearing an occasional playground fight ending in "You're a queer!" (which I thought meant "odd"), I'd never heard of a word that would telegraph man-on-man love. Gay, queer, and homosexual didn't exist in my vocabulary. When I was 12,

I once shouted out of the backseat of my 16-year-old sister's car, "Hey you queer hoppers!" as she drove by the only homosexual nightclub in Wichita. I had no idea what it meant, but she and her friends were laughing and being obnoxious and were delighted to see some "queers" emerging from the "Chances Are." I thought I was yelling at guys they had crushes on! I liked the word "queer." It sounded funny, and yelling it at men was exhilarating, but it had no connection to the concept of men loving men. And even if someone had told me what queer actually meant, it would have fallen into the same category as when my friend Sarah's sister instructed us on the activities involved with 69.

It would have been far too horrifying for me to comprehend.

When Connie told Sarah and me that girls sucked on men's penises until junk flew out of them, well, jeez! Sarah and I were forced to stab our fingers with a jackknife, press our blood together, and take an oath that "I hereby swear to God I will never put a boy's dick in my mouth and suck on it until junk flies out, and furthermore, no boy's face will ever come within two feet of my vagina."

This was serious business! Sarah's sister Connie had gotten married at 14 to a guy who was, like, 20! Apparently that was legal in Kansas. Connie knew all the ropes, all the tricks of the sex trade. She'd done it all! And she spilled it all to me and Sarah. Except for the queer stuff. She had no data about queers, and we didn't ask because we didn't know queers existed.

I had a slight inkling about lesbians, not the sexual part or what they were called, just the love part. My pediatrician had lived with her nurse for 30 years. My mom called them old maids, but I could tell that they were really in love with each other. I just thought "old maids" meant two women who'd lived together for a long time without getting married to men. Then there was one of my cousins, who had bigger biceps than my dad, cropped hair, and who strutted around like a dude. I just thought she was really athletic, which she was. My concept of dykes and old maids was skewed, and it certainly didn't involve sex.

But back to Jeffrey. He was about six foot three, I'd say, with black hair and cobalt blue eyes, the lethal combination of features that I can't resist. He didn't look at all feminine. In fact he was extremely masculine and charismatic. Ahhh, I would skip classes to watch Jeffrey dance or eat his lunch or just walk across the green-grassed campus. When he would walk past me directly and speak to me, I'd manage to eke out a barely audible "Hi," and when he said "Hi" back to me what he was really saying was "Hi Kirstie, I'm madly in love with you . . . Let's glissade our way through life and make stunning black-haired, blue-eyed dancer babies." At least, that's what I thought I heard him saying.

I'd known Jeffrey for eight days when he suddenly disappeared. He was nowhere to be found, and believe me, I looked and looked . . . and looked. No one knew of my torrid affair with Jeffrey, not even Jeffrey. So I had no one to talk to.

But there were two savvy girls across the hall from me in the dorm, Mary and Linda, who seemed to know everything about everyone. Although they were only 16 themselves, they were light-years ahead of me regarding life and sex and men.

"Whatever happened to that ballet guy, Jeffrey?" I cautiously asked with calculated casualness. "You mean that black-haired queer?" asked Linda. There's that *word* again. What's with that? Queer to me meant strange, odd, eccentric.

"Yes, where'd he go?" I asked.

"He went back to New York, I heard, to be with his lover," said Mary.

This was devastating news, although I feigned indifference until I just had to know . . . "Is she a famous ballerina, too?"

"Hahaha," they both laughed. " 'She' is a 'he' and yes, he's a dancer, too."

What???!!! What?! What??? What . . . what? What! What??!! I took a breather—*WHAT???!!!* What a lousy way to learn what queers were. What a crummy way to find out the dancing man of my dreams was the lover of another man.

After I'd gotten over Jeffrey, round about Thursday, I set my eyes on another guy, Ken. He was the total opposite of Jeffrey. He was a musician with lightish brown hair and lightish brown eyes, sort of an average beige-looking kind of straight guy.

Oh hell, you know what? Ken isn't even worth the ink and paper. Suffice it to say, he was just your average lower-level heartbreaker with a little dick, probably. I never got around to inspecting it . . . All I really remember is that I looked like a complete idiot at that art school. I had short, stupid hair, ridiculously cheap, unfashionable clothes, and was a massive goon ball. The only time I felt pretty at art school was when Jeffrey had said hello and flashed that big, beautiful gay smile.

The awesome outcome of my eight-day love affair with Jeffrey was that I formed superhuman gaydar. To this day I can spot a man who fancies the penis a mile away. I can even spot the ones who have imbibed in the wiener yet enjoyed the occasional vagina, rendering them bisexual. This sense of mine is laser accurate.

I prefer my men 100 percent straight, but wherever Jeffrey is now, he should know that although he broke my heart and abandoned me without saying good-bye, he gave me the skills to spot a queer from the moon.

> Very sorry can't come. Stop.
> Lie follows by post.
>
> —CHARLES BERESFORD,
> TELEGRAM REPLY TO A DINNER INVITATION

The Art of Male Visitors

I BEGAN HAVING male visitors when I was 14. My first visitor was a handsome, platinum-haired (from too much chlorine) swimmer named Kim. I was hugely crushing on him when I got the bright idea to phone him and invite him for the long weekend with a big school dance as the finale. Kim was 16 and god knows, I barely knew him. All I knew was that he was a swell swimmer and always wore Dante, this girl-dizzying cologne.

I had returned from art school, where I apparently learned all the ropes regarding men. I'd already had my heart broken by a gay ballet dancer. I'd already been humiliated by a redneck asshole. I felt like I was savvy enough to take on a weekend visitor. I'd also had many boys at art school fancy me and kiss me and ask me to write to them. So in my mind, men were "old hat," and caring for them and finessing them into loving me was pretty evident. I'd left for art school a child and returned a woman.

My mother said it was okay to invite Kim, but he would have to stay at the home of another male swimmer. Yes, I could see him every day and yes, he could join me across the street to babysit for the Clarks, but he absolutely could not sleep at our house.

I of course thought this was a dumb idea. Lillian Maxine Heaton, aka Mickey, aka my mother, clearly didn't trust me or know the ropes. I'd just returned from two months at art school, for Christ's sake, where I could easily have had sex if I'd known how. But my mother, unworldly as she was, had her stupid rules of proper conduct when menfolk came calling. My mother had not been to art school, she had not fallen in love with queers, she had not seen a boy almost jump off a building to his death because another art school diva had shunned him. My mother had only seen Kansas and my dad and tornadoes. She hadn't seen the world like I had. Her opinion was unfounded.

Anyway, I agreed that Kim would not stay overnight at our house, but I rolled my eyes nearly out of my head trying to comprehend how my mother could be:

A. My mother
B. So stupid

She was simply unsophisticated.

Kim arrived at my house that Friday afternoon, all the way from Oklahoma or Missouri, same difference, and had dinner with my family. I was embarrassed because my mother had prepared her "special" pork chops, which meant the ones cooked 40 minutes longer than required. The ones with bowed edges from being fried to death. The ones that were akin to leather soles. Those pork chops. Her theory was, "By God, THIS family won't get trichinosis." My mother was a nurse, you see, and knew every disease known to man and what every horrid thing—bacterium, fungus, and virus—could do to a person's body. I was never just "sick" as a child. If I had a common cold, I was dying of encephalitis, the disease she had warned us about the week before. I never had any common disease, and how many kids, at age six, are taught by their mothers to do tracheotomies in case a tornado causes a house to implode? Oddly, I CAN do a "trach" with a garden hose and a piece of glass. Slit that throat open right on top of the soft spot above your collarbone and insert a short section of garden hose or other tubelike thing and boom! Gregory House is in the room, saving that poor person's life. I learned a new medical procedure weekly from my mother.

I watched Kim eat the trichinosis-free pork chops and the canned peas. I gasped as he had to use the tea towel my mom threw in the center of the table for all to use, instead of individual napkins. *He's going to figure out we are poor!* We weren't totally poor, and I had no idea what Kim's social status was, but most swimmers I'd met were from wealthy families. They were from places like Mission Hills, Kansas, Tulsa, Oklahoma, and Oklahoma City. They were from oil families. The majority of the kids in the Wichita swim club were from rich families. Would this handsome boy from . . . from . . . the tristate area reject me because we were one overcooked pork chop away from the poor farm?

All through dinner, between poverty fears I'd get whiffs of Kim's bitchin' cologne, Dante. No man I'd ever met wore Dante. Certainly my dad hadn't been introduced to this pricey department store luxury. My dad wore Aqua Velva, and strictly because it was an aftershave, not a "signature scent."

After dinner Kim and I walked directly across the street to babysit Russell and Sharon Clark's kids. We played with them, watched TV, and had a big ole time.

After we put the kids to sleep we did what all babysitters who invite their boyfriends over do: we started to make out. Kim was the first guy to French kiss me, but my friend Sarah's sister Connie had told us what to expect: tongues. I sorta liked this tongue thing. It made me feel a little sexy and definitely made me realize I was in the big leagues now.

Like I said, Kim was 16 and had a lot more make-out experience than I. I was so happy I'd invited Kim for the dance the following night. All those other junior high girls would have the same 14-year-old loser townies we went to school with daily. Wait 'til they got a load of this flaxen-haired *man* all the way from Oklahoma . . . or Missouri. I would end up the talk of Mead Jr. High School, it was certain.

As we were making out there on the scratchy man-made-fibered sofa, Kim worked his magic lips over to my neck and nibbled awhile there, which I simply adored. Townies had never been so inventive. Then he made his way to my ear and blew a little warm air in there. This sent chills down my spine, as it does to this day. I was so, SO glad Kim had come all that way for the dance. Then he stuck his French-kissing tongue into my ear. *Ugh, what?* This was never part of my friend Sarah's sister Connie's menu. Sloshing around in my ear with his stupid "Okie" or "Show-Me" tongue was beyond the beyond. It was slurpy, and the slurping was magnified like listening to a conch shell screaming at you instead of whispering the sound of the ocean. Slosh, slosh, slurp, slurp, Jesus! Was Kim a serial killer in Oklahoma or Missouri? Where had he learned this carnival sideshow trick? It wasn't as disgusting as 69, but it was definitely the act of a rapist at least. I hadn't invited this cute boy to Kansas to feast on the inside of my ear! I was grossed out! It was like he was trying to "slurp" my virginity away. And that was the end of Kim.

The next morning I was so "sorry" to tell him about how terribly sick I was, with a terribly high fever of 104 degrees. I was even sorrier to tell him, "It looks like I won't be able to go to the dance or hang out all weekend. I might even have encephalitis!"

This is when I began to give serious thought to having male visitors. But as young girls do, after many years of life, they forget their solemn vows of never again having weekend guests. They even forget their blood oaths of never, never, ever doing 69.

In the past 12 years of being single, I have invited five male visitors to visit for between three- and seven-day stays. Although THEY thought they were having a grand ole time and that I was an excellent hostess, I can honestly and with great embarrassment say I have not changed since I was 14.

The only advice I can reap from these laborious encounters is: when you "fall in love" in a foreign country or in a different city, it's possible that exotic delicacies SEEM to taste better. Kinda like escargot—it makes a lovely appetizer but as a main course it makes you puke your guts out.

Always get married in the morning. That way, if it
doesn't work out, you haven't wasted the whole day.

—MICKEY ROONEY

The Art of Being a Bride

BOB ALLEY was my first true love. Of all the loves in my life, he
was probably best suited for me. And I for him. My maiden name
is also Alley, and to make it even weirder, my dad's name is Robert D.
Alley and Bob's name is Robert D. Alley; not the same middle names,
but Freudian enough nonetheless. Was it in the cards for me to become
Kirstie Alley Alley?

You really couldn't have found someone more spectacular than
Bob. He was handsome like the Marlboro Man, with long sideburns
and ringlet hair like Roger Daltrey, cofounder of the rock band The
Who. There was nothing it seemed Bob couldn't do. He could ride
a horse better than Little Joe on *Bonanza*; he had a pilot's license; his
singing voice was cool and on pitch; he was a great swimmer, a groovy
dancer, smart as a whip and funny as hell. He was the dream man of
most of the teenage girls in our high school, Southeast, and sought
after by dozens of beauties from other schools. His parents gave him

no curfew, so he could spend all night out if he wanted to, unlike my sixth-grader curfew of nine o'clock on school nights and midnight on weekends.

Bob was a year older than I was, was sexually active, and, well, just the hottest guy in the universe. He hailed from a wealthy family. His dad, Dr. Alley, was a renowned Wichita oral surgeon. I, on the other hand, was an idiot from a middle-class family, with limited abilities. True, I was a cheerleader, but not because I was beautiful or cool. Southeast's student body voted for me because I could jump five feet in the air and had had a lot of acrobatics training, so it was hard to ignore my impressive cheerleading skills as I handspringed my way across the gymnasium floor.

I'd cheered one Friday night at a game that took place at a rival school, East High School. It was the equivalent of my high school. There were only two public high schools worthy of attending in Wichita, Southeast or East, and if you were mandated to go to any other, you might as well have been a leper. There were always school dances after big football games.

Because I was a cheerleader people assumed I was popular. I was behind the gym after the game with a few of the actually popular cheerleaders, smoking, something that was strictly forbidden and grounds for being kicked off the squad . . . so, we were also drinking. Somehow I ended up making out with Bob Alley. It was random, and at first I couldn't tell whom I was kissing. It was dark and not uncommon in Kansas to just make out with whoever was closest. Although I was highly flattered that he grabbed me instead of one of the other cheerleaders, I didn't expect to see him again. He was WAY too cool for me, and I was WAY too dorky for him.

The following Monday I was bent over getting something out of my locker when Bob walked up behind me. "Hey, you wanna go out next Saturday?" Could this really be happening? Was he talking to me or was someone hiding in my locker? I snapped out of my reverie and realized I needed to give him an answer.

"Oh, this Saturday? Um . . . yeah I'm pretty sure I can do that—this Saturday."

"Good. I'll pick you up at seven. Dress warmly; we're going to a party out in the country," he said.

As he walked off I was already onto him and his devious little plan. How stupid did he think I was? I had no doubt that we would go to this "little party" out in the country, and we'd be the only ones there. He'd end up making out with me and then all his COOL friends would pop out of the woods and splash pig's blood on me and start laughing just as they had done in the movie *Carrie*. Of course *Carrie* didn't debut until 1976, and this was 1967, but perhaps I was prescient. I didn't know exactly how the charade would unfold, but I certainly knew he was setting me up just as that beige boy Ken had at art school.

Bob picked me up on Saturday and drove me to Augusta, Kansas, which was 20 miles away. As I had predicted—no one was there. "Wanna walk around awhile? Looks like we're the first ones here," said the spider to the fly. But I was so ready for what might happen. I had my moves all planned out. We walked around awhile, then he stopped by this big oak tree. I knew his next move was to lean in and pretend to be interested in kissing me.

It was too bad that he was an imposter. He looked so crazy handsome standing there in the moonlight. I glanced quickly, inconspicuously up into the branches, lest the evil boys were perched up there with their buckets of pig's blood or paint. But I couldn't see anyone; it was so quiet out there. Bob was being so sweet to me. He was so sexy. He leaned in for the kiss, but I blocked his fatal advance.

"Let's just wait for the others," I said cunningly, knowingly. An obnoxious smirk was plastered across my face. *This ain't my first rodeo, Hon. I've been shunned by queers and tricked by straight men with little dicks already. I GOT YO NUMBA, DADDIO*, I thought to myself. About that time six or seven cars and trucks came roaring up. Kids jumped out from everywhere. They had beer, stuff to make a bonfire, s'mores, hot dogs, and Jack Daniel's. They didn't have pig's blood or paint.

"Can I kiss you now?" Bob laughed. We did kiss . . . and kiss and kiss and kiss. From that day on we became inseparable.

That is, until this New York City Amazon rolled into town. She became hellbent on getting her claws into my man. How the heck could I compete with a girl like Katie Yeagley? All six foot one of her in bare feet. With her tiny-assed NYC bikini body and her shiny NYC black locks flowing down around her 19-inch NYC waist. To this day when I think of her, she always walks in slow motion, like she just stepped out of a Pantene commercial. Oh lord, if I'd been a man I would have jumped on Ms. Yeagley like New Yorkers jump into taxis. She had Bob in her sights, and it was clear this sniper never missed her target. She didn't look at me or flinch when she would pass Bob and me standing in the hall of our high school. All eyes were on her, and her eyes were on Bob. I always made sure to grab him and start making out with him if I saw her striding down the hall toward us with her long, fawnlike NYC legs. No one in Kansas looked like this bitch. No one anywhere looked like this bitch!

Bob would act like he didn't see her, but how dumb was that? She was 20 feet tall, for god's sake! You couldn't have been greener with jealousy than I was. And I knew it was only a matter of time before he succumbed to Ms. Manhattan. Bob was a year older, so he was graduating from high school a year before me. Ms. NYC was also one year my senior. Bob took me to his graduation bash out in the county by a huge lake. Of course my mother insisted I get back home before 10 because I had school the next day. And we all know how important that last day of school is compared to the threat of your old man banging the hottest girl in the universe. Katie was the focus of the party. Every girl there was clinging to her boyfriend for dear life. I was on the phone BEGGING my idiot mother to let me stay until the party ended, but she told me to get my ass home or she would ground me.

Reluctantly, I kissed Bob good bye, and I saw Ms. NYC grinning at me from across the lake. I was scared shitless of my mother, so I obeyed her orders and drove home. That night, about three hours later, I began to feel sick to my stomach. It was a feeling that I've since identified as the feeling I get when I'm being cheated on. I think we women have that sense about us—that keen perception when a man is not being faithful. It transcends mere speculation; it is our heart's radar system. I threw up most of the night. Bob didn't call me after the party, as he had promised he would, but I didn't call him, either. I fell asleep after wearing myself out bawling.

The next day I went to school. He of course wasn't there because he had already graduated. Katie wasn't there, either. When I got home from school, my mother told me Bob had called five times. I didn't return his calls. During that evening he kept calling. I didn't take his calls. I didn't take his calls for two days. Finally I agreed to talk to him. I could tell he was guilty as a henhouse fox and afraid he would lose me, which was probably why he denied doing "anything" with Ms. Thang in spite of being interrogated by me no less than 10 times a day. I never believed him, but I remained hopelessly in love with him. Two years later, in college, I agreed to marry him.

• • •

Bob and I hadn't lived together while we were dating. Even when we were in college together we had separate apartments or houses with our own roommates. I'd wanted to marry Bob since I was 17, like pioneer stock apparently, so waiting years was absolute torture. He was the first man I had sex with, *any* kind of sex, and unfortunately for both of us, intercourse only occurred a handful of times before we married when I was 20.

It took me *forever* to put out the first time. My mother had me convinced that girls who have sex before marriage were whores. True, I knew several whores who later in life became real whores. In fact one of them was a bridesmaid in my wedding and the other one taught me how to give a blowjob. She, Paula, later became a fairly well-known DC whore who made the news and became part of a genuine Capitol Hill scandal! I opted to not be a "real" whore, but instead swung the pendulum way too far to the other side. Poor Bob.

Although we had fornicated several times, we had never had "it's okay to have sex now" sex. It seemed after all those years of withheld, pent-up sexual urges, the honeymoon would have turned out to be a crazy "anything goes" romantic free-for-all . . . it seemed.

Bob wanted a sailboat, one of those small ones called a Sunfish. So he pled his case that if we didn't spend much on our honeymoon we could afford both a honeymoon *and* a sailboat. This seemed fine to me; I just wanted to go to a place that had an ocean—I'd never seen an ocean! I'd envisioned palm trees, white sand beaches, and moonlit nights for my first sexual interlude as a wife instead of a whore.

We chose exotic Galveston, Texas, as our honeymoon destination, mostly because it had an ocean and it was close enough to drive to. There was no Internet in 1971 and apparently no vacation pamphlets. Bob and I had bought a pinky-mauve-colored Rambler station wagon at a garage sale for $55. She was very ugly and as old as the price tag, but she was only $55! She was our first joint purchase.

After the wedding we spent our first night as man and wife in Wichita at the Howard Johnson's, where Bob had spent summers life guarding. When we got to the room, he went outside for a cigarette, and I called my dad.

"What are you doing?" I lamely inquired.

"Um, we're playing bridge. What are *you* doing calling me on your honeymoon?" asked the other Mr. Alley.

"Nothin', just sitting here."

God help me! I was barely 20, going on barely 14, perhaps one of the most modest, unprepared, geeky, daddy's girls anyone has ever encountered.

"You have a good time, Kirstie Lou, you're married now, go find your husband."

And that's how my dad broke up with me—on the phone.

The word "husband," which I'd been dying to hear for years, suddenly sounded like "go find the only person you're free to have sex with for the rest of your life." It was way too much for me to absorb. We were on our own, and there were no more excuses or reasons I couldn't be Bob's sex slave. I was panicking like a caged monkey. See, the thing is, Bob was really good at sex, well endowed, generous, and very capable in the bed. I, on the other hand, was the girl who'd spent four years staving off sex lest I become my mother's worst nightmare, a whore. I went to the Howard Johnson's front desk to buy candy bars. It took a long time to pay for them—when I returned to the room Bob was asleep. Phew!

The "phew" was short-lived. The next morning Bob confessed he had indeed messed around with Ms. NYC at his senior party. I cried . . . a lot. And screamed . . . a lot . . . as he had lied about it for the past two years. But I pulled myself together and decided to take the high road.

Four hours later, we drove to our honeymoon retreat in Galveston. It was dark by the time we arrived. I recall the lovemaking was lovely, the type young, modest newlyweds engage in. Sweet, satisfying, lovely lovemaking.

After we made love I locked myself in the bathroom and called my dad from the wall phone next to the toilet.

"Hi, Daddy, what are you doing?"

He chuckled, "Playing bridge."

"Oh," I said, "I miss playing bridge."

"How's Galveston?" Daddy asked.

"I don't know, it's dark, I can't see anything."

49

"How's your husband?" He asked AGAIN, as if to remind me he was no longer the only man in my life.

"He's good, he's sleeping. Who's your bridge partner?" I pathetically asked.

"Norma."

"Yeah, she's good but not as good as me . . . heeheehee . . . bet you wish I was there . . . hahaha . . . what do you have for snacks?"

"Kirstie Lou, go back to Bob. I'll see you when you come home."

As final as that! Now my dad had not only broken up with me, he was refusing to talk to me. I'd never before or since felt that betrayed and alone. Now I had been betrayed by two men.

When we woke up the next morning I rallied myself, and I'm pretty sure I instigated morning sex. Now that the other man in my life abandoned me, I was spurred onward to make a new life for myself as Bob's wife. I threw open the drapes with a flourish to take my first glimpse of a real live Hawaiianesque honeymoon ocean.

Ugh—the Galveston ocean looked like a lake. It had brownish, brackish water. No palm trees, no blue skies, no chicks in hula skirts, not even bikinis. The beach was not white or pristine. In the light you could see that the white bathrobes and towels were tinged with the gray-brown color of the ocean water.

My memory of my honeymoon goes black from that point; I truly can't remember another moment. The mind is like that, I think. When something is just too awful, it closes down to protect you from catching on fire.

I do remember our drive home in Rosie, the name we had christened our pink $55 Rambler station wagon. Rosie ran pretty well but had no air conditioner. Galveston in June, and all 11 other months, is hot as hell and so humid that your clothes stick to your skin. On this June day it was approximately 105 degrees. The sweltering heat was unfathomable as we drove along in our pink coffin. Bob and I stopped at a roadside watermelon stand and bought three ice-cold watermelons.

Bob had the guy cut one of them right down the middle. We positioned the cut half of the watermelon between us on the seat of the Rambler. As we drove along we scooped icy cold melon with tiny Dixie cups and slurped it to stay alive.

The drive from Galveston to Kansas is flat, brown, boring, and uneventful. Bob and I made up songs to keep ourselves amused. My favorite was "Dead Dogs and Tires," as there were several of each along the route, with the occasional dead armadillo. Bob has a very clever, acute sense of humor. He could always make me laugh until I cried. He was teasing me about how sad it was that all we had to return home to was a new sailboat after spending an awesome honeymoon in Hawaii.

Drenched with sweat, sticky from watermelon juice up to our elbows, we cruised along singing, already fairly bored of our "alone" time. Then suddenly, there they were! Two hitchhikers! They were undoubtedly stranded because their car had broken down in the godforsaken heat, although we saw no car. *My, they must have walked miles in the wretched sun, they clearly needed some Dixie cups of watermelon and a lift to the nearest gas station*, I thought.

"STOP!!" I screamed at Bob. "Stop the car! Come on Bob, if it was us out there, we would need help, too!"

It was 1971, or '72, or—hell, I can't remember. The point is, hitchhiking and hippies were the order of the day! I knew this because I'd seen news footage of Haight-Ashbury.

They came running up to the car and hopped in.

"Thank you, thank you," the weary walkabouts gushed. I noticed two things: neither of them had any teeth, and they had the distinct air of having escaped from a mental institution.

"Where you headed?" my friendly husband asked.

"Wherever you are!!! We ain't got no place to go—guess you're stuck with us!"

Although I was the opposite of street smart, savvy, or forensically trained, it was clear we were going to be murdered.

Bob and I survived our honeymoon and moved back into my parents' house for the summer to play bridge. In July we drove to Manhattan, Kansas, to find a place to live. That's where Bob would study veterinary medicine and where I would find a job.

College towns are infamous for nonexistent low-paying part-time jobs. They are also known for high-priced, limited housing.

Because of our vast array of pets, horses, dogs, cats, snakes, and raccoons, Bob and I quickly nixed the city life in lieu of country living. We found an 1865 stone farmhouse in Olsberg, Kansas, owned by a Mrs. Mildred Nelson.

Mildred was probably in her eighties back then and probably the most decent, sweet, generous person I've ever met. She could see we were a young, struggling couple, so she asked, "Would sixty-five dollars a month seem fair to you?"

The stone farmhouse had a living room, a huge dining room, a kitchen, a sitting room, two upstairs bedrooms, and one downstairs bathroom. On one side of the kitchen was a stove, a refrigerator, and counters with a sink. On the other side of the kitchen was a cabinet and a bathroom sink. The claw-foot tub and commode were behind a door by the kitchen/bathroom sink.

The house was heated by a wood-burning stove and a gas heater in the living room. I'm pretty sure it was the first gas heater ever invented.

Mildred told us that before we arrived in the fall she would have the $65-a-month stone house spruced up. I should mention, it was a $65-a-month stone house sitting in the middle of 80 acres of land! It had barns, stables, and outbuildings. All of it just for us. The big yard was lined with a Victorian iron fence butted up against 10-foot-tall ancient lilac bushes. The smell of newly mown hay and lilacs filled the air of Mildred's house, once inhabited by Mildred and her husband, Peter.

Mildred and Peter could not have children but were happily married until his passing, whereupon Mildred moved into town (which was a quarter mile from the farmhouse, with a population of 108). Of course

Olsberg's population of 108 didn't all live "in town," and a few had died that year so how accurate the census was remained a mystery. When a baby was born in Olsberg, Kansas, Bob and I would joke about running out with a bucket of paint and changing the sign to 109.

We gave Mildred our deposit on the stone farmhouse—$20—and went to the "big" city, Manhattan, Kansas, to find me a job. I thought the ad said "receptionist at a dry cleaners," but that quickly shifted to "laundry worker in a sweatshop" where the average temperature was 105.

I took the job. I would start in September.

Bob and I spent the rest of the summer playing bridge, riding horses, sailing, and loving each other like love stories in the movies. The summer of our first year of marriage proved to be magical.

When we arrived at the stone house with our stuff that fall in Olsberg, Mildred met us at the door. So sweetly she said, "Welcome to your first home. I hope my choices of wallpaper are suitable for you." Every room had been freshly painted and sweetly wallpapered with delicate, old-fashioned pristine papers. Each room a different paper that collectively made the 19th-century home look like a dollhouse. It was breathtaking. The only thing Mildred had asked me when we first rented the house was what colors I preferred. I had told her pale yellow, pink, green, and lavender. Each room was clean, soft, welcoming, and the perfect setting to become "fancy," something I had always wanted to be.

I will never forget how Bob looked standing there on the porch to our new "mansion." It was evident I had married the man of my dreams and probably every other girl's. God! Life was about to explode into our glory days!!

I began by making our house "fancy." My grandmother had passed away and left me all of her antique furniture: a modest but lovely dining room set, table, eight chairs, a sideboard, a hutch, and an antique six foot tall RCA Victor radio/record player. We went to an estate sale and bought furniture for the living room. We hit pay dirt, this 1940s four-piece set of sofa, love seat, and two comfortably worn burgundy velvet chairs. We were getting fancier by the day. Bob and I would lug all the treasures in a borrowed truck.

The stone house didn't have pretty hardwood floors, so when we put our new finds atop the bland worn-out carpeting it looked shabby, not shabby chic, just shabby. I started collecting carpet remnants from the trash bins in Manhattan, Kansas, carpet stores. It was the 1970s, baby, and patchwork was king. We took all the multicolored, multitextured pieces and fashioned them into a carpeted patchwork quilt floor. The carpet of course was all brand new, just in pieces. We cut them in shapes—squares, rectangles, and triangles. When we were done it gave a groovy, mod look to our 1860s dollhouse—the perfect blend of antique and modern.

There were no window treatments in our house, but my mom had bought me an early birthday present of fabric and fringe. It took several days, but I made curtains for each window. Bob stayed busy mowing, weeding, and edging.

There were plenty of wildflowers to fill Ball jars and vases. We had finally hit the ranks of "fancy." We were the fanciest self-made newlyweds I'd seen or known. While our friends starved, living in expensive, overpriced apartments in the city, we flourished on our 80-acre country estate. Married life was not only nirvana, it was supremely fancy.

On one September morning, Bob and I drove into the city for his first day of vet school and my first day at the laundry. Rosie was running beautifully, our lives were in order, and everything was going as planned. I kissed my handsome husband good-bye, and we went off on our separate ways.

The laundry was enormous, probably a 20,000-square-foot brick building. It was fronted by a tiny dry-cleaning store, which of course also took in laundry. Out of the 100 employees, 50 percent were mentally or physically challenged, 30 percent were ex-cons, 18 percent were prostitutes, and 2 percent were the huge black guy who carried a .45 and me.

I instantly made friends with .45; I was naive, not stupid. This sweatshop was filled with washers, dryers, and mangles, which are enormous ironing tables with conveyor belts and rollers. The temperature of the room ranged from 100 to 120 degrees, depending on the workload inside and the temperature outside. We prayed for snow no matter what time of year.

My fanciness was not an asset at the laundry. Turf wars and teams began to form. My team was comprised of hookers, crippled people, and the guy with the gun. Lest this get confusing, I'll refer to us as the Crips. The mentally insane and the ex-cons formed the other team; I'll refer to them as the Crims. There was a rhythm to this madness. Turf wars didn't involve murder. The weapons of choice were linens, or at least that's what I kept telling myself.

At one end stood the team with the unironed, damp laundry, whose job it was to feed the sheets, tablecloths, and pillowcases into the massive, dangerously scalding eight-mangle machine. Awaiting the linens was the team whose job it was to rapid-fire fold the laundry, lest all the laundry flip onto the floor, getting them fired by the dreaded lead girls. It's all fun and games for the feeding gang, but it creates fury in the folding gang. Things get nasty fast. The feeders shove the linens into the mangles as fast as they can. The folders frantically try to keep up. The meaner the feeders, the faster they shove. However, the gangs rotate every two hours, so the feeders can't be too obvious about their war games. And if they have been terribly evil they know they need to brace themselves for the ultimate in laundry wars, the illegal double-layered linens! The Crims were made up of convicted felons and lunatics, so legality meant little if nothing to them.

At the end of each day, .45 would walk me to my car to make sure

I didn't get raped or murdered. It was deeply appreciated. Each night Bob and I would drive the 20 miles back to our stone house wiped out, me physically, Bob mentally.

On week four I was offered the lead girl position at the laundry, aka the girl who was going to end up gang-banged by Christmas. I said good-bye to .45 and resigned from the laundry the next day.

Being in veterinary school is not an easy task—it's actually brutal. Bob worked his ass off in school, and I worked my ass off keeping a fancy home. I became a nanny, and my work life immediately became better.

Bob and I lived in the stone farmhouse until he graduated and became a full-fledged veterinarian. We said good-bye to the place that had been our first as husband and wife, good-bye to Mildred, good-bye to the bushel loads of lilacs, good-bye to the ghost who lived in the cellar, good-bye to the 107 people we left behind in Olsberg, and good-bye to the Billy Graham revival that occupied weeks of our lives since we only had one TV channel. We packed our dog, cat, and raccoon and were on our way to California. After all, there was gold in them thar hills.

By this time I had less confidence than when I began my marriage, not having to do with Bob and me, but with myself. I was scared to death to leave Kansas. I had no skills or training. Bob was now a doctor, his brother was an oral surgeon, his brother's wife was a scholar, and I was nothing. I knew I'd have to work in California, but it seemed I wasn't even fit to be a dog groomer, and thought myself too stupid to be a mailman, fearing I couldn't pass the civil service test.

But here before us was our future: Bob's looked bright and shiny; mine looked vacant. I had exiled myself into the oblivion of just being "Bob's wife" and I was terrified.

Marriage is a wonderful institution, but
who wants to live in an institution?

—GROUCHO MARX

The Art of Tornadoes

BY THE time I was 24, I'd been married to Bob for four years. I was restless and bored out of my mind. Sex had become a torture, a kind of looming task that I was unwilling to participate in. Bob was the only man I'd had sex with. I wasn't looking for someone else to shag. I was just chronically inventing ways to get out of "doing it": ironing at three in the morning, feigning illnesses, can't "do it" on my period, arts and crafts, gotta get up at five o'clock to get to the beach, back pains, deaths of pets, sad news of the uncle I'd never met passing away, it's too hot in here, I electrocuted myself, I fell off my horse, the raccoon bit me, you hurt my feelings, I'm gonna throw up, I can't get over Ms. NYC, we have guests, the dog fell off the roof, the chinchilla is eating the wrong food, I have to mow the yard, I can't find the goose, my stomach is going to explode, I think my IUD is lodged in my uterus, we have no electricity, the shower is leaking, and "Hey, how 'bout that Halley's comet?"

I kept thinking about the second time I had sex with Bob when we were in my mom and dad's room after they had left town to attend my cousin's funeral. What happened to the girl who was dying to have sex with Bob, even when Jesus was warning her not to?

There was this gilded oval–framed photo of Jesus Christ above their bed glaring at us. I was trying to be sexy and cool, but I seriously couldn't fornicate in front of Jesus. I grabbed the portrait of the Savior, walked it into the bathroom, and turned it facedown on the counter, freaking out because the tile was cold and it seemed a horrible way to treat Jesus. I spread out a bath towel, nestling Jesus on the terry cloth, then covered the frame with another towel. Then I started worrying I was smothering Jesus, so I removed it. I turned off the bathroom light, and pondered whether Jesus hated the dark. No, these were not the calculations of a seasoned vixen, these were the thoughts of a 17-year-old girl who wanted to be a woman.

So there I was in 1974, being the woman I'd always dreamed of being, with full permission to bang my brains out . . . but I didn't wanna.

Bob and I were living in California. My mind was still like a 14-year-old, my body was like, well, not a 14-year-old . . . I had curly, flowing hair to my boobs, with an athlete's ass that had finally molded into the tiniest, tightest pair of Fiorucci jeans made. My once-embarrassing swimmer's six-pack had now smoothed out to a concave slice of heaven—I thought the California boys were day-trippin' at the sight of me sauntering down Hermosa Beach. There was no doubt in their minds—or mine—that I was "the shit."

I had resisted all advances, and by resisting I mean I'd flirted with every beach boy in my path but never acted on it.

Bob and I had bought our first house, overlooking the ocean in Redondo Beach. We had a sleek, new white BMW. He was a partner in his veterinary practice, and he was breathtakingly handsome in his

Dr. McSteamy sort of way. He was instantly an excellent veterinarian, and he was working really hard and assuming tons of responsibility.

I, on the other hand, was restless, useless, jobless, sexless, lifeless, bored, with no direction. I was a great cook, funny, highly creative, with a fine ass that I didn't want my husband to touch. I was worthless, actually. I'd become worthless.

One day, while looking for a new cat in the *LA Times* classifieds, I noticed an artist advertising for a model. His name was Putt. I interviewed with him and got the gig of posing for his latest oil painting.

He was a fine artist, he really was, but I made a bad decision to pose for his painting. If I recall correctly, Putt painted Western scenes; thus I was in some stunning dance hall gown, one shoulder up, the other draped down to expose one nude breast, a sultry painting. I guess we could say this painting was the modern-day version of a sex tape floating around in someone's living room or gallery now. But I quickly learned that husbands don't like their wives posing nude, even for accomplished artists. Of course I already knew that, didn't I? To this day, I think I did it as some covert revenge for Bob cheating on me with that NYC beauty queen my junior year.

My husband was furious when I told him, and rightfully so. He thought I was at home cooking his dinner, I'm sure, instead of posing seminude for a local artist. It was also so unlike me, as I was modest to the point of Victorian prudishness.

This marked my turning point—I'd degraded myself, and Bob helped me degrade myself a little more. He called me many names; the most impressive one started with a *C*. I knew what I'd done was wrong, that I wasn't a nude-y kinda girl. I felt like shit, like the whore my mother predicted I'd become. It really screwed with our marriage.

We decided to go home to Kansas for Christmas. I had all these decorated pillows there that I'd made when Bob and I were in college, and a Wichita friend of mine named Carmen had made terrariums.

Apparently she was as bored and hard up for some goal in life as I was. She said, "Kirstie—let's take your pillows and my terrariums and sell 'em at the holiday showcase in Wichita." Out of storage flew my 150 handmade pillows to be put on the open market, but we needed a BIG vehicle to transport all those pillows and 10 bulky, ugly terrariums.

Carmen's husband, Dick, had a friend with a Bronco, so come Saturday morning, along came Jake—a handsome, twinkly-eyed, pseudocowboy rich guy. He just "got me," you know? He "understood me," "appreciated me." Good ole Jake. I loved his name: "Jake." He'd never been married, never found true love, and he was just the kind of midwestern bad boy I'd been fantasizing about. The one all the girls in Wichita wanted . . . Jake.

Why wouldn't they all want him? He was 27, blue-eyed, with a big smile, cowboy hat, custom boots, and a ripped body. He appeared to be a cowboy who'd just gotten off his horse, scrubbed up, and come to town for dinner. In point of fact, he was a highly educated heir of a prominent oil family in Kansas—the recipient of a hefty trust fund, compliments of his grandfather and Standard Oil of Ohio. Jake—he was so strong and helpful and happy. Attentiveness is and was his most obvious trait. He didn't have me at "hello," he had me at "howdy."

I sold all of my "before their time" designer pillows and spent Christmas with my husband and our families with visions of this new guy Jake dancing in my head. Bob went back to California to his practice, and I stayed in Kansas for another week. Oddly I found a penchant for the game of backgammon at Dick and Carmen's parents' house. The best player? Of course it was Jake. We spent several nights studying that backgammon board, with me doing my best Faye Dunaway impersonations à la *The Thomas Crown Affair*. I dazzled the cowboy with my coy smiles and my infinite wit, but I left it at flirting. Soon it was time to go back to California and my husband.

I blocked Jake out of my mind, didn't talk to him for six months, and that summer Bob suggested we go home for a vacation. I loved his family, especially his mother—she was a role model for me. We swam and did skits, ate the finest food known to man, played games and a lot of bridge, rode horses, and flew around in Dr. Alley's plane. It was perfect; I loved my husband, and I had since I was 16 years old. All was well.

Bob had to head back to Cali to work, and I decided to stay another several days to spend more time with my friends. I'd made my decision to be a good girl, and that summer Jake had faded out of my mind.

Kansas is notorious for tornadoes. They are destructive and devastating, perhaps a prelude to my own life.

Carmen, Dick, and I were all hanging out at his family's house— it felt like my second home, a huge College Hill estate in the heart of Wichita. They were a family with five sons, each one hotter than the next. The home was warm and inviting, with animals all around, dogs, cats, and raccoons. Dick's parents, Don and Maxine Aldritt, were fun—not hipster fun, just warm and adorable. They let their children have full rein. There was always tons of home-cooked food around, and articles by Louis Comfort Tiffany and Maxfield Parrish adorned their house. There was a huge swimming pool with a tall cabana that horrified us girls when the boys dove from it into the pool. This place was what I imagined the Kennedy compound in Hyannisport was like, without the ocean and the Catholics. I remember sitting at the kitchen table while Maxine was making brownies. We were playing backgammon . . . and in walked Jake.

My heart started pounding like a damn drum. His white shirt so crisp and clean, rolled-up sleeves, revealing his tanned perfect forearms and his understated stainless-steel Rolex. Jake had the most beautiful hands and chest I'd ever seen. I can still envision his tan forearms covered with golden-blond hair. His eyes looked bright blue like my dad's against his dark skin. Immediately, this girl was gone.

He told us to turn on the TV, that a tornado was headed toward Wichita. But the combination of our impending doom and the sight of his tan neck against his white cotton shirt made me feel the need to breed.

About that time, loud crashes of thunder shook the Aldritts' house. You have to witness a Kansas storm to know its full impact. The wind whipped up and was immense, and the lightening was like a thousand transformers blowing at once. I've been terrified of storms my whole life, especially tornadoes. I'd seen Udall, Kansas, flattened to the ground when I was eight. Tornadoes are vicious and unpredictable.

I snapped out of my crush coma, and true fear set in. But a moment later I had the insane thought, *Oh my god, it's Jake. I need to brush my teeth so that I have fresh breath when I flirt with him before we die in a twister.*

While he was in the living room messing with the TV I seized the moment. *Oh my god, I probably have brownies in my teeth.* I scrambled in my purse for a toothbrush and ran across the kitchen to the sink. Under the cabinet was a tube of toothpaste. I began brushing wildly.

Oh my god.

I can't have brownies in my teeth!

I can't let Jake see brownies in my teeth!

Jake can't see me brushing my teeth!!!

Oh my god, he looks so flippin' handsome!!!!!

I scrubbed my teeth double-good in case I wanted to whisper anything to him. Brush brush brush!! Suddenly, my mouth began to burn. No, really *on fire* burn. *What the hell!??!* My freaking escalated into a frenzy. I grabbed the tube of toothpaste—*OH MY GOD!! It wasn't toothpaste at all!! It was Bengay!!* Seriously? I'd brushed my teeth with an analgesic heat rub used to relieve muscles and joint pain?! *Fuck!!* My mouth was on fire!! And my lips were crimson!

I was rinsing my mouth with cold water like a fool as fast as I could as Jake walked toward me.

I burst out laughing, probably drooling like a dog as I offered up the Bengay and toothbrush. He burst out laughing, and there we were, crying as the house was preparing to implode.

All senses were heightened: fear of the tornado; lust for the cowboy; burning Bengay mouth. And that was just the beginning.

The storm alert had turned into a full-blown tornado warning, and in Kansas that means air-raid sirens blaring and TV storm trackers shitting their pants trying to act calm.

"Get in the basement!!!" Mr. Aldritt yelled. The noise of the storm was deafening. All the Aldritt boys were sitting on their asses, listening to Stevie Nicks.

"Get in the damn basement!!!" Mr. Aldritt shouted. You didn't have to tell me twice, I was scared shitless. I ran for the stairs!

"I'm getting the raccoons!" hollered Mike Aldritt.

"Forget the fucking raccoons," Jim Aldritt bellowed.

"I'm not coming in the basement without the fucking raccoons," Mike protested.

"Bring the damn raccoons," Mr. Aldritt conceded.

"What about the dogs?!" Mike pleaded. "And the cats?"

"Okay, everybody grab a fucking animal and get down the damn stairs now!" Dick screamed at his brothers.

This gave me ample time to situate myself in the basement underneath the staircase and snuggle up against Jake. I was half freaking out for real and half feigning a starlet-movie freak-out. If I had spoken, which I didn't, I would have said, "Rhett, don't let me die in a cyclone . . . Rhett, I need you, I love you, this is a sign from God. Oh, Rhett, protect me from the dreadful storm!" And Rhett would have said, "Frankly Scarlett, I DO give a damn!! There is never tomorrow, only today . . . and there's no place like home." The frenzy was so vast that even Rhett had gotten his movie lines mashed together, but I didn't care, I just didn't care!!!!

No dialogue was needed in this scene. This performance began my acting career and would have won me an Oscar if cameras had been rolling. I was clutching Jake, who was wrapped around me like a tortilla on a burrito. There were raccoons flipping out, dogs barking, cats hissing, five brothers laughing, Carmen telling them to shut up, Don and Maxine wondering why they had so many kids, the wind droning like a train . . . and then, as quickly as it had come, it went. Dead calm.

It was nothing new to any of us Kansans—just another night in ITA (Wichita), the Air Capital of the World.

Noah's ark, family, and friends danced up the basement steps to the kitchen. When a tornado doesn't actually kill you, you suddenly feel like the Berlin Wall just came down: exhilarated. Fleetwood Mac was blasting from the living room—"you can go your own waaaaaay"—and that's exactly what Jake and I did.

"Storm's over, let's go out by the pool to smoke a cigarette," he said. There were those tan hands. There was that crisp white cotton shirt. There were those stick matches that Jake was striking on the zipper of his Levi's jeans. He was holding the flame up to my smoke, and lordy lordy, it was all too much. I delayed a beat to let him light my cigarette, and the match went out. He leaned forward and kissed me hard on the mouth, and it was probably the most perfect, memorable kiss of my life. The "forbidden" kiss—and then it hit me: *I've kissed someone. I'm a married woman and I've kissed someone.*

The next day I did more. As Jake lay on top of me for most of that Sunday afternoon, making out like teenagers after the prom, I thought, *Oh well, at least we didn't have sex. We just parked our bodies face-to-face— and smooshed. Okay, okay, that's not horribly horribly bad . . .*

But as I got on the plane to leave Wichita the next day, I thought . . . *I am a whore . . . My mother was right. She raised a whore.* It left me but one choice—I had to get a divorce—which I did.

I took nothing; I was the bad one after all. To this day I cannot believe what a cold, callous, heartless ass I was to my husband. I didn't just break his heart, I thrust my hand into his aorta and ripped it from his chest, something I've punished myself for a thousand times over, and something I've regretted my entire life.

All of my justifications came floating to the top: *Well, he cheated on ME and didn't admit it until the day after we were married. Well, well, well, well, well . . .*

It never really works to cause immense pain to another and then justify your actions. However, I didn't learn that till much later in life . . . much later.

I became insane with long intervals of sanity.

—EDGAR ALLAN POE

The Art of Wallpapering

I F EVER there was a man who deserved the title of saint, it was Dean White. Not to imply he's dead now; he's very much alive and very much a part of my life.

When I moved in with Jake, before I was officially divorced, he suggested I decorate our duplex. Jake had money and I had talent. We made an appointment with Dean's Designs, a fashionable interior design firm in Wichita. Jake and I were new in our relationship and were on the wavelength of newlyweds, although we were just shacking up.

Dean—"Deano" as his children call him—was the top man (owner). We made the appointment, and it was love at first sight.

Dean was a terrific guy, one of the most naturally funny people I've met. He showed us all the design books that met the description of what we wanted. I chose this and that fabric. Those pieces of furniture, carpeting, and lamps. I was having so much fun with Dean and Jake, just designing away.

Although I studied interior design in art school when I was a teenager, I was far from a pro. I only knew I had a knack for it and loved designing. At the end of our decorating sessions, about three weeks after our first encounter, Deano said, "You're really good at this! You want a job?" I thought he was kidding but, yes, I did want a job as an interior designer.

I said, "I'm not trained, you know."

He said, "Who cares? You're good and I'll train you in the bullshit of all of it." We laughed, I said yes, and Monday morning I showed up for work as one of Deano's new interior designers.

Of course I'd never ordered anything in my life. I had no knowledge about purchase orders or working with clients of legit interior design firms. Dean's wife, Joyce, thought I was a lunatic and thought Deano was probably loony for hiring me, and she was right on both counts. What Dean and Joyce didn't know was that I had a budding cocaine habit.

Deano and his secretary, Betty, set up a section of his large store as my "design office." It was small, but wow, how did an idiot like me land this primo job in the first place? Dean immediately got me clients. It was crazy! I'd meet them at their homes and ask what they liked and tell them what I thought would be "lovely." Then I'd go back in the store where Betty would help me order everything.

This was all going swimmingly, and I had five clients within a month. Joyce was not as suspect of my lunacy as she'd been the month before, and Dean was getting rave reports from my clients.

Then Dean gave me a client named Paul. Paul was a well-known, wealthy businessman who owned an enormous plumbing-supply store. When I first met Paul, I thought he was gay. When I next met with Paul, I knew he was a raging middle-aged cocaine addict. Paul remains on my top-ten-weirdest-people-I've-ever-known list. How he ran the biggest wholesale plumbing-supply house in Kansas, I'll never know.

After meeting Paul I told Dean, "Paul is a total freak." Dean replied that he already knew that and that I was the only one who could handle him. *Why Dean? Because I'm notorious for handling freaks?* I thought. Anyway, it was work and it was a client and he was rich and on good days he *was* coherent.

One day while I was having the drapery woman hang drapes in Paul's bedroom, he took me aside, way aside, into his garage where he kept his Bentley and his Benz.

"You're doing a great job on the house, Kirst." Sweet Jesus, what a red flag it is when people call me Kirst. It culls them from the normal folk instantly. "You're doing such a great job, Kirst, that I got you a little gift." He handed me a crystal Art Nouveau box with an enamel lid. The box was double the size of a cigarette pack. It *was* stunning, and I'm sure it was the real thing, an antique.

He said, "Go ahead and open it. What's inside is even prettier." So I opened it. Probably five ounces of cocaine filled the lovely box to the brim. "I just had it flown in from California," he said. "Do you like cocaine? Have you ever tried cocaine?"

And here's where I broke my professional bond with Paul. "I've tried it a couple of times. It's sorta fun." I blushed. Jeez! I'd never seen five ounces of California cocaine! I bought my stash by the gram in little folded papers. "Thank you, Paul, would you like to do a bit with me?" I knew cocaine wasn't called "bits," it was called lines, rails, bumps, blow, etc.

"Yes," cunning Paul said, "let's do a 'bit.'" We snorted a quarter of the Art Nouveau box—enough to kill us both twice.

The drapery lady finished up six hours before we were done. Paul ended up offering to have me design a yacht and his showroom by the time I left, but he never tried hitting on me or approaching me for sex. Although he said he wasn't gay—he claimed he had sex with hookers—he was definitely a very twisted gay man. He also liked to seduce fairly innocent girls with drugs.

Another time the wallpaper guy didn't show up at Paul's house to wallpaper the kitchen. My friend Lucy and I were loaded when I got the call, both high as kites, and we went over to Paul's to assess the situation. Now, I had wallpapered rooms when Bob and I were married and were living in the house we shared briefly in Redondo Beach, California. After assessing Paul's kitchen, I decided it was a good idea that Lucy in the Sky with Diamonds and I do the job ourselves.

"Hell, Lucy, we don't need to take down the old paper! Let's just hang on top of it." This sounded like a champion idea to Lucy as she dipped her little fingernail into a ziplock bag of cocaine.

This was supereasy wallpaper to hang. We didn't even have to use wallpaper paste; it was prepasted. All we had to do was run the paper through water and hang it. Lucy and I went out and got all the right tools, brushes, sponges, straight-edged razors, and such. We snorted a few long lines of coke off the kitchen table, and we were ready to go. I'm a Kansas girl, a jack-of-all-trades, and that's how we roll in Wichita.

Lucy pulled the paper through the water, and I hung it. Strip after strip we went. The cocaine added to the speed of the hanging. It only took about three hours. Hell, we were done by noon.

We grabbed ourselves a Diet Coke and sat down at the kitchen table to go about the business of a "job well done" coke-snorting frenzy. About 15 minutes into the coke-a-thon I noticed the paper behind the refrigerator had begun rolling down from the ceiling.

"We gotta glue that down up there. Damn preglued paper!" As I was Elmer-gluing the strip back up I heard a ripping sound, like the sound of tape being torn from a dispenser. Piece by piece the wallpaper began rolling from the top by the ceiling and peeling down until it lay on the kitchen floor. It was as astonishing as it was horrifying.

Two things occur when you're high on blow. Everything is hysterical and everything makes you paranoid, usually in that order. Uncontrollable laughter could have been heard from Paul's kitchen for upwards of an hour, followed by a paranoia rivaled only by a serial killer surrounded by the FBI.

We—I—had hung the prepasted paper over vinyl paper. It was ruined. This was a conundrum. It would take four weeks for the new paper to get to Kansas, and it was expensive. Paul could easily come home at any minute in a coke rage. Our hearts were pounding. We could see Paul driving into the garage. We were terrified.

Paul walked in and said, "What's up, ladies?" I blurted out how stupid I was and what I had done. I waited for the explosion to ensue . . .

"Got any coke?" he calmly asked.

"Yeah, we have a lot of coke."

Then . . .

"Let's do some blow!" he cheerfully decreed. He could have cared less, and he never reported me to Dean. He just had me order more paper, which he insisted on paying for.

The real wallpaper guy took the old paper off and did the job correctly.

I learned one very important thing that day: if *you* are a cokehead, it's good to have a cokehead for a client. And always keep blow handy for emergencies.

"How's it going with Paul, Kirstie?" Dean would ask from time to time.

"It's going great, Dean, but he has some wacky ideas about what he wants," I replied.

"Oh, that reminds me," Deano continued, "Paul wants his entire basement and boat done in red, white, and blue."

"Red, white, and blue? Are you kidding me?! It will look like it's been decorated by Uncle Sam, for Christ's sake!" I was livid. My reputation was at stake. True, all that cocaine stuffed up my nose could have ruined my rep and put me in prison but I was willing to take that risk. I wasn't willing to be known as a tasteless designer.

Dean said, "Clients know what they want, even if they want shit." We laughed. "It's your job to make them want what you want them to want." And that became my new mantra. I became proficient at making people want what I wanted them to want. It works in more arenas than design!

Dean taught me everything about interior design. He took me to markets in Dallas and Carolina. I was rarely, if ever, high on any of our trips, and Dean and I had some of the best times of my life together. Joyce, Dean's wife, was on our trips, too, and tried to like me, but she was perceptive and knew I was not fully trustworthy. Bless her heart, she was spot-on.

I'd taken flower arranging in college on my way to flunking out, and I loved flowers. Dean owned the biggest flower store in Kansas, which was, and still is, on the bottom level of his design/furniture store. Dean let me hang around the professional flower arrangers, probably called florists, but that word reminds me of funerals, so I never use it.

During Mother's Day and holidays, Dean—who was a flower arranger extraordinaire—would come hang with me and teach me, again, everything he knew. I learned to make huge Christmas bows that to this day my friends beg me to make. I learned how to stick flowers in Oasis foam and how to effortlessly remove rose thorns with my bare hands.

I used to create the most delicious floral arrangements in teacups: delicate lilies of the valley flown in from Switzerland, accompanied by violets. They were superb—tiny masterpieces. Dean would ooh and aah over them, but then break into a roaring laugh and announce "Jesus! You're looking at a two-hundred-dollar arrangement! Jammed in this tiny-assed teacup!" My arrangements were not cost effective, not even close.

I worked for Dean White for almost four years. He never got angry with me and never found fault with a single thing I did, even though he had grounds to fire me, even jail me.

Dean is the kind of man who doesn't think anyone is "quite right," but he doesn't care. He never judges people. He himself is eccentric and wild. He's held court with kings and queens, nobility, trailer trash, and bums. Dean is the Kansas version of Will Rogers: he never met a man he didn't like.

Dean opened all kinds of doors to me. He introduced me to anyone in his path and told them how swell I was. Before Dean came into my life, I had the confidence of a wallflower at a cotillion. Dean believed in me, he validated all of my rightnesses, and ignored the wrongs. Dean was the first man in my life to give me a taste of how exciting life could be. He was by far the best boss I ever had.

Dean is a beloved family man with three sharp, productive children, Mark, Brad, and Michelle. He was a devoted husband to his wife, Joyce, for over 30 years. Sadly, Joyce passed away from a brain tumor.

I was filming a movie in Canada when it happened, so I flew Dean in to be with me for a week. He was in bad shape when he came to me, sort of like I was when I came to him. We have remained lifelong friends, and he goes down in the annals of my life as the first man to give me hope, confidence, and a glimpse of what was possible. He was the guiding light that let me know I could be, do, or have anything I wanted.

Everyone needs a mentor in their life, that person who sees your potential buried deep underneath the rubble. That person who is willing to water you long enough to see you bloom.

For me that person was Deano.

I never told my own religion nor scrutinized that of another. I never attempted to make a conflict, nor wished to change another's creed. I am satisfied that yours must be an excellent religion to have produced a life of such exemplary virtue and correctness. For it is in our lives and not from our words that our religion must be judged.

—THOMAS JEFFERSON

The Art of Not Dying

'D DONE enough cocaine to kill several people. I weighed 112 pounds. I couldn't *be* anywhere comfortably. It was 1979 and I was engaged to Jake. I had the most gorgeous eternity ring, chockfull of half-carat diamonds circling the band. We didn't have the term in 1979, but I was a hot mess. I looked sexy and cool, but I was a complete lunatic.

Paranoia had set into my life and I was losing my mind. I couldn't stop doing cocaine, yet I would sit around like a frenetic Chihuahua taking my pulse between each line to see if I was going to die. I called in sick to work three times a week. The high from the coke lasted less than

30 seconds, but I persevered for the high I'd gotten when I first snorted it. My eyes looked like a cat being chased by a dog—glassy, wild, and involuntarily quivering in the light. I was fucked up.

I lived in lazy Wichita, Kansas, but was pacing like a caged tiger, so I drove to my friend's farm 50 miles away in Harper. When I say I couldn't be anywhere, I mean it literally. I was crawling out of my skin. I couldn't be in the yard, bedroom, or kitchen, agitated and wringing my hands, feeling the anxiety of not belonging anywhere. Every space was too big. Every space was overwhelming. My friends Carmen and Dick helped me pitch a canvas tent on their living room floor, and that's where I resided for four days, eating Beanie Weenies, a gone-mad camper who couldn't exist outside of the tiny green canvas walls.

● ● ●

One day my drug buddy Bruce, who had access to prescription drugs because he was in med school, drove to Harper with Valiums to "take the edge off me." Valium really works well for people on a short-term basis, when they have received a severe mental shock, like a death, or for people like me who'd shocked themselves into a drug-induced insanity.

The Valium cooled my drug-withdrawing jets as I began to unravel and sort out my whacked life.

I emerged from my Coleman tent on the fifth day. I'd come close to having a psychotic break, but thankfully didn't go over that cliff. There were so many decisions to make. What the hell was I doing with my life? I was surrounded by druggies, destroying my body and my mind. When you're at the bottom, the good news is there are only two options: death or life. I had to choose.

The first decision I made was to survive. I wanted to live, and I didn't mean just breathe. I wanted to change. I wanted to be happy.

A friend had told me about this book, *Dianetics*. She sent it to me to read. You probably think this story goes on a straight path of organized sanity from this point forward; far from it. I decided to read it when I returned to Wichita, and I did—while I was snorting cocaine from a silver tray and drinking limeades.

Hadn't I learned anything in Harper? Yes, I'd learned to always take Valium to come off the agitating high of cocaine.

I had a white bedroom: white walls, ceiling, carpet, and bath, and I draped myself on my white chaise longue with my white cocaine to read my new book, *Dianetics*, by L. Ron Hubbard.

I didn't know L. Ron Hubbard from Adam, and the only thing I knew about Scientology was that they drove some rad cars that I'd seen parked in the lot of a Scientology place in Redondo Beach. Whenever my husband, Bob, and I would drive past it I'd make a mental note, *Scientology equals Porsches and Mercedes*, while the Methodist church I was raised in equaled Chevys and Fords. If anyone had asked my opinion of Scientology in 1973 I could have commented, it's the religion of nice rides.

Religion is a goofy subject. Religions are based on beliefs, faith, and teachings. All of them that I've looked into have been interesting. They fascinate me. I was raised Methodist, which, in our house, meant going to church occasionally and listening to the preacher's stories. Baby Jesus was a hot item for me. Baby Jesus, conceived immaculately, was riveting and opened up all sorts of questions for me. I loved the Ten Commandments; they were definitely rules to live by. But my parents could answer none of my questions about Christianity, and when I asked my dad if he believed all this stuff, he said, "I don't really know what I believe."

As I sat there snorting line after line of cocaine and reading *Dianetics*, I began to wonder: *What was true? What was real?* All I knew was that I believed Jesus did exist. He was a good person. The things he did for mankind were on track with helping people live better lives, so I liked him. The concept of him being the son of God made sense. But the concept of accepting him as my savior or else I would be doomed to eternal hell didn't. That sounded more like something a person made up. I'd read Revelations—God said he was the Alpha and Omega, the beginning and the end. I certainly believed in God and still do, so I liked that passage in particular.

It was curious to me because Jesus has only been around 2,012 years. What happened to all the billions of people who had lived and died before him? They didn't have a savior, at least not Jesus, so did they all go to hell? Or was that a new concept that arrived with Jesus? My Christian friends have told me that if people are exposed to the word of God and don't take Jesus as their savior, they will end up in hell. Maybe that's not what all Christians believe, but it did concern me and provoked more questions. Did all those Buddhists and Hindus and Jews and Muslims, all good people, go to hell just because they believed in something other than Christ being their savior? This seemed too cruel. This made no sense and seemed un-Godlike. That's what led me to know I wasn't a Christian. It may be true, but it wasn't true for me.

I examined several religions and found I believed in parts of them but not all. It became evident to me that people believe what they believe, have faith in what or whom they have faith in, based on what is true for them. Not by indoctrination or by beating concepts into them but by free will and selection.

Dianetics made me aware of one distinct factor: I was really fucked up and was killing myself spiritually even more so than physically. Not only was I betraying others, but I was giving my own moral code and integrity a thrashing. So the first thing I hoped to get out of *Dianetics* was a certainty of my own truths, and to become honest. I wanted to become sane and helpful, useful to the world around me. Of course I knew I'd made myself nuts by doing drugs. But what had provoked me to do them in the first place? That's what I hoped I'd find out from Mr. L. Ron Hubbard by the end of *Dianetics*.

• • •

Scientology has been cloaked in mystery fabricated by the press, mostly. It's actually analytical and easy to understand. It does not include aliens, although I'd love to meet a few and believe we are not alone in the vastness of the universe.

My goal is not to convert anyone. It is merely to tell you why I chose Scientology as my religion and how the man who founded it affected my life. If you're just reading this book for funny stories and sexual escapades, skip this chapter!

All religions sound a little wacky if you take them literally and if they don't happen to be your own. Take communion, for example: Wine symbolizes the participation in the blood of the Christ. Bread represents participation in the body of the Christ. That's enough to scare the hell out of any kid who takes it literally. Believe me, if this were a Scientology practice, the front page of the tabloids would read "Scientologists Practice Cannibalism."

People fear religions, and why wouldn't they? People have been deceived and duped by religions throughout the history of man. They've been beaten, burned at the stake, gassed, eaten by lions, had their heads shrunken—just to name several atrocities—in the name of religion. Of course little of it was part of any religion. It was just based on man's fear of other men and their ideas.

People don't like when other people don't do what they want them to do or believe differently than they do. It makes them nervous. It rattles their own sense of being right. Mankind feels safe around people of like mind, especially in regard to religion. They think something awful will happen to them if they find themselves not believing what they once believed. This makes them feel alone and lonely. It excludes them from their group. So they kill the people who are different or reduce their freedom or enslave them in an effort to make them comply. The funny thing is, humans are tough motherfuckers and even at risk of death, they will adhere to what is true for them. They will fight for freedom of thought. They will die fighting for it if they have to. But most wars are simply about money, power, greed, insanity, and control of territory. Instead of tolerating differences, wars became about eradicating people who were different.

Yet man continues to believe what he believes no matter the duress of the suppression and punishment. This is how you know that inside man's body is a spiritual being seeking truth. I believe it's not his first rodeo. He's recycled himself in and out millions of times in search of his own answers. Each being is an individual, not a collective, so he therefore seeks his own individual truths about himself.

You can sometimes beat a man into submission if you beat him long enough and hard enough, but if someone rescues him and takes him to a safe place where he would not be punished any longer, he will tell his rescuer his deepest beliefs. They don't vanish because he was persecuted. They are still there, unwavering. We really need to stop trying to squash people's faiths and beliefs, mainly because it has never worked and never will. Man thrives on freedom and his own truth. And oh lord, I'm not defending crimes or insane actions in the name of truth, so don't jump there. People who kill, steal, molest, rape, or commit any other crimes should be put somewhere to prevent them from harming the rest of us. But even criminals or the dangerously insane won't get better if they are punished, beaten, and controlled in bad ways. How great would it be if people were actually rehabilitated? Economically it would be more cost effective. And for the sake of the idiot next time around, even if he weren't released back into society this lifetime, he might come back a better human being.

• • •

Now on to demonstrating how L. Ron Hubbard influenced *my* life directly.

He taught me that I could change. He taught me that other people could change. He taught me humanity and responsibility. I learned that man is basically good, as opposed to basically evil. Although humans can get pretty screwed up, at their core they are good and trying to right their own wrongs. This gave me a different viewpoint of myself and others. It let me see that if man *was* basically good, he himself would seek to punish and stop himself from harming people. This seemed true—criminals leave behind all sorts of clues when they've stolen something or killed someone. They leave fingerprints when they could have just worn gloves like OJ. They leave trinkets, receipts, DNA, witnesses, and videos. They know what they're doing is wrong, and because they are innately good, they set themselves up to be caught and punished. If man were truly evil, he wouldn't be so careless and stupid. It's evident, even if it's vague, that he wants someone to stop him from committing harmful acts if he can't or won't stop himself.

The first thing I learned that truly helped change my life was that no matter how badly I've screwed up, I can always change my condition in life; I *can* get better. And so can everyone else.

We've usually been punished enough in our lives. Punishment does not make us better. It can cause us to suppress what we wanted to do, but it creates little lasting change. Knowledge, justice, and understanding can help us change.

When I began doing Scientology, I was a drugged-out mess. I understood hell—depression, anxiety, addiction, failure, and loss. Well, at least, I understood that I'd experienced a fair quantity of each. Through the teachings of L. Ron Hubbard I gained a different point of view of these age-old problems. Depression, anxiety, loss, addiction, sadness, hate, and self-loathing are not new subjects.

You may or may not know this about people who practice Scientology: we don't use psychotropic drugs, electroshock therapy, or lobotomies to get better from those illnesses. Why is that? It's certainly not because we are a group of millions who haven't experienced all or part of their symptoms. It's not because we don't believe that all these things exist or that they are not real. Try to tell a man he's not chronically depressed or a new mother she doesn't really have postpartum depression, and you might get shot. They do exist. They are real. They are painful, debilitating, gruesome, and at times unbearable. I don't know anyone who wants to have these crippling disabilities. So the issue is not whether those symptoms exist, nor an accusation that they are fake. The issue is, what do you do to get rid of them?

Addicts crave drugs and booze, among other things. They 100 percent know they are killing themselves slowly or rapidly by using them. People who have suffered great losses in their lives know with certainty that they are so depressed that they literally can't get out of bed, can't function, and can't control their emotional and then physical pain.

A mother who has lost a child cannot be talked out of her grief, nor can she be drugged out of it. Even psychiatrists and pharmaceutical companies will admit that their drugs will not cure anything and that they relieve symptoms in less than one-third of their patients. Their only solution is to change the drug and prescribe a new one or double-, triple-, quadruple-down with additional psychiatric drugs, or add treatments such as electroshock therapy.

Granted, if someone is in a state of shock after being the victim of some gruesome crime, or overwhelmed by unfathomable loss such as the death of a child or loved one, they could be in such a state that they can't function. In these cases, mild sedatives such as Valium might, for a short period of time, ease the feeling of being overwhelmed. Painful emotion can be camouflaged or suppressed, but drugs will not eradicate the loss or violation.

So the big question arises: what the hell does one do if experiencing some or all of these issues? It's not my job to diagnose mental disorders, nor do I want to. It's also not my business to evaluate the paths other people take or the choices they make to help themselves or their loved ones. I do not presume to know what is right for everyone. The choice is always their own. It was my personal quest, as I suffered from anxiety and depression, to find alternatives to drugs. It's also fair to say

I suffered from chronic anxiety prior to taking cocaine. For my own answers, I researched different options and different schools of thought. Being an ex–drug addict, I wasn't necessarily looking for the next drug to solve my problems, even if it wasn't a street drug.

I discovered two distinctly different schools of thought on the subject. One school of thought is that of psychiatry, medicos, and Big Pharma. The other is the school of thought I discovered in Scientology. The first school has concluded that these diseases are genetic and/or problems of chemical imbalances in the brain, such as low serotonin levels. Because their assumptions are based on the body itself, their solution is to first treat the body with talk therapy and powerful mind-altering drugs that affect brain chemistry. If that doesn't work, it's on to electroshock, and as a last resort, a lobotomy (currently called psycho-surgery), whereby holes are bored into the brain with lasers. Many of you might think I'm nuts for insinuating people still get electroshock in the year 2012. You might even think I made it up! Jack Nicholson's character received electroshock in the 1975 Academy Award–winning movie *One Flew Over the Cuckoo's Nest*, and after that electroshock took a dive. There was such an outpouring of public outrage at the brutality of electroshock that it was renamed electroconvulsive therapy (ECT). According to Mental Health America, 100,000 Americans yearly receive ECT. The tally is one million worldwide and includes the elderly, pregnant women, and toddlers.

I didn't invent psychiatry, psychopharmacology, or psychosurgery—they evolved. According to Medco Health, a leading prescription drug supplier, one in five American adults is now taking psychiatric drugs, to a total of 49 million Americans. That number does not include the 10 million American children currently taking psychiatric drugs. Worldwide, 120 million people are taking psychiatric drugs (including those 49 million American adults). If this is not considered an epidemic, I don't know what would be.

So there we have the psychiatry school. Recapping, their tools include analysis, drug therapy, ECT, and psychosurgery. Their bible is the *DSM* (*Diagnostic and Statistical Manual of Mental Disorders*), which cites 374 mental disorders and their symptoms. Phew!

Then we have a school of thought that is 180 degrees opposite, and that school is called Scientology. You see people with the same disorders come through the doors with their multitudes of manifestations. But what happens within is different. Mr. Hubbard has no dispute with the various bazillion diagnoses within the pages of the *DSM*. Anxiety, depression, grief, psychosis, and more all exist, and we can see they do with our own eyes. But what I learned from Mr. Hubbard, and what I've now experienced myself and witnessed in thousands of others over my 33 years practicing Scientology, is those people can be made better, dramatically better, without drugs, without analysis, and without psychosurgery or ECT. Seems impossible, right?

The function of Scientology churches is to make the able more able. They are not rehab facilities for criminals or predators. There is a social betterment program called Criminon based on the writings of L. Ron Hubbard and geared to help rehabilitate criminals in prison, but it is not part of the church.

Dianetics was fascinating, but was it just fiction or did it work and do what it said it could do? I'm a curious girl by nature but wasn't necessarily adventurous. I was cautious yet willing to observe. This is a good quality I believe, so I decided to take a look for myself. By the time I headed out to California to see if Scientology was real or fake, I was a colossal skeptic—another good quality.

I'd gone to a psychologist for about a month before I read *Dianetics*. His best advice was to stop doing cocaine and do manual labor, like cleaning my house and mowing the yard. He also advised staying away from my mother for a while. I immediately did all those things and felt better. On subsequent visits, though, he began to analyze me and tell me why I was the way I was, and he lost me. It didn't help that he was wearing socks with sandals. And it really didn't help that his evaluation was dead wrong. No, I hadn't been molested or wanted to screw my dad, nor was I a bedwetter.

In Scientology it is theorized that you and you alone know everything that has happened to you, and also what you've done to others, even while you were unconscious. So I surmised that at least my experiences belonged to me, and yes, I could remember most of what had happened to me. And yeah, I could kinda see how, under the right circumstances, I might be able to recall what was going on while I was sedated. I mean, I was there; Dr. Socks with Sandals wasn't there, that's for sure. So I decided to go find out for myself, and against all odds I made it to Newport Beach from Kansas. It took 26 days to make the 19-hour drive because I had to score cocaine along the way, or not along the way, as I backtracked and zigzagged my way across the country.

• • •

I arrived, immediately got loaded, and called the Scientology place.

"Hi, it's me, I'm here."

"Hehe, what took you so long?" Jim, the person on the other end of the line, chuckled.

"Family problems," I lied.

It really doesn't seem like I could have been more screwed up and still standing. I was drugged out, depressed, riddled with anxiety, and laced with cocaine, Valium, Percodan, and some drug I snitched from my sister's medicine cabinet. My weight was 112 and I was five foot eight. I'll admit, if you didn't look at my glassy, dilated eyes, just from the neck down, I looked badass in my skintight Fiorucci jeans and five-inch heels. But my mind and spirit were as dead as dirt.

"When are you coming in?" Mr. Scientology asked.

"Um, in a few days, I need to get settled in."

"Okay, whenever's good for you. Oh, one question, when was the last time you did drugs?" (You can't do Scientology counseling if you're on drugs—mind-altering drugs, that is, and my stash was definitely mind altering.)

"Yeah, let me see," I pondered, "I think, um, yeah, yeah, it was . . . it was six weeks ago." It was actually five minutes ago.

"Good, then you can get started," he responded.

Yes, yes, I couldn't wait to get started . . . As soon as I hung up I got started all right. My drug dealer guy had just flown in to LA to assist me. Oh yeah, I forgot this part. I'd just broken up with Jake before I left Kansas. It was sad for both of us, but the day Jake left Wichita to work on an oil rig in Texas, I slept with Greg, my drug dealer. How could that have slipped my mind? Greg brought all sorts of pre-Scientology party favors, including heroin. I did enough cocaine to kill four people, plus Valium, Percodan, hash, and booze. But I didn't do the heroin, thank god. I just sat there and did lines of coke while Greggy chased the dragon. It was quite spectacular, as I'd never seen anyone smoke heroin before. Then I topped it all off with Dalmane—you know, to take the edge off?

Three days passed, and I got a call from Jim the Scientology guy.

"Hey, Kirstie, how ya doin'? Are you coming in?"

"Um, yes, I'm just getting situated here. I have an idea! Jim! Why don't you come to the beach with me?!!"

"What time?" he calmly asked.

"Now! Come now! It's insane here! It's gorgeous!" I asserted.

Something deep inside me was trying to save my life, but it certainly didn't seem to be me. Jim was this really big, tall guy, sorta handsome, really funny and easygoing. We mostly just joked around for two or three hours. It could have been six minutes for all I knew.

"So, you wanna come with me and see what Scientology is?" he asked.

Now that was the million-dollar question. Did I? I mean, I'd just driven 17,000 miles to LA and all. I'd just broken it off with my boyfriend of four years. I'd quit my job and sold my stuff and packed what was left in my black BMW. I'd lugged my dog and cat to California and told all my friends I was going to LA to go "Clear," the object of Scientology counseling. I'd endured my mother throwing a dictionary at me on my birthday, demanding I look up the word "cult." Hadn't I put everyone and everything on hold just to have a shot at being sane and happy? Why yes, I had. So, DID I wanna go with Jim? Why not?! I was out of coke and I'd just sent Greggy packing to Hawaii to visit friends and advised him to read *Dianetics* because I was so hip to the subject.

"Yeah, let's go." I rallied from my drug stupor.

I had Scientology counseling that next week, and after my first session I have never wanted to do another drug. Of course it was a lucky break and probably not something you would see happening every day in Scientology, but it happened to me.

Apparently I was ready to confront the dreadfulness called *me*, and I prevailed. I never turned back. Every day I worked on some part of my screwed-up life until the anxiety dropped away. I handled all the losses of people I'd loved who had died. The depression went away fairly quickly as I discovered the reasons I'd been depressed in the first place. It was like digging for gold. First dirt, then mud, then bits of mica, then bedrock, then bingo! I would find smatterings of gold—I would find the truth.

The reason Scientologists and L. Ron Hubbard don't support mind-altering drugs is because they only prolong or obscure the truth. They impair a person's ability to find and dissect the truth of how they got in the state they're in. Mr. Hubbard's philosophy calls for zero tolerance of the Scientology counselor evaluating *for* the person or invalidating his answers. The person must come to his or her own conclusions, with the assistance of a counselor guiding him through, kinda like a tour guide. But the counselor is ONLY allowed to acknowledge those conclusions, never interjecting his own personal opinions. Hubbard's philosophy is analytical, gentle, and effective. It feels like peeling an artichoke, pulling back the leaves one by one, only experiencing the pricks of life, not the degree of physical or emotional pain one felt when it originally happened. It is so full of care; you just peel the leaves back and back and back, one by one, until you get the reward deep inside. In an artichoke it's the heart, and in Scientology it's the truth. Scientology isn't addressing the body. It is addressing you as a spiritual being.

I've known hundreds of people who have been diagnosed with chronic anxiety, clinical depression, bipolarity, ADHD, psychosis, and hyperactivity. They, too, went in and peeled the artichoke, leaf by leaf, with no invalidation, no evaluation, no interpretation, no drugs, no hypnosis, no lobotomy, no electroshock, and no restraints. But don't take my word for it. Ask them. It was their journey, not mine. I've often thought it would make for an interesting research project. There are millions of Scientologists out there, and they and their children don't take mind-altering drugs to end their mental suffering. I think it would be terribly important, even to the medical community, to find out how and why.

So there you have it: the flip side of the "How do you help someone become sane and happy" coin. There are really no similarities to psychiatry whatsoever. The schools truly are 180 degrees apart from one another. I chose Team Scientology.

• • •

Mr. Hubbard did not profess to be a god or a savior. Scientologists do not worship him or pray to him. He is not a deity. In fact Scientology does not deal with the subject of deep-seated concepts such as God. A person will believe what they believe, and that's how it's possible for a person to practice their own religion while practicing Scientology. They usually just don't conflict.

Many people ask me why Scientology is a religion. My answer is that it deals with you as a spiritual being. Yes, there are real things that attack the body, including cancer, diabetes, polio, viruses, infections, encephalitis, and the bubonic plague. People die from these or get treatment and recover. But Scientology deals with the spirit and its effect on the mind and the body. Mr. Hubbard taught me how to situate myself and view all aspects of life and then act according to what I observe and know. And to participate in life!! It's not much good to sit on top of a mountain and contemplate life. It's also not much fun.

He showed me how I can make my dreams realities. How to climb out of the rabbit holes that I'd plummeted into along the way.

Before I started Scientology, my life was myopic. I could barely see in front of my face. I would never have dared to dream of becoming an actress; by age 10 I'd had that thought thoroughly smashed out of existence.

L. Ron Hubbard has had a profound effect on my life, and I consider him one of my best friends, although I never even met him.

> All discarded lovers should be given a
> chance, but with somebody else.
>
> —MAE WEST

The Art of Making Love to an Unfortunate Man

BEFORE I was an actress, but after I moved to LA and stopped doing drugs, I began dating. I remember this one particular "date" vividly. I've told this story before, but some stories just bear repeating . . . I mean, REALLY bear repeating.

He was on a Harley-Davidson, and I was in a $16,000 stereo system disguised as a convertible Toyota Celica. He and I zigzagged flirtatiously, winding around each other on a well-known canyon road in LA. He motioned for me to follow him—something I was not inclined to do, but it was springtime, my top was down (no pun intended), and after all, he was an actor I'd seen before. So I accepted the invitation and followed.

He spent the afternoon boxing with a friend of his, and I was the audience—very macho stuff, that boxing, and admittedly it was sexy watching two guys beat the hell out of each other. He asked me out for the coveted Saturday nighttime slot—reserved only for important dates.

During the evening it became quite clear that he was somewhat of an idiot and that the boxing had been the high point of our tryst. He drove me home, and to be polite (the downfall of my personality) I agreed it would be fine for him to come inside for a late-night coffee. I don't drink coffee, didn't know how to make it, and really wanted to get rid of the actor, but it did sound like the civil, adult thing to do.

After I pretended to drink the coffee, he made a proposal: "I want to make love to you." All of my friends had recently told me, "God, Kirstie, you don't have to marry a guy just because you sleep with him." Now, that sounds like very hip single-girl advice, doesn't it? Actually I aspired to be the kind of girl who could participate in lovely casual sex and then just move on to the next casual sexer—so in this five-second period of time I made my decision.

"No, I don't think that's a good idea . . . we've only just met and as fun as this date was, I think the timing is not right." Man, that sounded smooth! I was shocked that this came out as if I were so, well, experienced! But then an odd thing happened—something I'd really never seen before. The actor began to weep. Great big crocodile tears.

"Wow—I just feel so close to you—I just . . . well . . . I know it's corny, but I'm falling in love with you."

Corny? Hell, no! Not for me. Love? Love, did he say? Well, even though I thought he was a complete idiot, "love" might be at stake here—love, marriage, children, ding dong! I might be passing up my future as Mrs. Actor!

"All right," I said, "I didn't know that's how you felt."

He took my hand and walked me up the badly carpeted chocolate-brown steps to my bedroom. He undressed me. I knew my body rocked, so I proudly stood there like the model-slash-goddess-slash-stunner I thought I was.

Then it was my turn. I took off his shirt to a previously choreographed rendition of the song "Ring My Bell." I unbuckled his very groovy biker belt and let the pants drop dramatically to the floor. I slid ever so stealthily, like an Abyssinian cat, between the TJ Maxx sateen sheets. He equally professionally slid in beside me nose to nose, eyes to eyes—and my hands (as they say in romance novels) began to read his body.

Then a strange thing occurred. While I was reading his body I realized he had no hair on his chest. Or his arms or his legs, actually. No, he wasn't a chick—not that that didn't cross my mind. I began to sweat, and the anxiety began to sweep me away. In my head I thought, *Shut up, shut up Kirstie. So what if he's hairless, so what? Stop only thinking about the physical. Get into it, for god's sake!* I slipped my hand ever so gently down his throat, across his barren chest and nonexistent treasure trail onto what could best be described as a small child's thumb. Or should I say, small child's erect thumb.

Panic and terror blasted through me in waves. I'd read about something like this, with Jean Harlow and her husband who committed suicide because of his miniature equipment. I didn't want the boy to kill himself . . . or did I? At one moment it seemed that one of us surely would after this encounter, and I was certainly too young to die. Thoughts I'd never had raced through my head: *Is this for real? Is this guy a chick with a dick? Does this moron not know he has the world's smallest johnson—by Guinness standards? Would he not think it appropriate to announce beforehand, "Hey, my penis is the size of a cheap eraser, so before we embark I'd like you to have the opportunity to decide whether or not to proceed?"* But the most pressing thought was, *How in the hell am I going to get him off with a baby cock like this?!*

I calmed myself before taking control; I knew I'd gotten myself into this mess, and hadn't I heard on *60 Minutes* that many serial killers had no hair and little wieners? Oh my, back to the responsibility; but wait, he was beginning to speak. Maybe he would explain that perhaps he'd had polio in the penis as a child or maybe talk about his time in 'Nam and how Agent Orange had caused all of his hair to fall out and his watson to shrink from its original size to that of a toddler's. Instead he said—with bold virility—"What does baby want?"

Did I hear that right? Yes, I did, because he repeated it with more masculine bravado. "What does baby want? Tell Daddy what baby wants."

Oh yes, it was all I could do not to scream, *Baby wants a cock! Jesus, it doesn't have to be a porn cock but come on, asshole, Baby wants a fucking real, at-least-average-sized cock!*

Instead I kept thinking of poor Jean Harlow's husband—the shame and degradation and of course, the suicide. He had his last actual fuck, as I personally believe suicides are, in fact, the committer's final grandiose "Fuck you!" Nevertheless, I did always worry about penile suicide prospects. It haunted me for years, actually. Poor Jean Harlow's sad, tiny-tallywackered, suicidal husband.

I said casually, as if I'd experienced this kind of thing hundreds of times in my work as a prostitute, "This is what baby wants" and put my fingers in a peace sign between my legs. I deduced it was the only possible hope to get this guy off and out of my house.

He complimented this ingenious idea. "Oh baby, you've been around."

Of course, I thought, *in my line of work, you need to know all the tricks of the trade—after all, you never know when your pimp might set you up with something that makes a preschooler's rod look like John Holmes!*

After he finished fucking the peace sign and I finished faking the most pathetic orgasm to date, even by fakers' standards, he rolled off me in baby dick bliss. "Damn, baby—damn that was good!" Of course it was, buddy boy, but just remember if it hadn't been for Mr. Sad, Dead, Suicidal Harlow and his tragic farewell, you, your underdeveloped appendage, and your overdeveloped ego would never have come close to heaven's gate, peace sign or no peace sign. Peace out!!!

There is no end. There is no beginning.
There is only the infinite passion of life.

—FEDERICO FELLINI

The Art of Champions

I T SEEMS most people set a timeline on the pursuit of a given task.
In 1980 I was on the verge of giving up on becoming an actress.
I'd given myself exactly one year to "make it," and it was the end of the
tenth month—late October, jeez. I'd come so close, so many times to
being the female lead of this or that big movie, but it was always between me and one other "famous" girl. But the truth was I'd never been
hired for anything, movie or television, not even a guest shot.

Some would encourage me by telling me that getting close was the
step right before being the victor. This all sounded swell, and it encouraged me from time to time, but being the runner-up for a huge movie
roll was akin to being runner-up at the Preakness. Who gives a damn?
No one knows who the runner-up to the Preakness was last year, right?
Except the guy who sold the horse after the race.

I was so close to sticking my tail between my legs and running back
to Kansas. I had almost no money, even though I was working three

or four jobs. None of my friends were actors. I had zero connections in the acting world. I'd gained 14 pounds and had gone from a whopping 116 pounds to a behemoth 130 pounds. I'd just broken up with my well-meaning, hot boyfriend, Doug, who wanted me to stay with him and draw faces on his penis at bath time and support him while he became a manager, a gem dealer, an art dealer, or a minister. Granted, his dick was as talented as a triple-threat actor, but at four-thirty on a Saturday morning, I broke up with superdick. I surmised that I only had two months to make it as an actress and there would be plenty of great cocks in my future. Little had I known that "great" cocks really are an oddity. Good ones are fairly common but great ones are extremely rare. But I digress . . .

His heart was slightly crushed, but honestly our fights consumed a good six hours a day and the other eighteen were spent shagging. You can imagine that this left little time for rehearsals, acting lessons, and auditions.

He couldn't quite understand that our split was final, so for a while he would break into my house nightly at around 3:00 a.m. He'd make me sit in a chair while he lectured me as to why we needed to stay together. This would go on for two hours as he paced and smoked 87 cigarettes. I'd zone out and nod off, which provoked him to yell really loud. I'd jolt to attention, but I needed sleep! I finally changed the locks and ignored his late-night rants while pounding on the doors, and finally he gave up. I felt sad for him, as I did still love him, but it had come time in my life that work—my craft—had to take precedence over dicks and . . . well . . . dicks.

I had to take off those pesky 14 pounds. I HAD to weigh under 118 pounds! Because when I was 16 I weighed 116 pounds, and it was the number I'd arbitrarily decided was the perfect weight for a five-foot eight-inch woman with medium bone structure. It was also the bottom number on one of those weight charts in the back of *Vogue.* I began the Beverly Hills Diet, which I think consisted of pineapple, papaya, and chocolate cake. Every moment was spent working out, dieting, turning down dates, and staying holed up in my house rehearsing lines for auditions.

I remember feeling extremely disciplined, something that was fairly foreign to me.

I had this agent, Steve Dontanville. He had told me he wouldn't sign me to the Paul Kohner Agency he worked for, but that he would send me out on things. This was sorta cool of him, since I was a "nobody" who had done "nothing," including not going to drama school. I knew he didn't rep me because he was hot for me. He batted for the other team and had no interest in my big boobs.

So Steve called one day and said, "I've got a meeting for you tomorrow. It's a long shot, but it's the female lead in a forty-million-dollar movie and they like your picture. Oh, and it's to play a Vulcan."

Wow! This sounded like a ridiculous opportunity. I'd gotten very close on other big movies. I was never sent out for a small part; Steve only sent me out for female leads. I liked thinking it was because I was too hot for character roles. It spurred me on.

It was one of those rare moments in my life when I felt überconfident. I'd whittled my ripped body down to 116 pounds. Since I'd not been going out, I was well rested and not hung over. I sorta looked bad ass.

Although I was extremely poor, I decided to splurge on an outfit that would dazzle the Paramount casting people: a short turquoise sweater and slim, tight turquoise jeans, size 2 or 4, with four-and-a-half-inch-high gray pointy-toed boots. My ass was the size of a 16-year-old boy's, but more curvy. In 1980 I had as close to perfect skin as a girl could have. I was 29 years old, although my agent thought I was 23. I didn't correct him and besides, the DMV had screwed up the date on my driver's license. Instead of putting my correct birth date 1951, they put 1957.

Steve sent the script over so that I could learn the lines I needed for the audition. I worked hard on them, and I felt awesome. Oh yeah, and although I thought *Star Trek* was lame, I'd seen all the TV episodes because Bob loved them and I liked lying around with him watching TV. By proxy, I knew everything about *Star Trek*, but mostly Spock, who was the only character I paid attention to. I liked his "no emotion" dilemma.

It turned out Steve Dontanville was partly wrong: I was going out for the role of Lieutenant Saavik, a half Vulcan, half Romulan. So here was this girl, half Vulcan, no emotion, half Romulan, known for anger and rage. This had the makings of one hot-tempered sociopath.

I was stoked. I could also emulate Spock, as one of my eyebrows naturally arches up when I speak, especially if I'm querying something, and I had dark hair and, and, and . . .

It dawned on me driving to my first interview, *Seriously, who the hell could play this better than I?* My answer was no one.

I drove to Paramount, long boob-length hair blowing in the wind, top down on my Toyota convertible with the $16,000 stereo called my car, wearing a turquoise sweater, little turquoise jeans, big turquoise sunglasses, and spike heels. That day, I was one badass bitch and no one was gonna take down this role but me.

I gave them my name at the guard gate at the gloriously infamous Paramount studios. The guard said, "Yes, Miss Alley, here is your parking pass." "Miss Alley." Oh jeez, my Romulan blood was beginning to boil, in a good way.

Here I was, this girl from Kansas who, a year and a half before had been a cocaine addict in Wichita. Here I was with my parking pass, and guards calling me "Miss." It was explosive.

I started across the lot in my four-and-a-half-inch heels and my little-assed jeans. He'll never remember this, but Eddie Murphy walked past me, and I think he checked out my fine ass. Anyway, I pretended he did, which gave me even more confidence.

I walked into the casting agent's waiting room, and the receptionist asked me to take a seat. There were only about three other girls in there. This is when I decided to do something that I have done in every waiting room with every actress over the last 30 years. I beamed them. I just looked straight at each girl with my green eyes and got the idea of boring a hole in their brain with the concept, *Yes, I'm a badass, and you don't have a prayer in hell of getting this role, so you might as well pick your ass up off that chair and head on outta here.* I accompany this high beam with a smirky smile that makes Jack Nicholson look like a schoolgirl. It worked then and has since. I feel them quiver, quake, and begin to dismantle themselves. I've never revealed this weapon, trick, evil intention, whatever the hell it is. It's just my own private Idaho when I go on auditions.

Don't feel too sorry for the other actresses. Believe me, I learned this trick the hard way, from some of the most ruthless brain-beaming actresses in Hollywood. It's an old trick, really.

"Kirstie Alley? They'll see you now," said the receptionist.

Oh god, how I hated the sound of my name rolling off her tongue.

Two syllables and two syllables, Kir-stee Al-lee. How stupid, the sound of my name. Not like the actresses I adored, Meryl Streep, two syllables then one syllable. E-liz-a-beth Tay-lor, four syllables and two syllables. Cath-er-ine De-neuve, three syllables and two syllables. See what I'm saying here? Kir-stie Al-lee: two syllables and two syllables, almost rhyming, for god's sake, and sing-songy, as my third-grade teacher had said in criticism of my poetry. I thought long and hard about changing my name to a different-syllabled combination: Kirstie Streep? Too obvious. Khristina McKay? Too *Wide World of Sports*. Kirstie Collette, my name combined with my sister's—yet still stupid because two syllables and two syllables, and not in a cool way like Mar-lon Bran-do.

Nick Meyer, the director of *Star Trek II: The Wrath of Khan*, offered his hand for me to shake.

The casting director said, "Nick, this is Kir-stie Al-lee." My confidence took a slight dip, but I feigned holding it together.

What I wasn't aware of was that Nicholas Meyer would become the first champion of my acting career.

Nicholas Meyer was cool-looking, with jet-black hair and cool blue eyes. He wasn't tall, but he was one of those guys that exuded stature and, god help me, mega-intelligence. He was intimidating, in-tim-i-dat-ing—five syllables.

He was also a genius. His IQ would have made any Mensa member quail. And he had a charismatic, glorious smile. Thank god I knew my lines cold, because the sight and presence of him would have given me early onset amnesia.

"So Kirstie [Al-lee]." He didn't say my last name, but he didn't have to, it was implied, "Where are you from?"

"Wichita, Kansas."

This was the time in my life when I was very clearly a Kansas girl. Many Kansas people do not extend answers to questions. Examples: "How are you?" "Fine." "You like it here?" "Yes." "How long have you lived here?" "A year." "What do you think about Hollywood?" "I like it."

So this was the entirety of my interview with Nicholas Meyer. Shockingly, he said, "Okay, let's read this." And we did.

Up went my eyebrow, curbed was my emotion, with just a hint of rage underneath. Yet when we got to the last scene, where Spock dies, I had a light mist in my eyes (contrived) and a slight break in my voice.

"Hmmm, I liked that," Mr. Meyer said. "Can you come back Wednesday?"

Can I? Can I? Can I? Yes, I can—Yes I CAN!

• • •

"How'd it go?" my nonsigning agent asked when I got home and called him. There were no cell phones in 1980, so you had to drive all the way home to tell your agent the good or bad news.

"How'd it go? It went great!" I said. "They want me back on Wednesday."

"Okay," he responded. "I'll call the casting director and get the time."

There were no computers in 1980, no Google or IMDb. There was no hotline into what the directors had done, or whom they were married to, or what schools they went to. It never crossed my mind to research directors or producers because things like that didn't exist at that time. There may have been some actresses who were more savvy than I was, but I certainly wouldn't have thought of it. I just ate a lot of pineapple and worked out like a lunatic and studied my lines.

I had a date later that week with a guy who was ultrahandsome and had been asking me out a lot. He was hard to resist because he was seriously hot, but I kept turning him down, and unlike most boys I turned down, I told him the truth. "I'm up for this role in a movie, and I don't wanna blow it. I don't want to drink or stay out late, I just want to get this role." He was an actor who had done his fair share of work, so he would laugh and flirt and say, "You can do both, you know." I would whinny like a horse and respond, "Let me just get this role and then we'll go out." He was very hard to resist, but I vowed to stay steady on the course, be good, keep my integrity, and *Rocky* my way to triumph.

I read for Nicholas on Wednesday. He had more people in the room, most of whom were producers. He smiled, he was happy. Oh, and I wore the same turquoise sweater and tiny turquoise jeans. I had no money, and it was the only sexy outfit I had.

He asked if I could come back a week from Friday and read again. "Yes, I can!"

By Monday of that week and after a very long boring weekend alone, working out and eating pineapple, actor boy called. John was his real name (and probably still is).

"You wanna go out Friday?" I thought, *What the hell*, I will have already read my final time for *Star Trek* earlier on Friday, and I would want to celebrate and make out with John and eat something, anything other than pineapple.

"Okay, cool, we'll go out on Friday."

"Eight?"

"Perfect."

I spent all week exercising, working on my scenes, and eating papaya. On Friday I picked up my turquoise outfit from the cleaners. I was now superstitious about it and decided to just keep wearing what was successful.

On Friday I did my final reading, and I nailed it. Nicholas was amazing. He was sweet and professional and presented me to all the new producers like I was a seasoned actress. Nicholas knew I had never had a single job as an actress, and I'm sure he was smart enough to know that everything on my résumé was a lie—all my "productions" of fake plays and all my "film parts" in Kansas, for god's sake, that never existed—and yet he still presented me like I was a great actress and a pro.

I HAD done a great job on that reading. Nicky told me I did, and I could perceive that glorious energy that flies around the room when people are really interested in you.

I felt so happy, so proud of myself that I'd worked so hard on the script and had forgone parties and bad food to get that role. My integrity was intact. I hung my turquoise outfit in the closet; it was like my talisman. It hugged me tight and carried me through the auditions. Yes, I'd earned the date that I was going on in six hours, and I was also getting a free meal at a nice restaurant, and I was fucking hungry!!!

I got all fixed up, fresh clothes, not my "uniform" that I'd joked with Nicholas Meyer about in my meeting earlier that day. I told him it was the only thing he would see me in until I donned a *Star Trek* outfit, so could he please speed it up. I was ridiculously happy.

At about seven o'clock I started feeling really weird. I couldn't tell if I had food poisoning, which was doubtful since I'd had no food. Then

I began feeling really anxious, like I was going to have an anxiety attack. It escalated. God, it felt like what I envisioned a nervous breakdown feeling like. Shit, I was going nuts or getting ready to have a stroke or coming down with some bizarre strain of exotic papaya disorder.

I went in and lay down on my bed. It was getting really bad, and I was getting scared. I gave my roommate, Alice, John's phone number and asked her to call him and apologize. I begged her to let him know I really was sick and wasn't faking and felt horrible about canceling. She came in afterward and said he was cool and that he said if I needed anything to let him know. Jeez, cool, hot, AND considerate? There I was, ready for the asylum.

About 30 minutes later, Alice walked in and told me my sister was on the phone. I said, "Oh god, tell her I'm sick and I can't talk right now." But my sister said, "Get her on the phone!!"

She told me our parents had been in a car wreck; that our mother was dead and our father was in the hospital dying.

Suddenly, everything went still. There was no more anxiety, no more instability, no more sickness, just dead calm. As horrifying as it was, my perception now matched the truth, and I understood what had happened.

I don't have a perfect recall of all of the next week because it felt like being swept up in some time-stopping bog where every moment was in slow motion. I flew all night to get to Kansas, on borrowed money.

It took three or four planes to get to Wichita, which is ironic since Wichita is the "Air Capital of the World." I didn't speak to any of the people who sat next to me on any of the legs. I couldn't speak and I couldn't hear. My only interest was getting home.

What do you do when parents die? You do what adult children of dead parents do: you make arrangements. Our mother was dead, but our father was struggling for his life. So we straddled that fence of making arrangements and grieving for our dead mother and spending the rest of our time by our dad's side at the hospital.

On one of those days, it seemed like a Monday, my agent called me. Not because he knew what happened but because he needed to schedule yet another audition for fucking *Star Trek*. Oh my god, I'd forgotten all about *Star Trek* and Hollywood and agents and Nicholas Meyer and countless producers and the pearly gates of Paramount.

"Steve, my parents were in an accident, my mom died. My dad is in intensive care, and I can't come back for a meeting."

Steve was shocked, of course, and very sad and respectful of me but he was, after all, an agent.

"They want you Wednesday for the final audition with all the producers and all the brass at Paramount. This is the critical meeting and the last audition. It is between you and two other girls." I told him that my mother's funeral was on Wednesday and that my father could be dying and that I would not be going to LA until after my mother's funeral and unless my father was out of intensive care and doing well.

Steve said, "Okay, let me figure this out. I'm not going to tell them about your parents. You have never had a part, you aren't even in the Screen Actors Guild, for god's sake, and you just lost your mother. There is no way Paramount studios will ever entrust a forty-million-dollar movie to an actress with all that shit happening in her life."

I said, "Steve, as soon as my father is out of intensive care I will fly to Los Angeles. You tell them that. You tell them I want this more than anything but not more than I want to see my dad well."

He said, "You're not gonna get it, then," and I said, "I understand." And then I laughed, "*I* wouldn't even hire me."

So Steve called them and told them the whole story, and Nicholas Meyer said, "We will wait for her."

When Steve told me this, for the first time since the accident I fell apart. I could not believe the kindness and the humanity of Nicholas Meyer, the producers, and Paramount studios. You hear lots of horror stories about Hollywood; I'm happy to say I've never encountered them. Can you imagine the sheer gratitude that I experienced when these powerhouses, knowing full well what had happened, sweetly said they would wait for me?

I was shattered in the best possible way I could have been shattered. The juxtaposition was mind boggling.

I came to my senses and thought, *By God, if those people can be so nice to me right now, I can do my part to make this go right for them.*

I grabbed my eight-by-ten head shot and drove to the hospital. I walked into the intensive care unit and held up the glossy for my dad to see. He was on morphine, and I assumed he was unconscious. But I was banking on the power of the soul. I was betting that I could reach way in there and appeal to the being who is my dad.

"Daddy," I said with the photo held in front of him, "I have a chance to be a movie star, and I really want to be a movie star, but unless you get well fast and get out of here I'm going to miss this opportunity. Thank you."

At 2:00 a.m. my father pulled out all of his tubes. His doctor called me and said, "The son of a bitch pulled all the damn tubing out so we are going to watch him and see how he does."

The next day, they wheeled my dad out of the ICU. He looked at me and said, "So you're going to be a star."

Never underestimate the thinking capacity of an injured or unconscious person. The body might be unconscious, but the being is not. And I guess you should also never underestimate the strength and determination of an actress. We make sharks look like kittens.

We chose the casket and arranged the service for my mother. I had the horrible task, against my will, of telling my father that my mother was dead. But it was part of what children must do when parents die, and when our family needs us.

My brother, my sister, and I attended the funeral without my father. When I flew back to LA the next day to audition one last time, I felt a resolve that I've rarely felt. If I got the movie, swell. If I didn't, I was moving back to Kansas to be with my dad for the rest of his life. I really didn't care which way it went but I was hoping to have it all.

This audition was different than the rest, other than my turquoise sweater and tiny jeans. There was no chitchat, and a quiet reverence hung in the air. I began, and the last scene I read was Spock dying. When I teared up this time, it was real. Somehow my performance was flawless.

Nick said, "Thank you, please wait out in reception."

I did. Less than five minutes later Nicholas called me back in the audition room. "You got it, kid. The part is yours." I broke down and sobbed.

This was the best Hollywood story in Hollywood.

"Now get back to Kansas and take care of your dad," Nick said.

To have been championed as Nick Meyer and all those Paramount bigwigs championed me was uncanny. To know the pressure a seasoned actress would be in under normal circumstances taking on the lead in a $40 million film is one thing. But to hire a first-time actress who just lost her mother in a tragic accident was nothing short of extraordinary.

It is impossible for me to express the gratitude I feel for Nicholas Meyer. He is brave. He is the true definition of a champion. I am forever indebted to my little turquoise pants and to Nicholas Meyer. Thank you. Against all odds you chose me. I will never forget you.

> Don't leave a piece of jewelry at his house
> so you can go back and get it later. He
> may be with his real girlfriend.
>
> —AMY SEDARIS

The Art of Shagging Next-Door Neighbors

THIS IS another one of those stories I've told before but COME ON! This book is about how men have influenced my life! I would be remiss to leave this humiliating gem out of my jewelry box.

Seven hundred and fifty dollars was the price tag of the little suede pants that were tugging at my heart strings. They were fawn-colored, slightly rough suede with long fringe all the way from waist to ankle on the outside seams. Low-cut, lined with buckskin-colored silk, size 2.

I had gotten my first movie, *Star Trek II*, and was paid a little money, so although $750 was still outside my price range, I knew I would not, at least, go without food as I'd done in the past when something had struck my fancy.

I had an enormous crush on an actor from the movie *Animal House*. We'll just call him Tim Matheson because that is his name.

Tim and I had several odd dates. When I look back on it, I believe I was the "I don't really have another date, so I'll call her" girl. At times it seemed we were quite smitten with each other, but he was never as smitten with me as I was with him.

I'm more than willing to be self-deprecating when I relay my stories, but I don't like to speak about other people unkindly. However, I consider Tim fair game.

Tim had asked me out for New Year's Eve. Now, this was a huge step in our weird relationship. New Year's Eve is a coveted date slot and we girls are no dummies—we know the significance of a New Year's Eve date. It means you're practically married.

Tim called: did I want to go out the night before New Year's Eve, also? It was his birthday, the eve before New Year's Eve. Okay, now I was the gangster of love! I was not the expert of trysts, but wow, the night before New Year's Eve, his birthday, AND New Year's Eve? He was clearly my next husband, right? He said, "Yeah, then let's go somewhere New Year's DAY!" It seemed that old Timmy boy had fallen as hard as I had, after all. It seemed inevitable that it was only a matter of time before I became Mrs. Animal House, Mrs. Tim.

Tim and I actually looked like brother and sister. We both had dark hair and light eyes and black lashes and brows. We were both tall, with good teeth and nice smiles. Mine wasn't as flashy as his, but this is my story. Our *Animal House* children would, without a doubt, look like clones of us, as we looked like clones of each other.

I went back to the little suede pants shop and resplurged on a sweater to accompany the little suede pants. It was a sort of raspberry-colored mohair with raspberry-colored fox fur inset into the shoulders of the sweater—I wasn't a card-carrying member of PETA yet, so please forgive me. Remember, this was the early eighties, and shoulder pads ruled. But these raspberry fox–adorned shoulders didn't need pads.

They were so fluffy on their own that they achieved double-shoulder-pad status. My flat, hard, tan stomach peeked out from the two-inch gap between the raspberry sweater and little suede pants. Raspberry fox sweater—$545. Then there were those boots I'd seen at Fred Segal. Raspberry kid-leather four-inch heels, inside zipper from ankle to knees. Raspberry boots—$375. Underwear—raspberry lace bra and bikini pants, add an additional 200 bucks. My assistant Kelly makes fun of me every time I say "bikini pants," but that's what we called them back then. Perfume—the only kind I wore was Casaque, clean yet hauntingly sexy—$100 an ounce.

Tim did not have to pick me up for his birthday date, our pre–New Year's Eve date, as Tim lived next door to me. That's sort of how I met him, and that's what we really had most in common: our addresses.

Chestnut perfectly waved and ringleted hair down my back, raspberry fur sex-kitten sweater, little suede pants, raspberry killer boots with four-inch heels, yummy lingerie, and sensual scented Casaque—that, all topped off with tons of black Bridget Bardot eyeliner and pale, very pale titty-pink lip gloss. No wonder Animal House was hot on my trail—damn booty—I was one of Hollywood's finest up-and-coming ingenues, although I was 30 years old. But everyone thought I was 23. I liked to keep telling myself that.

I strolled next door to Tim's. We had Champagne and laughed that giddy Champagne laughter. He took me out to dinner and then, of course, we came back to his place. Tim and I were pretty excellent lovers, really; we had no trouble getting on the same wavelength. Tim lit a fire in his bedroom. It was a funny house—his bedroom was upstairs but was the ONLY thing upstairs. No halls, no guest rooms, just one big bedroom with a master bath attached. It was a tricked-out expensive house. Tim had worked a lot and was not short on funds. It was unlike the small house that my two roommates and I rented next door. Tim's house was the pièce de résistance of the block, and it also had a lot of land, I'd say about three acres.

As I stood in front of his fireplace in his upstairs-only bedroom, I stealthily peeled off my raspberry fox sweater, then unzipped my little suede pants and pulled them over my kid-leather raspberry four-inch-heeled fuck-me boots. There I stood, raspberry boots, bra, and bikini—PANTS. Raspberries took on a whole new meaning.

Tim and I made passionate love, then Tim served up a tray of fine pastries from Michel Richard. We decadently lay there dining on éclairs, napoleons, and petits fours. It was 30 minutes until midnight—30 minutes until Animal House became a year older.

But I got a weird feeling in my gut. Not like an "I've just been laid feeling"—no, something much different. A sort of nervousness, like when my mother had been killed in a car wreck. I excused myself to the restroom. I was pacing about for a while, trying to figure out why I was nervous, yet still noticing my fabulous, just-laid tousled hair trailing down almost to my waist. I thought, *Damn, I look good after sex, damn!*

I noticed outside the window that I could see my roommate Callie talking on the phone in our house next door. It made me laugh—here I was naked and had just been banged, and there she was yapping away on the phone to god-knows-who, slurping down a Diet Coke with lime. I tapped on Tim's window and tried to get her attention, stupidly thinking she would hear me and look up. She didn't, and she didn't. I'd calmed down a little bit, didn't feel quite so anxious, so I went back into the bedroom to be with Animal House. Five minutes until showtime. Five minutes until Tim's birthday.

I sat on the edge of his bed naked, *Barbarella*-haired and all. He lay on the bed naked with my hair cascading down his chest.

"Tim," I said. "I think I should go home, I feel a little weird."

"Oh come on, Kirstie," he said, "it's almost midnight, it's almost my birthday. Stay all night with me, let's make love again as my birthday present." One minute 'til midnight.

Oh Tim, oh Animal House, oh you black-haired, blue-eyed god of col-

lege girls everywhere—of course I'll stay and birthday-fuck your brains out. I'm falling in love with you, Animal House, truly I am and you've become awfully interested in me lately. Of course I'll stay, hell I'll stay forever and forever. I can watch my ex-roommate Callie talking on the phone each night out our bathroom window in my old rented house next door!

We began to kiss a deep, hot, desperate kiss of young, deep, hot desperate lovers. Bong, bong, bong, bong, bong, bong, bong, bong, bong, bong, bong, bong. The clock downstairs in Tim's living room struck midnight. I came up for air. "Happy birthday, baby—happy birthday." Yes, Tim was riveted by me, mesmerized by my wonderfulness. I had him in my tight little grasp. He was quivering, smitten with my majestic beauty and expertise lovemaking.

Just then I heard something way out of context. *Knock, knock, knocking on heaven's door.*

"Tim?" this voice said.

"Lissette?!" Tim nervously blurted out.

I sat up and turned my body to the left. There stood this beautiful blonde girl.

"Tim?!" she said, more desperately.

"Lissette?!!" he said more horrifyingly. It was a very bad rendition of George and Marsha. I decided, as I was between Lissette and Animal House, to become invisible. So I did. I just made myself invisible. I disappeared into another dimension. *God, Tim, say something besides "Lissette" for Christ's sake. Say, hey, get outta here—say, who the hell are you? Or what are you doing in my house? Say something, say something, I can't stay invisible much longer.*

Lissette ran down the stairs in a burst of hysteria and screaming, "Oh my god, oh my god, how could you do this?!!" Tim was up in a flash, frantically putting on his jeans.

He said to me, "Stay here, don't leave." Hmm, *stay here, don't leave?* Remember Tim's bedroom is the only room upstairs? Was I going to leisurely saunter down the stairs to greet a hysterical Lissette who would possibly pull out a knife and stab me?

Yes, Timmy boy, I'll most certainly stay right here, but hey, who in the hell is Lissette anyway?

I put on my raspberry lingerie, my raspberry mohair fox-trimmed sweater, my soft kidskin raspberry four-inch-heeled boots, and finally my beloved little suede pants with the delicate long strips of suede fringe dripping down from my thighs to my ankles.

I could make out some of what pretty Lissette was saying: *Engaged.* "Engaged" was the word that specifically stuck in my mind. And "How the fuck could you cheat on me like this?" was another show-stopper.

Tim was screaming, "I'm sorry, I'm sorry, calm down, I'm sorry." Lissette was screaming at the top of her beautiful blonde lungs. Then she ran outside and her wails trailed off.

A perfect time for my exit, I thought. *I'll just run down the stairs, out of the house and quickly fly inside my rented house.* I began my descent, but whoa, Lissette was back. The wailing was coming closer and closer, *damn*! They were back in the house. I hauled ass back up the stairs into Tim's infidelity love nest.

This scenario occurred over and over—in and out, in and out of the house Lissette went like some misguided cuckoo clock. I became desperate, choking for oxygen. It was surely only a matter of time before Lissette went totally psychotic and decided to take her pain out on the bitch upstairs who was screwing her fiancé! It turned out that beautiful blonde Lissette was actually engaged to Animal House and that she had traveled all the way from New York City to stand in her soon-to-be betrothed's front yard and wait until the clock struck midnight, then bound in and wish Tiny Tim a happy birthday! How the hell any bitch could or would trust ole Timmy boy is beyond me, but apparently Ms. Soon-To-Be Tim did, and in fact, she truly believed he would just be waiting like a good little boy on a Saturday night, all snuggled in his footie jammies, drinking hot chocolate and eating animal crackers.

And what about him? Did it not occur to him that at least his fiancée would be giving him a call on his birthday?! And what the hell was he going to say he was doing the next night? New Year's Eve? Out with the boys? Home in bed again? What?!

Oh god, I had to get out of there, and pronto! I ran to the bathroom and looked out the window. Callie was still on the phone. A solution hit me like a ton of bricks. I'll have Callie bring a ladder over, and I'll go out the bathroom window while Lissette is wailing in the living room. Yes, yes, good plan. Good plan, Kirstie, good thinking even under extreme duress.

Dial 854-3317—beep, beep, beep, beep. *Damn busy, of course busy, I can see her mouth moving, for Christ's sake. Okay, emergency interrupt, that's it.*

"Hello, yes operator, I'd like to make an emergency interrupt to 854-3317. Yes, I'll hold. I'll hold."

But the operator said, "I'm sorry the party will not give up the line." And why wouldn't the party? Callie, my friend Terry, and I each made at least three emergency interrupts a day, trying to get the other of us to hang up the damn phone!

"Operator, please try again, please tell the party this is a real emergency—a real emergency and I must get through."

"I'm sorry, the party says they are in the middle of a conversation with a new hot guy and will not be able to give up the line at this time."

Fuck you, Callie, fuck you, fuck you, fuck you! Can't you see me in this window? Can't you tell a real emergency call from the countless fake emergency calls we make during the day? It's midnight, for fuck's sake. No one makes fake emergency calls at midnight, you fucking idiot!

How far down is it, anyway? If I jumped, I mean. Would I break something or only sprain something? Let's see, Lissette murdering me or a slightly sprained something—okay, I'll go with the sprain.

I opened the window, shimmied out in my little suede pants, hung on tight, and lower, lower, lowered myself. Thud, raspberry kid-leather boots four-inch heels, sucked three inches into the sod below, cushioned the blow. It was hard to pry those four inches out of the mud, and damn, one heel broke at the quick—shit! Raspberry mohair fox-appointed sweater—snagged on a holly bush. Stretched way, way out. Look to the left, look to the right, no Lissette, no Animal House, and I hobbled for my life next door.

Hobble, hobble, hobble, door locked. *Oh shit, door locked and purse is still in Tim's love den—shit!*

Around the side of the house to Callie's window, bam, bam, bam, bam, "Callie!" Loud whisper-scream so Lissette wouldn't hear me and proceed over yonder and beat the shit out of me.

I heard Callie: "Oh god, I've gotta get off the phone and call the police—someone is outside."

I was still pounding on the glass, wondering if blondes do have lower IQs. Around to the front door. Ding dong, ding dong, ding dong, as I peered into the entry hall door. I could see Callie crouched on the floor calling the police. *Oh god, Callie, you can't be this stupid, you really can't.*

Around to the back of the house I ran. Maybe we'd left the back door unlocked as usual. As I ran to the back door, the inevitable occurred—not Lissette as expected, no, something more lethal to little suede pants. The sprinkler went off. The sprinkler sprinkled my little suede pants until they were drenched and cold and sagged around my oh-so-perfect size-2 booty—like poopy diapers on a toddler.

The back door was unlocked. The police were called off. Lissette went back into Animal House's house and all was quiet this birthday eve. This eve of New Year's Eve.

Tim came over the next day and explained a few things, including he didn't really think it "appropriate" to have our New Year's Eve date now with Lissette and the engagement and all. You think so, mother-fucker? You really think it "inappropriate"?

Tim and Lissette were soon unengaged, and I was soon in love with another actor, trading Animal House in for a Hardy Boy.

Tim taught me something I could never have learned the easy way . . . don't trust actors no matter how many éclairs they offer you.

Art is what you can get away with.

—ANDY WARHOL

The Art of Anal Sex

"NO!"

I've already told you. The only way to
a woman's heart is along the path of
torture. I know none other as sure.

It is always by way of pain one
arrives at pleasure.

—MARQUIS DE SADE

The Art of Pain

THE ART of living with a perverted man is both precarious and
dangerous to the soul. Being with one is a bit like being owned
by a rabid dog, albeit with black latex. It's not my intention to "out"
the assholes who tried to destroy me—unless it makes for a funny
story. It's not my intention to make the girlfriends I confided in hate
the men who have done cruel or bizarre things to me—they already
hate them. I guess my intention is to warn women about men like this
next one.

At one time or another, most strong women are drawn to one of
these guys. If you LIVE through it, you will have funny stories to tell.
But most don't. This chapter is out of sequence. Kinda like my life was.

I'm the girl who developed the "one hit" theory at an early age. True, women can miscalculate the sanity of their male choices, but five minutes after he gives you that first hit, punch, trip, or shove, you should head on down the road.

There are, of course, exceptions to every rule. As an example, I've had two men hit me, well, sorta. One flogged me with a beach towel and the other slapped me after I slapped him in the face because he said Ann-Margret was sexy.

I've had men do the occasional "puffing up," like an ape. This posture makes a girl think the gorilla is going to give her a pounding if she doesn't shut up and stop taunting it. And yes, I've had the walls behind me slugged, instead of my face, which proved painful to the fists that mistook cement for Sheetrock.

There was the one guy who used to hit the bed close to where I was sitting, making it clear I was the real target and not the Tempur-Pedic. I also have to admit I've been grabbed hard a few times. But that's the extent of my male-inflicted physical abuse. I must admit reluctantly that I've given a few "reasons" to be more physically aggressive. When I go in for the kill I can antagonize a saint.

I remember when Parker was throttling me with a beach towel after he overheard me tell another actor "I love you" on the upstairs phone. While I was getting a soft thrashing I was thinking to myself, *Should I cry "abuse"?* My answer was no. If I were him, I'd have strangled me.

So, I can unequivocally say, I've never been physically abused by a man.

But the most damaging abuses, in my opinion, come in the form of invalidation, nullification, and trickery.

One man in my life was a master of said abuses to the nth degree. Let's just call him "Christian Black," for the sake of his undeserved anonymity.

Black was devastatingly handsome with a devastatingly enormous penis. He was a creative genius and unfathomably charismatic.

I've since learned from other powerful women that this is the lethal combination. If you throw in richer than dirt, it is the crowning blow. Black was not that, but he possessed the other qualities in spades.

I met him on the set of a famous TV series. I wasn't in the production; I was just visiting a friend.

If Black had lasers for eyes he would have bored a hole through my soul. Instead he just used his normal eyes and his devastating smile to lure me in his direction. All he said to me in that first encounter was "Hi, I admire your work."

Really? I thought, *I admire your Marlon Brando dimples. I have no idea who you are so I can't admire your work but I highly admire that you look like an aquiline Greek god.*

The next time I met Black was in the lobby of a hotel. I was leaving for Italy the next day to put a charity project together.

He walked right up to me. "Hi, remember me? I'm Black."

Wow!! Do I ever!! Of course I remember you! You're the most handsome man on earth, you crazy fool! As I came to my senses, I answered coyly "Oh, hi Black."

"May I sit down?" he politely asked.

"Of course," I coolly said.

"What are you working on?" he asked.

"Oh, I'm going to Italy tomorrow to do some charity stuff, and I'm trying to figure out the exchange rate of the dollar versus the lira." What transpired next was subtle, yet slightly insightful.

He said, "I'll come to Italy and help you."

I laughed, "Oh you will, will you?"

"Yes, I will." He smiled. "I like what you're doing. That's all. I'd love to help you," he said.

And there it was; hook, help, and sinker. I'd never had a man use "help" to lure me in.

I was curious about this "help" he had offered, and I showed him a map of all the places I was going in Italy. But I was running behind and had to get packed and do my errands before I departed, so I told him I had to leave.

At the end of our conversation he closed with "If you need any help, I'll come over at the drop of a hat."

And there it was again. He didn't have me at "hello," he had me at "help."

I turned down his offer, as I was already going to Italy with another man. I went to Italy for three months and forgot all about Christian Black.

So I did my charity work while I traversed Italy, giving the term "under the Tuscan sun" a new and dangerous meaning. The person I'd gone with threatened to break up with me, saying, "There is no oxygen in your universe, no room for *anyone* else." He was right; I had sucked up all the air and was fighting for more. When we got back from Italy, we broke up.

Black must have heard the rumor. He called me and asked me to come to his house to tell me about the Italy trip. I told him I was doing errands and could only stop by for a few minutes, but he said that worked out perfectly because he had to go to an event.

I was sitting on the edge of his bed as he was getting ready for his engagement. As he passed by me, he gave me our first kiss: a little tiny, soft kiss on the lips, followed by probably about nine little tiny rapid kisses, barely-touching-me kisses.

My first make-out encounters have always been, *There you are, here I am BAM!* Full-on making out.

But not from this gentleman. It threw me into a dreamy tailspin. I felt dizzy and in a slight drug delirium, like I'd just taken a couple of Quaaludes. My heart pounded like I'd been kissed for the first time. Then he was off. I just stayed still, perched on the edge of his bed. I sat there for a long time wondering *What the hell just happened?* I was under his gentle, charismatic spell.

If there's one thing I've learned about the "Blacks," it's that they are slow, gentle, subtle, and endearing. The agenda is laid out like sweet agave nectar—clean, clear, easily digested.

Perverted men never have a *P* branded on their foreheads. They've had lots of practice enticing butterflies into their web. Every step is calculated like lining up dominoes, delicately ensuring the rows don't topple into a cascading avalanche.

But how could I have known this? I was the girl who thought kinky sex was "doing it" any other way than missionary. I once had a guy smack me on the ass when we were kissing, and I fled his house immediately, knowing he was a perv. It helped that he whispered, "Daddy needs to spank his bad girl," but I had that radar, that instinctual red flag that pops up, that is innate in women. The flag that tells us this guy is nasty and this would be the tip of the nasty he'll become. I didn't hesitate with this guy, "Reed, I said I gotta go, I'm late."

Women have built-in danger barometers. Or it would seem. For the straight-up freaks, the antennae work well. But for the masters of sexual manipulation and deception it seems the bells, whistles, flags, and radar are rendered useless long before they go in for the kill. It's like the way a wave erodes a shoreline: it happens slowly, and then before you know it, the foundation of your house is crumbling.

Christian Black had a room in his house that was essentially a dungeon/shooting range combo. It was decorated with a dental-office chair, an S&M black leather swing, and other gadgets of pain. There were no windows . . .

"What the hell is this?" I asked when he took me in there on our first real "date" to shoot .22s in his basement firing range. Oh lord, at this point in the story I can hear all the girls who've fallen for this dude screaming, "Oh my god!! I used to date that guy! I know Black!!"

"Oh, this shit?" he laughed and explained. "I just did an indy film in here, just haven't gotten rid of it yet."

Phew, I thought, *phew!* What was I thinking? *Of course, that's it. There's the logical answer I needed. Phew!* I really did believe him. After all, he was the guy who had done nothing with me but give me nine tiny kisses, as gentle as a baby's kisses.

"When does the movie come out?" I asked.

"Um, uh, the movie should be released in about six months, a cool movie—I play a perv."

I teased, "Now, you're sure you're not into this kinky stuff, right?"

"Yeah, right! This is where I bring all my victims," he laughed.

He laughed. *My god, how funny my new love was. How funny and witty and handsome.* I hadn't seen his enormous dick yet, or I would have included that, too.

It all made sense to me, it truly did. S&M was so far from my reality that it wasn't even a thought. And zero flags went up, zero bells chimed, nary a bleep on my superb radar.

Just an acting role. Just an indy movie. Just a shooting range where we spent hours firing hundreds of rounds into paper targets. He didn't even kiss me.

I was madly in love. He was just mad.

The sick threads of his web had begun to attach to my mind.

He never did anything or tried to do anything to me with that equipment or in that room, which was further evidence he was telling the truth. He was a "good" guy. Or was he?

The first time we made love (I hate that term), it was mind- and body-blowing. He smelled like a combination of sugar and clean sweat. He was loving, gentle, and a bit of an expert. I remember vividly when I laid eyes on his cock-a-doodle do, I thought I had hit the mother lode. In my not-so-vast dick experience, I'd only encountered what I would call "regular dicks," not tiny (except for the hairless man), not huge, just regular, except Doug who had regular length but mighty girth.

But this thing was off the hook! At first I was afraid of it, like a mighty monster unleashed in the room. I wondered, *Will something like that fit in something like this?* But the prospect of it was exhilarating. I'd only heard stories of huge-dicked men like Lee Majors and John

Holmes . . . and all black men. I thought, *Well . . . either I'll die being ripped apart, which will make for a unique* Enquirer *story, or I'll figure how to work into it.* And you know, you DO have to work into it. Sorta like a born-again virgin, I was.

It was all straight-up, straight sex. Except for the adjustment of Black's blackman dick, it was same ole, same ole. Oh, and did I mention that he was really good at it? The best; no one else had ever come close. Wild and strong, he threw me around like I was Tiny Barbie. All was good in the big-dicked hood.

And this normal yet stunning sex went on every night for about three months. Tiny kisses, deep kisses, incredible, creative, passionate, "I love you more than I've ever loved anyone" sex.

I was at the top of my game in all senses. Hit movie, hit series, movies "on the table" for my hiatuses, in my prime, in my zone, madly, deeply in love.

As he began to make love to me on that November night right before Thanksgiving, I was at the pinnacle of love and trust for this man. *I've finally done it right*, I thought. *I never imagined life could be this unique and glorious*, and *I've finally found the person that I'm willing to do anything for. I'm willing to share the oxygen.*

As I was lying there in some lovesick delirium I felt his hand move around my throat. *Whoa, what's this?* I thought. Then his other hand slipped over my mouth while strategically pinching the air off in my nose. My first reaction was to start laughing; I just couldn't stop laughing and giggling because I couldn't imagine it was anything but a joke.

I remember the look in his eyes when he pulled back from me and asked, "Do you think this is funny?"

I immediately became introverted. *Oh, god, had I insulted him? Had I made him feel like I thought he was going to hurt me?*

"Er, uh, well, no, not funny, but it's uh, no, I don't think it's funny."

He put me in my place, didn't he?

But he wasn't hurting me, and we began making love again. His hand went back to my throat, his other hand across my mouth to keep me from breathing. There wasn't a lot of pressure on my throat—he wasn't actually choking me—but there was definitely too much pressure.

I kept fighting off laughing, but again I started giggling. I wasn't afraid at all. I just thought it was funny, that he was kidding me, playing with me. And again he drew back and asked, "Do you think this is funny?"

This time I couldn't stop laughing, and I said, "Well, it better be funny, or you're getting off on killing me!" Hahahahahaha.

His eyes looked like he snapped back into his head, like he snapped out of this peculiar trance.

He started laughing, too. "I'm just fucking with you!"

And I believed him.

Of course he was just fucking with me, otherwise I was with someone who liked choking women. Someone who got off on pretending he was killing women. Wow! Phew! That was a close call!

We giggled together and made love and slept like babies.

A few weeks later, there was that hand around my throat again, there was that trancelike look in his eyes, and there was that other hand cutting off my ability to breathe unless I turned my head and gasped for air. And after a few weeks of this, the girl who laughed before had changed. I didn't laugh. I didn't feel like laughing, and my thoughts had shifted to *I was too straight before. Too dull, too regular, too mainstream, not hip, not cool, not edgy, not Hollywood.*

And that seed that was forming inside my mind, like a malignant tumor, began to grow.

What was once funny and unreal began to be normal, escalating, and varied.

Bizarre sex toys, riding crops, weird role-playing, wigs.

We never spoke about it, and I never queried it. We began fighting, outrageous fights. At first I delighted in the fights, and anything became fair game, except physical abuse.

I felt like a modern-day version of George and Martha in *Who's Afraid of Virginia Woolf?* Our fights became epic! I'd never rolled like this! With other men I was analytical and civil. It seemed so boring compared to flipping tables over, crashing vases, clearing entire table-tops with my arms, screaming at the top of our lungs, and my favorite: bolting out of the house, yelling, "I'm fucking leaving you!"

The more bizarre our fights got, the more perverted our sex life became, including the "rules." Rule number one: What he did to me couldn't be done to him. I was tied up. He was not allowed to be. I was choked and "play" suffocated. Never him.

I followed the rules like a good little slave.

His secret weapons were:

1. You're getting fat.
2. You're older than I am.
3. Why are you wearing that?
4. Why don't you do what you did to me two weeks ago?

When I would say, "I don't remember what we did two weeks ago, could you tell me?" his answer was "No, if you can't remember what I like, then forget it." There were many more rules, equally lopsided.

He was insanely jealous of my fame, and he pouted or caused an enormous fight if I didn't wear hats, wigs, or dark glasses to conceal my identity when we were out.

He didn't like any of my friends, and he frequently protested that they all hated him. So he set about his agenda of culling me out of my herd so that I belonged only to him.

He made Mickey Rourke in *9½ Weeks* look like a novice.

I became introverted and diminished. What started as a wild, cool, controversial game was turning into a living hell. Every fight and every weird sexual experience was followed by "I love you, baby, you know that, right? You know how much I love you."

I would always answer the same thing, "Yes, I love you, too," with all the zeal of a zombified robot.

My daily routine was to go film. I'd get up in the morning, we would have an intense psychotic fight, and I would get in the car and cry and shake all the way to the studio. My driver, my assistant LeeAnn, would say the same thing every day: "You'll work it out, you always do." Ten minutes after I hit the studio, one of us would call the other and beg forgiveness and everything would fall calm again. I would have an amazing day filming, but every day one of the actresses would ask me, "Is someone hurting you?"

"Of course not, who? Who would be hurting me?" was my reply. Each day the actress would ask me this same question, trying desperately to get me to simply take a look at him. She never said his name or mentioned him in particular, just "is someone hurting you?"

But endless flowers, diamond-encrusted crowns, exotic gifts flooded my dressing room and life.

There were hundreds of perverse sexual encounters, all followed by me feeling more and more and more dead. It never dawned on me to tell anyone what was happening, because by then it was "normal." It was probably what every Hollywood couple did behind closed doors.

The only reason I'm not going into all the perverse details of my life with Black is because this book is not intended to be erotica.

My intention is to alert young girls and not-so-young alike to hold dear that keen antenna that warns you of danger and that it won't remain keen if you, yourself, chip away at it. I'm sure most thieves don't start by robbing banks; they start by stealing from their little sister. It's like acid erosion. The acid's intention is erosion. The perverted man's intention is to destroy the woman, second by second, minute by minute, slowly eroding her good sense, her morals, her soul. The target is not to sexually pervert her for the sake of sexual perversion. It is for the sheer pleasure of using sex as the tool to destroy her life.

These men know that they themselves are worthless with no power. They despise creativity, power, talent, and success in others, so they seek to destroy the other because she is a constant reminder of what he is not.

Beware the person who uses sex, drugs, and pain to dominate you. You are signing your own death certificate if you comply. And believe me, death is the goal, no matter how gentle the tiny kisses.

While with Black, I all but destroyed my career. His poison wreaked havoc on my body. I had four concussions, six bouts with pneumonia, injuries and types of accidents I've never had before, and countless weird illnesses.

I take full responsibility for my journey into hell. I spent a good three years making amends, rekindling all my friendships and rebuilding my life.

The more responsibility I took for what I had become, the more well I became.

I'm a lucky person. I reestablished my relationships, and they grew stronger than before.

I have not seen "Black" since I walked out the door. The only time I hear about him is in a phone call or letter from one of his unfortunate subsequent victims.

He was not, and is not, unique. He represents all men like himself whose destiny includes the destruction of women.

His existence in my life is only relevant to me helping other women, especially young women. Especially in a society and within a time that glorifies men like these in novels, movies, and television.

Right and wrong do exist in this universe, and the way to prove it is to observe one's happiness at any given moment. Right decisions create life, love, beauty, and solutions. Wrong ones create chaos, pain, and death, if only of the mind and spirit.

To suppose that men like Christian Black are heroes and role models is as ludicrous to the outcome of a woman's life as is the notion that Ted Bundy was a nice man, other than killing all those girls.

I think it's important for women to be aware of men like these and the real damage they cause when they affix themselves to you. They are calculating. They are lifeless. Black's real name has no importance. He exists only if I let him. He only existed because I allowed him to. I harbor no animosity.

He is invisible to me now.

Why slap them on the wrist with a feather when you
can belt them over the head with a sledgehammer.

—KATHARINE HEPBURN

The Art of Closure

PARKER IS the man I spent the most years with. I dated him
for two years and was married to him for fourteen. During
those years, I experienced the most stability, the most peace, the most
gentleness, the most learning. Yet Parker is the love of my life whom I
know and understand the least. Parker was and to this day remains an
enigma.

I was 30 years old, and I'd just been told I was starring in my first
movie. It was my first real job as an actress. The night before I began
filming *Star Trek II: The Wrath of Khan*, I decided to go out and celebrate instead of learning my lines, a very bad habit that has remained
with me through my entire career.

I was, of course, on top of the world! I was the James Cameron of
women. I was the "Queen of the World!"

My girlfriend Mimi Rogers and I started off at a chic, hip restaurant
in West Hollywood called Kathy Gallagher's.

Mimi and I walked in, dressed to the nines. I'm five foot eight and she's five-nine. We had no question about "if we were pretty," and the adrenaline surging through me knowing I was the female lead of a $40 million film in 1981 was, in itself, an aphrodisiac.

Our table wasn't ready, so Mimi and I perched ourselves at the bar, directly in front of the entrance doors. There was a huge mirror covering the wall in front of us, behind the bar.

We had been sitting there for about 10 minutes when my attention went to the reflection in the mirror. Parker Stevenson, his best friend, Wally, and two blondes were walking in. It was like time stopped. I'd never seen eyes that blue. Parker gave a new meaning to the word "stunner." I paid no attention to the date he had on his arm. After all, I was 14 hours away from being a movie star. I kept my eyes focused on him, and out of the corner of my mouth I whispered to Mimi, "For him, I would die."

I don't think he saw me or noticed me at all. The maitre d' escorted the quartet to a nearby table. When the maitre d' led Mimi and me to our table, we had to pass Parker's. I've been told since I was five years old that I have "bedroom eyes," so I tried to flash the bedroom eyes at Parker when I walked by his table, but he was consumed with Blondie.

Kathy Gallagher's was the stomping ground of young actors, directors, and pervs. It was a restaurant, but also the gateway to the after-hour hubs, sort of the Stargate to the stars.

Mimi and I were whooping it up with the likes of 10 or 15 well-known movie and TV personalities. Nonstop flirting was the agenda (and remains the agenda to this day in hip Hollywood hot spots). Kathy's wasn't a meat market, per se, just a portal to the next location.

This guy heads for our table. It's Wally, Parker's best friend. "We're going to the Daisy after dinner, if you girls wanna join in, come on by." Wally wasn't talking to me, either; he knew one of the other girls at our table.

I casually asked my new "connection" after Wally left, "So, um, who's that guy with that guy who just left the table?" To this day Parker doesn't know that I asked about him.

"Oh, that's Parker Stevenson. You know who Parker Stevenson is, right?"

"Yes! He was the star of a John Knowles novel-turned-feature-film."

"You idiot!!! He's one of the Hardy Boys!" she said.

"I know that," I quipped. But I didn't really. I remembered him from the movie *A Separate Peace* in a riveting performance as the troubled, introverted Gene. And I remembered trying to decide which WASP I had a bigger crush on—Gene or Phineas.

"So! You guys want to swing by the Daisy after dinner?" the blonde clone of all blonde California bombshell clones asked.

I gave my typical noncommittal answer, "Maybe." Maybe? Maybe, my ass! If I could have had Scotty beam me up to the Daisy I would have already been waiting there an hour early to greet Parker Stevenson at the door!

Wow! I knew it was going to take some hooch to relax me a little. Take the edge off, cool my jets, whatever you wanna call it. So I began drinking. It worked, I got a little buzz, and my fake confidence started to kick in. About two hours later, over walked Wally, Parker, and their two blondies. "So, you guys gonna come to the Daisy?" Wally asked our table's spokesperson. She replied, "Yes, I think we might stop by." It seemed Parker made eye contact with me, yet because my eyes were slightly glassy by then, it was hard to tell. But maybe he thought my bedroom eyes were ultrabedroomy . . .

About an hour later my friends and I, all girls, came flying into the Daisy. I'd left my car parked in Kathy Gallagher's parking lot because I was too buzzed to drive. I get buzzed on half of a drink, so whenever I drink ANYTHING I don't drive.

The Daisy was hopping, filled with famous actors, sports figures, blonde clones, and the usual clubbers. Mimi and I sat at a table with a few girls, the tennis pro Spencer Segura, and some other rich guy whose family owned everything Doheny. Doheny Drive, Estates, and Mansion. Ned was a real rich guy—a real rich, drunk guy.

I couldn't see Parker and his blonde Barbie anywhere, but I was getting a lot of attention, as someone, not me I swear, brought up *Star Trek* and that every ingenue in town wanted that role. This chitchat boosted my ego and confidence even more.

Then it began: the blonde waitress saying, "Round of drinks from Mr. Stevenson," as she lay a silver tray of tequila shots on the table. I was honestly, at this point, so full of booze that I became confused as to whether it was me Parker was interested in or one of the four hot girls sitting at the table with me, including my hottest, best friend, Mimi Rogers. Another round came, then another. I was filled with curiosity real, fake, and chemically-induced. I excused myself from the table, walked to Mr. Stevenson's table, politely thanked him, took his hand, and said, "I want to talk to you." I walked him to the dance floor and we began to dance. It was some awful '80s tune. Then out of the blue I just grabbed him and shoved my tongue down his throat. It was a terrific icebreaker, and I thought it was a good way to find out if it was me he was interested in.

Then I did something I've never done before or since. His date came up to Parker and said, "We're leaving." I didn't even let Parker speak. I said, "That's cool, 'cause Parker's leaving, too—with me."

What??!! Seriously???

I'd never been that brazen. I was the girl who sat around aloof, beaming men with my bedroom eyes, then looking away.

I know by today's "let's all get drunk and fuck everybody" standards this seems tame, but to me, it was monumental! All Lombard and Gable! Now I was doing what REAL actresses do!

Parker didn't protest. He apparently thought I was the cat's meow. Actually, I think he thought he was going to have a three-way with Mimi and me.

When we got to the parking lot of the Daisy he said, "Where's your car?" I'd honestly forgotten, and so had Mimi. But then I remembered that it was at Kathy Gallagher's.

He said, "Why don't you guys come to my place for a drink?" Yes! Because I really need *more* alcohol . . .

We walked into swank Shoreham Towers, behind swank Spago, Wolfgang Puck's first swank LA restaurant. Parker's penthouse was straight-up *9½ Weeks*, all gray flannel, Le Corbusier chairs, gray on gray on gray—on gray.

This Kansas girl had never seen nothin' like this.

When Mimi excused herself to the restroom, Parker said, "I'd like you to stay. I'll have a cab take Mimi home. I'll take you to your car tomorrow."

What?! I may be an actress, but I'm no LA ho. I don't do one night stands, Daddio . . . well at least not since that guy with the toddler dick, I thought. "I'm so sorry, I just can't, I have to be at Paramount at eight tomorrow morning."

How freakin' fun was that to say?! I was born for this movie star lingo.

I kissed him good night. He said, "Can I have your number?"

"Sure," and I gave it to him. Mimi was sober by the time the cab drove us back to Kathy Gallagher's to get my car, and I was sober-ish, too.

The parking lot was locked! I started to panic. Mimi said, "Just take a cab in the morning," which was now four hours away. That gave me two hours to sleep and two hours to get showered and changed. Cabs in LA, by the way, are expensive. Not like the $10 fares in NYC. So I woke up at 6:00 a.m. and in true Hollywood fashion, called Paramount studios and asked them to "send a car for me." Those were the good ole days, my friends, no questions asked. They sent a car for me.

Parker and I began dating immediately, not exclusively but frequently. He had some mud wrestler and an Italian contessa on the side, and I had a famous actor and an ex-boyfriend on the side.

After six months of dating, I THOUGHT we were exclusive. Apparently half of us weren't, so I almost broke up with Parker. It shattered me and led to an insanely long grudge. Probably THE most important lesson I've learned about men is that if they cheat on you, you either work it out and forgive them—I mean TRULY forgive them—or you end it. I stayed midway, in a split decision. "I love you, I forgive you, not really, but I'll try to, not very hard, and we'll move on, no fucking way, I'll make you suffer for a very long time." And for a very long time I did. I never fully trusted him, and I gave him plenty of reason to stop trusting me.

Still, Parker and I eloped in 1983 to Neil and Leba Sedaka's house in Westport, Connecticut. I was midway through shooting a TV series and we had a few weeks off for Christmas. I'd been married before, and we didn't have time for a proper wedding with both sides of our families flying to wherever. So we decided to elope to Connecticut, then drive to Philadelphia to be with his family for Christmas.

We got married on the morning of December 23, 1983, and our justice of the peace was a woman who read Kahlil Gibran. Leba Sedaka had made the house into a fantasyland. There was a crystal-adorned Christmas tree, and the setting looked like *Dr. Zhivago* meets Currier & Ives.

As we were about to get married, the snow turned to rain, and Neil Sedaka stood before us and sang "Laughter in the Rain." His audience was just me, Parker, Leba, the justice of the peace, and Kahlil Gibran. An hour after we married I called my dad. He was happy for us; he loved Parker.

Parker and I were polar opposites. I'm rowdy and impatient. He's conservative and "lovely." I use that word in quotes because Parker used to use it a lot to describe things, "It's lovely." I'm a Kansas girl, and I'd never heard a man say the word "lovely," but I found it refreshing, artistic, and "lovely."

We first moved into a Richard Meier–type white-on-white-on-white modern house. It was a sexy house, and it looked like it was built for adult brats. We fit the bill.

Our relationship was interesting: we were close but not close. We were always friendly and respectful, but we were not each other's confidants. I don't recall us discussing the deeper aspects of life. Both of us were always busy working, and my career was on a full-fledged roll. I bounced from movies to miniseries to movies to *Cheers*. Parker and I had our share of ups and downs, but mostly it felt safe and consistent. People like me can do with a little conservatism in their lives. If you hooked people like me up with other people like me it could end in a free-for-all.

Parker had gone to Princeton, and he was a preppy guy. He had been in a singing group there, the Tigertones. Everything about him was fancy, and his family hailed from blue-blood Philadelphia. They were on the Social Register, a far cry from my midwestern roots. There once was a photo of Parker and me in Las Vegas from when we were dating. He was wearing a suit, and I was in a red dress with a neckline that plunged to my navel. Within 24 hours he received a phone call from his mother. "Who IS this GIRL?!" Parker liked my shocking wild ways, and I was enamored by his East Coast Ivy League intelligence. We were definitely the odd couple, but it somehow worked.

Parker is hard to read, and he keeps it all close to the vest. If you suspect something is bothering him, you have to draw it out of him like a splinter from a foot. And when he does talk, he won't reveal much. It was never easy to decipher the truth with him. Not about big, secretive, bad things, just the kinds of things people bitch about to each other on a daily basis. "Man, that idiot at work pissed me off!" was the kind of thing I would share. Parker would pace or sit on the porch and smoke cigars and ponder life, which looked painful to me. I wished he would just run out to the middle of the yard and scream now and then, for his sake.

Over the course of our 14-year marriage we gave each other unique gifts. I gave him a red Ferrari Berlinetta Boxer for Christmas when I had precisely $67,000 in my bank account. The Ferrari cost $65,000, leaving me $2,000 to pay bills. Parker started buying me pets while we were dating. The first animal he surprised me with was Cinderella, a giant brown English lop-eared rabbit. Throughout the years we were married, my dad referred to Parker as a saint for putting up with my menagerie of creatures. Funny—Parker bought me most of them, including my first pair of ring-tailed lemurs, Ricky and Lucy. And one Christmas morning, when I headed down the staircase of our beautiful Encino bungalow, I was met by a tiny gray miniature horse standing in the entryway, which I named Buckwheat.

During the *Cheers* years, a lot of cash was rolling in. I was doing 24 episodes a year, then movies in my hiatus. That left two months every summer to go somewhere. We bought a 22-bedroom "cottage" on the coast of Maine. It was perfect! With all that work going on during the year, it was hard to make time for family and friends, especially if they didn't live in LA. Maine was the perfect place to congregate. We had upwards of 30 people as our guests at one time, and the place was spectacular. There was a deepwater mooring dock and a clay tennis court surrounded by Essex Green Victorian lattice. There was shuffle-board, a pool hall, croquet, a swimming pool, a children's garden. It was magnificent. While Parker took interest in boats and more boats, I spent my days arranging flowers and planning meals for our guests. It sounds so perfectly Americana. So Martha Stewarty. I dressed the part wearing Laura Ashley dresses and big brimmed sun hats. Parker took me aside once and said, "You do know I didn't marry an East Coast girl on purpose, right?" But it was SO exciting to be who I wasn't. I'd never been exposed to these kinds of people, with their pink shirts and those pale yellow pants with whales on them. I'd never experienced cocktail parties where people still actually drank martinis and ate Ritz Crackers with cheese spread and olives on them. True, I have a bad habit of becoming a chameleon when I'm with a man. I tend to get all caught up in HIS lifestyle. With Bob I became a little hippie. With Jake, cowboy chic. With Parker, naughty coed mixed with Gibson Girl. But I'm an ACTRESS, for crying out loud!! What good is life without drama and costumes!!?

In 1992 we adopted our first child—William True Parker. We called him True.

In 1994 we welcomed our daughter, Lillie Price Parker. The "Price" part was the surname of his mother's side of the family, and I was mad for his grandmother Granny Price. She was delicate and strong at once—just like our Lillie seemed.

In 1996 I took the kids to Italy. I was restless, again. It seemed I could only withstand a 14-year stint before I would experience the heebie-jeebies of marriage. But at least I'd done better than the first time I was married; that time I'd only lasted four years.

When I was married to Parker, life seemed to go along smoothly. Then BAM!! I'd meet some handsome temptation, and I was off the rails for a few months. Then I'd sort it all out and go at the marriage again for another four years. And so it went. Until the last time.

I never cheated on Parker but I called my marriage quits in 1997. The way I handled it was not ideal by any means, and I can say the same for him. It got a little nasty. We were both jerks. I've since tried to make up the damage I caused. Just because I didn't want to be married to him any longer didn't mean I stopped loving him. The picture of our life that I painted intentionally has the gray side omitted. Hell, we never got that dark to begin with. And it's a good policy to never speak unkindly of your children's other parent. I know divorced couples can end up despising each other during or after a divorce, and they can also end up being friends and laying down their arms. It's now been 15 years since Parker and I divorced, and I'm sure we've both learned a lot about ourselves. What I learned, FINALLY, from my life with Parker is to knock off flirting with men while I'm attached and to stop dramatizing being the victim of an unfaithful mate. We ALL make mistakes. NONE of us is perfect. And forgiveness and understanding are key. I'm not my father. I believe that marriages can be reconciled if infidelity has transpired. But I am like my father in realizing that infidelity is calculated and premeditated. Dicks don't magically fall into vaginas. There is an evolution.

Since my breakup with Parker, I'm proud to say I've achieved the ability to be in a relationship without flirting with other men and without having one bag packed and my foot out the door.

And my greatest dream, for our kids' sake, is that some year down the road we can have a big old-fashioned Christmas together. All of us.

MAGGIE

Oh, I'm more determined than you think.
I'll win alright.

BRICK POLLITT

Win what? What is, uh, the victory of a
cat on a hot tin roof?

MAGGIE

Just stayin' on it, I guess. As long as
she can.

—TENNESSEE WILLIAMS,
CAT ON A HOT TIN ROOF

The Art of Art

I COULDN'T GET a meeting with the late, great theater director
José Quintero for the life of me. My then-agent couldn't even get me
in the door. José was casting Tennessee Williams's *Cat on a Hot Tin Roof*
and I was hell-bent on playing the lead role of Maggie, even though
I'd never acted in the theater. The play was to be performed at the re-

nowned Mark Taper Forum in LA. The role of Maggie was coveted by every 25- to 35-year-old actress in the world.

José Quintero was born on October 15, 1924, in Panama City, Panama, and he directed his first play in 1949. He was a founder of the Off Broadway theater Circle in the Square, where he directed regularly from 1950, establishing the house as a major center for serious theater. He was best known for his productions of 20th-century plays, especially those of Tennessee Williams and Eugene O'Neill. José was virtually responsible for the success of many Eugene O'Neill plays that had flopped in their first Broadway productions. Among them were *The Iceman Cometh*, *A Touch of the Poet*, and *A Moon for the Misbegotten*, and all of them starred the acclaimed actor Jason Robards Jr.

José knew and worked with acting greats such as Colleen Dewhurst, Vivian Leigh, Geraldine Page, Jane Fonda, Ingrid Bergman, Warren Beatty, and Dolores del Rio. José was the quintessential actor's director. The quintessential director, period.

José battled alcoholism, and with the help of his life partner, Nicholas Tsacrios, he was able to defeat his addictions in the 1970s.

Okay, phew! So that's part of José's bio. I want you to see how ludicrous it was for me, a girl who'd never done a play except for playing the sun in the first grade and forgetting my lines, to think I could not only get in the room with the great Mr. Quintero but think I could land the role of Maggie and become a theater star.

So this agent just couldn't get me a meeting. And hell, I actually knew this play. I'd seen the movie, for god's sake! Seriously, I was desperate to play this role that all actresses dream of playing. I'd even heard actresses talking about the damn play in odd locations; Lesley Ann Warren was sitting behind me on a plane discussing with someone how much she wanted to play Maggie.

But I couldn't even get a flippin' interview. One night when Parker and I were at dinner with his agent, Chris Barrett, I was lamenting, "God, *my* agent can't even get me in the door for this *Cat on a Hot Tin*

Roof thing." Chris said to me, "I can get you in the room, I represent José Quintero."

What?!! What?!!! What?!!

"However," tricky Chris continued, "if I DO get you in the room with José, I'd like you to consider letting me represent you. You don't have to say yes right now, I just want you to consider having me as your agent. If you decide not to, I will of course still get you in the meeting, in fact, I'll get you the meeting first, and then you can decide about me down the road."

Wow! How cool was that? This was all after *Star Trek* and during filming a not-so-great ABC-TV series called *Masquerade* with Greg Evigan and Rod Taylor. It was a fairly dumb show, with us running around in disguise when we were actually CIA agents.

So it meant *if* I got the role, which everyone except me knew I wouldn't, I would have to be doing the play simultaneously with shooting the series.

Chris called the next day to schedule my meeting with José Quintero. It was pretty obvious that José was just doing Chris a favor by seeing me, but this happens every day in Hollywood. People call in favors, and if you're the unlucky end of the favor, the director, producer, or casting people just go through the motions with you, never intending to give you a shot, simply carrying out their obligation to see you.

What I wore to this meeting was very significant to Mr. Quintero's first impression of me. I wore white leather pants with white high-heeled boots, a white turtleneck sweater, and a white leather jacket with lots of zippers. In short, I looked like a very white Hells Angel. José, being Panamanian, looked and sounded very exotic. He was an exceptionally deep and emotional person, and he was kind but appeared sophisticated and a bit erudite. I was married to Parker, so erudite men didn't scare me.

He asked me to tell him a little about myself and my "body of work." I told him about *Star Trek* and briefly about the movie I'd recently done in Greece. It was one of the worst movies ever made, and I can't really talk about it or the director will sue me. But it was simply awful!! José didn't need to hear how awful it was, though, he simply needed to hear "feature film in Greece," which sounds fairly impressive from the biker in white.

"And theater?" He gently smiled. "What have you done in theater?"

Gulp—the answer was "played the sun in first grade" but I knew that would never do with an icon of José's status.

"Why, Mr. Quintero, I've done everything Elizabeth Taylor has done." (Elizabeth Taylor was the star of *Cat on a Hot Tin Roof*—the movie.) He smiled and was probably fucking with me.

"Oh really? Excellent. What Elizabeth Taylor plays have you done?"

"Oh you know," I prattled on, "*Suddenly Last Summer, Cat on a Hot Tin Roof*, and . . . umm . . . *Butterfield 8*."

"Oh my . . . that's quite a lot, and so you've already played Maggie? That's quite impressive."

Yes, it was quite impressive. I could tell he was *very* impressed indeed!

He then had me read for the role of Maggie the Cat, and I felt I did a bang-up job of it. Being from Kansas, that faint Southern lilt is pretty easy for us.

He thanked me, and I thanked him.

What actors must have and are dying to get after meetings is feedback. If you are really lucky, *they* call your people. If you're not really lucky, *your* people have to call them and pry the information out of them.

Well, they didn't call Chris. He had to call José and ask, "How was she?" The actress is never sitting in the catbird seat when the agent has to make the call, so Chris is on the phone relaying this data to me. "He said you were very good but he was afraid of you—did you wear some motorcycle getup to this meeting?"

"Yes!" I protested, "But it wasn't black, it was white and it was really soft kid leather!"

"Well, José thinks you are very tough and scary."

Oh jeez, I'd blown it because I'd looked like Easy White Rider? Oh, for god's sake, why was I so stupid?

"However," Chris went on, "because he thinks you are an interesting actress, he'd like to see you again tomorrow afternoon." And as I started whooping and hollering he added, "Wait, wait, I'm not finished, when you go in there tomorrow he would like you to wear something feminine and soft. Something a lady would wear."

I wore a soft voile pastel flowered dress, dainty little T-strapped pale pink high heels. My makeup was 1950s style to look like Maggie's, as *Cat on a Hot Tin Roof* was set in the South in the '50s. My hair was more styled than I usually wore it, and I didn't chitchat with José when I walked into the room. I just read with an actor he had in the office.

I didn't chitchat on the way out either. I just said, "Thank you, Mr. Quintero, for the second opportunity." I seemed to have the slightest hint of a Southern accent in my voice. It was sweet, ladylike, feminine, and soft.

The next day *we* didn't have to call *them*. They wanted me to try out on the stage of the Mark Taper Forum, not so that they could see if I could act but to see if they could hear me, since ALL of them actually knew I'd never done theater.

Before I began to read, José whispered to me in his low, sultry Latino, Antonio Banderas voice, "You see that man standing at the back of the theater?"

"Yes," I said.

"That is Gordon Davidson. This is his theater. Speak to him. Make sure all of your lines can be heard by him. But do them exactly as you did them for me."

"Thank you," I whispered back.

That night I got the call from *them*. "José loves you, Gordon likes you a lot, too, but says you're not a big name." I interrupted, as usual, "But I will be a big name after I do this and blah, blah, blah."

"Let me finish," as Chris always had to say to me, "but José championed you. He told Gordon he would not do the play unless Gordon hired you as Maggie . . . so you have the role."

I wept like a baby for an hour, half excited for getting the opportunity to play this once-in-a-lifetime role and half because I couldn't believe the courage and conviction of a director to actually back out of a very publicized production if he didn't get the leading lady of his choice. I was dumbfounded. So was Chris. So was every big-named agent and actress in town. HE CHAMPIONED ME!!!

I kept thinking, *How have I gotten so lucky in my life to have two champions fight so hard for me when I didn't seem like the girl they should be fighting for?* First Nicholas Meyer on *Star Trek*, and now the great José Quintero in the theater. I cried for a few more hours.

When I showed up for the first day of rehearsal, José met me with open arms and whispered, "There was no other person to play this role—you were born for it." Then he taught me something very particular. He said, with a glint in his eye, "Although you have done all of the same plays as Elizabeth Taylor, it's important you take voice lessons so that you don't blow your voice out during the run of the play."

I smiled and said, "Yes, that's a very good idea, Mr. Quintero."

"Please only call me José," he said.

"Thank you, José, I'll begin voice lessons right away."

My Brick was played by the exceptionally talented actor James Morrison. He was dreamy and the perfect person to play the troubled ex–football hero. Pat Hingle played Big Daddy and Alice Ghostley played Big Mama. I was blessed to be in the company of such legendary actors.

The play was a tremendous success with valentine reviews. We couldn't have written them better ourselves. After opening night José presented me with a gift, which was an original poster from the 1950s of Elizabeth Taylor in *Cat on a Hot Tin Roof.* I cherish it. But even more amazing was the friendship and love José and I developed. He was an extraordinary director, precise and emotional. He didn't tell you how to act, he radiated emotions out of his soul to express his feelings. You could feel it as surely as you could feel someone punch you in the face. The best single word I know of to describe José is "exquisite." His eyes were black and mysterious. His skin was dark and his face chiseled like an Italian or Spanish aristocrat. He was deeply intelligent and tortured, always somehow tortured by his own demons. His humor was dry, yet dramatic. He could mimic anyone, especially women, so he was funny in a unique way that separated him from all other people.

He was a homosexual man, brought up for decades in a world that would not tolerate homosexuals. His friends were Truman Capote and Vivian Leigh. He loved his partner of many decades, and Nick took good care of José until the very end. When José died in 1999, Nick lost the love of his life. I lost my best friend.

José was a haunting person. When I think of him I think of the emotion, the angst, the magnitude of feelings he had toward people and life. His eyes were haunting, and at the same time seductive, then sparkly.

The entire world is a better place because of José. The world of theater lost one of its brightest lights, and all actors should know José's name and be thankful he did the groundbreaking for the theater and for homosexuals.

His name was José Quintero, and I'd like to take this moment to whisper to him, wherever he is, "You see that man up there in the last row of the theater? That's you. I hope you can hear all my lines. I tell you I love you every day. Oh, and PS . . . I'm doing a new Elizabeth Taylor play at the Mark Taper Forum . . . *National Velvet.*"

> It would take too long to explain the intimate alliance
> of contradictions in human nature which makes love
> itself wear at times the desperate shape of betrayal,
> and perhaps there is no possible explanation.

—JOSEPH CONRAD

The Art of Temptation

THIS ONE is a tough one to speak about.

I was in love with him while we were both married. I had never fallen in love with a married man, nor had I ever had a crush on a married man or a date with one. I considered it taboo, and I still do.

This man and I never had sex or did sexual things, but I consider what we did more dangerous and more of a betrayal to our spouses. I got used to not being with him, but I never stopped loving him.

We had all been summoned for a huge cast table reading in 1984. The cast truly was enormous, as we were about to embark on a six-month journey through a miniseries called *North and South*. It was as comparable in magnitude as its predecessor miniseries, *Roots*. So in the first reading, there we were, actors, actresses, producers, directors, writers, and TV execs all gathered around an endless conference table.

Maybe I was dreaming, but I felt something pulling me to look to my left, just a "look over here" kind of pull. I looked to my left but didn't see anyone looking at me. Then I leaned in to see my script, and there it was again, someone wanted my attention. I looked to my left again, and there he was, Patrick, just sort of grinning at me. He was at the opposite end of the table, so it was clear he had a powerful ability to pull one's attention. I turned back for a brief moment, but quickly looked away. I didn't peer at him again throughout the lengthy script reading.

When we were finished and everyone was getting up to leave, Patrick walked by me and said, "I admire your work. I look forward to filming with you." This is the standard line most actors say to most actors when they embark on a project together. But the *way* he said it, in his low-slurred-mumbly kind of James Dean/Elvis–speak . . . Ooh la la.

Whoa, Kirstie, make a note. Do not get silly about this one, this one is dangerous. This one is married. This one's trouble, stay clear of this one.

And that's how Patrick Swayze and I began our relationship.

• • •

North and South and later, *North and South, Book II*, was the saga of the Civil War and its relationship to two families. I played Virgilia Hazard, of the Philadelphia Hazard Ironworks family. I was dying to play this character. She was not only from an affluent Northern family, she was an abolitionist. She also denounced her family, ran away, and married a black slave. Hot stuff for TV back in 1986! Patrick played the son of a Southern plantation family. He became besties with my brother George Hazard. Their North-South relationship as friends worked beautifully until the Civil War began. Thus the conflict. Then all hell broke loose.

It was a funny production, part of it anyway, unintentionally, I'm sure.

The producer was a flamboyant gay man, so all of us rich girls were drenched in lavish jewels, and instead of the modest higher-neckline dresses of the period, we were decked out in reproductions but with plunging boob-revealing necklines. All of the actresses would sit around and laugh as we looked at old photographs or paintings from the Civil War period. The hair was not cool and sexy, the jewelry was petite and reserved, and the dresses were exquisitely tailored but never revealing, even for the rich folk. But Chuck, the producer, opted for opulence. We once calculated the value of the family jewels dangling between our boobs. In 1862 they would have been valued at around $45 million! Ha!

We wore authentic corsets with our gowns. Corsets were designed to be worn from one to three hours, depending on the occasion. Poor women's corsets laced in the front so that they could lace them themselves, while rich women's corsets laced in the back because they had servants or slaves. We worked 12 to 16 hour days in the corsets, sometimes under the beating Charleston sun. By the end of week two and throughout the production, most of us stopped having periods, half of us had passed out, and the rest were just mean as hell. Sunday go-to-meetin' corsets were not made for the arduous hours of filmmaking. But they did make our 24-inch waists compress to 19-inch waistlines. The point is, although we didn't look all that authentic, we looked hot!

The men looked hot, too, especially Patrick, who had ridden horses his whole life. He was a beautiful rider. So when I laid eyes on him with his long brown hair flying in the wind, galloping down a mile-long tree-lined drive toward the antebellum mansion where we were sitting between takes, it took my breath away. It took it so far away that I immediately went in the house to get away from him. There are hot men, and there are dangerous men—he was both.

· · ·

The expansive *North and South* and *North and South, Book II*, casts were mind boggling:

Elizabeth Taylor
Patrick Swayze
David Carradine
Lesley-Anne Down
Johnny Cash
Hal Holbrook
Gene Kelly
Robert Mitchum
Jean Simmons
Forest Whitaker
Lloyd Bridges
Olivia de Havilland
Jimmy Stewart
Wayne Newton
and so on.

I sat with Jimmy Stewart one day. He is on my top-ten all-time-great-actors list, and he was nothing short of stellar. We talked about our animals, and he told me he and his wife had monkeys, too. The monkeys had a special outdoor/indoor cage, and at night the Stewarts opened the cage into their bedroom where they played with the monkeys and let them leap around.

I was so honored to have met and spoken with such icons as Olivia de Havilland and Jean Simmons. It's where I first met Elizabeth Taylor, who later became a friend. The same with Gene Kelly.

Between *North and South* and *North and South, Book II*, the filming spanned an almost-two-year period.

I got married in 1983 while I was simultaneously doing a TV series and *Cat on a Hot Tin Roof* onstage. I'd done *Star Trek II* in 1981 and I was slightly crushed out on my young, bisexual costar Merritt Butrick, who became my friend. Sadly, he died of AIDS in 1989 at the young age of 29.

I'd done a movie in Greece while Parker and I were dating nonexclusively and made out with my leading man, Joseph Bottoms. My leading man on my short-lived TV series was Greg Evigan, and although he was very hot and sexy, he was also very married and taken.

What I'm trying to say is, I hadn't been in a position such as I was in in *North and South*. It was my first experience going on location for a long period of time. When we were filming, I was away from home for at least four months, which turned into six. Other than the film in Greece, I'd only filmed in LA. Parker cheated on me when he went on location to film. We weren't married when he did, but we were exclusive. So with this in mind, I guess I figured I had a "get out of jail free card" in my hip pocket.

The danger of Patrick was looming. He was married, but he exuded "anything was possible." I purposely avoided him at all costs for the first few weeks. I would go to dinner with the entire cast but wouldn't go out afterward. Then came the night that I agreed to go out for a few hours. We all danced into the wee hours, which worked for my character. The crazier she became in the story line, the more broken down she looked.

The shift occurred one night when we all went out dancing after filming and Patrick and I got drunk and decided to stay a little longer than the rest. This was several years before he made the movie *Dirty Dancing*, but when I tell you we were dirty-dancing that night, I can tell you it made that movie look like *Singin' in the Rain*.

He walked me to my room that night and said, "I'm falling in love with you."

Knowing he was drunk, it had little effect on me. Knowing we were both married apparently had little effect on me, either. After all, I did have that free pass in the hip pocket of my very tight, very sexy Fred Segal jeans.

The next day we were all off work. We congregated in my hotel room in Charleston. We had about 300 boxes of these tiny paper fireworks things; I think they're called poppers. They are small amounts of gunpowder or something, about the size of a pea, wrapped in tissue paper. If you throw them at something or someone, they pop really loudly. Most kids have two or three boxes of them to spook people. We had 300 boxes!

Everyone was emptying the boxes into this one huge box about the size of a large hatbox, and we ended up with 3,000 individual poppers. It was rush hour in Charleston. The streets were packed with people below my third-story hotel room, and we were positioned at the open window. When the crosswalk light turned green, we would unleash 100 poppers. When they hit the ground, they would POP! All the people were freaking out, laughing, ducking for cover. We increased the artillery to the "500 popper drop." SNAP! SNAP! SNAP! It sounded like a thousand tiny firecrackers going off. Patrick was exhilarated!! We all were in ecstasy torturing the poor rush-hour Charlestonians. It was juvenile but it was pre-9/11 and before the days of mass shootings. The people laughed when they realized they were poppers. Life was different then.

Most of us were in our early thirties but acted like 12-year-olds. There was a sense of summer camp each and every day, but we were getting paid for it. Hot summer nights, reminiscent of Tennessee Williams finest plays.

Patrick and I rarely worked in the same scenes. When we did, we milked it for all it was worth. In the story line, Virgilia and his character, Orry Main, were archenemies. But we decided that the subplot was that we were enemies with a hidden passion for each other. When we were on screen together, even if it was a scene filled with anger and adversity, our motivation was that of lust and submerged attraction. Lord! The extent an actor will go to justify his or her indiscretions is endless.

"I hate you!" (I really love you.)

"Get out of my house!" (Stay in the backyard and wait for me.)

We had it down to a ridiculous tee.

There were many days we never saw each other, as we would split up and film in different locations. Every time I laid eyes on him, it left me breathless. Then our spouses came to visit and threw monkey wrenches into the budding affair.

It was especially stressful because I was still in love with my husband, and he, his wife. They'd been in love since they were teenagers. And the worst part was, she was this beautiful, terrific person. I instantly fell in love with her myself.

One night we were all at dinner, Patrick, his wife, Parker, and me. Parker was so handsome and charming; she was engaging and so damn likable. Rightfully so, I felt like a horrible person. We hadn't kissed or had sex, but we had dirty-danced and professed our love, which is probably much worse, much more dangerous than a one-night stand.

They seemed so pure and good, and we seemed so dark and naughty, which felt pathetic. I don't know the exact mechanism that kicks into gear to make all your integrity and scruples go down the drain. Well, actually I do, but when I was in the grasp of the forbidden, it used to turn me on. Ahhh, what a tangled web we weave . . .

I spent time with Parker, Patrick with his wife. I can't speak for him, but I couldn't get him out of my mind. And all the while I knew I'd never seen a single affair that turned into a lasting relationship.

Filming and lusting for each other went on for months. The emotions and dialogue escalated daily. One night, toward the end of the shoot, I got fairly drunk, dirty-danced for hours, and then succumbed. We made out with each other. I decided it was a swell idea to just go for it and have sex. Now, this never happened to me before or since. Luckily, from some sector of the sane universe, came the voice of reason. Not my voice.

"Patrick, I wanna make love with you, I don't care anymore, let's just do it!" That wasn't the sane voice of reason I'm speaking of, but here it comes. He started laughing . . . laughing!

"No! Come on, you're drunk, Kirstie, you don't really wanna do it. You're not that girl, you will regret it for the rest of your life. If we're going to be together, we're not starting out like this," he said.

I was pretty shocked. No one had ever refused to have sex with me! Especially someone who had daily conspired, even originated the idea of leaving both of our marriages to run away together.

I sobered up, lickety-split. "Seriously?" I said. "You seriously don't want to have sex with me?"

"Of course I *want* to have sex with you, fool! But you're the girl who freaks out and frets over hand holding. Can you imagine what this would do to you? It would eat you up."

With all the crazy shit I'd seen Patrick do, and in spite of the stuff I surmised he had done, he was spot on.

What the hell is it about me that provokes men to protect me from myself? I know men refuse sex with women (rarely) when they're not interested, but that was not the case. He couldn't keep his hands off me. He'd spent every waking moment with me for months.

Five minutes later I was in the bathroom, almost on my knees, thanking god he hadn't gone along with yet another of my swell drunk ideas.

I was near hysterics at the thought of almost having to tell my husband I'd cheated on him or look Patrick's wife in the eye, knowing I'd banged her husband.

There was a knock on the hotel door. It was my driver. I hadn't realized it was 5:00 a.m. and I was supposed to have left for the set at 4:45.

"I'll be right down, Jimmy," I meowed, looking like a cat had dragged me in.

Thank god I was shooting a scene in an insane asylum. I needed no makeup, and my eyes were black and swollen from crying. I've never been more grateful to a man for rejecting me.

There were two weeks left of shooting. Patrick and I spent every second together. The desperation was frenetic, with that sick indulgence that infidels wallow in. He asked me one last time to divorce my husband and make a new life with him.

He was very persuasive. The decision of whether to run off with him was torturous. But isn't that the point of affairs? To be tortured? To take no responsibility for preexisting relationships?

I began to realize that although I might be willing to destroy my own marriage for him, I wasn't willing to destroy his for me. I also knew in my heart that we might last two or three years, but we weren't cut out for a life together. Patrick and his wife had something few people ever find.

No matter how much he told me he loved me, or how many romantic plans he devised, I knew that married people go through endless temptations during their marriages, especially actors. Some succumb to affairs. Some leave their spouses for another, only to find out it wasn't really love. Some have sex with other people and confess and patch up their marriage. Some are left behind even when they wanted to patch it up, and the other person wasn't willing to give them another chance. And some, like me, even amid the throes of love and passion, could see the truth.

As Patrick saw in me an inability to live with myself if I'd cheated on my husband; I saw an inability for him to be genuinely happy, for any length of time, with anyone other than his wife. I also knew he'd been drinking a lot.

Patrick did not let go of me easily. We spoke many times after we filmed. I found it painful and tempting, but I refused to meet up with him. It was still too dangerous and besides, at the end of filming I did what I always did, I confessed it all to my husband and went about the business of loving him and trying to be a good wife.

Over the years I saw Patrick three times. Once when I won a Golden Globe and once at a premiere. We just smiled at each other. The last time I saw him was at an event for Muhammad Ali, about six years ago. I was single. I walked to my seat at the banquet table. The hostess seated me next to Patrick and his wife. When she excused herself to use the ladies' room, he turned to me and said, "There's not been a day I haven't thought about you." I just smiled and thought, *You asshole, don't even start.*

The last time I saw Patrick's wife was when she kindly asked me to speak at his funeral. There, I spoke my truth.

"No matter what Patrick said or did, no matter what occurred in his short, wild, dramatic life, it all boiled down to one thing, his passion for the love of his life—Lisa."

> Here's all you have to know about men and women:
> women are crazy, men are stupid. And the main
> reason women are crazy is that men are stupid.
>
> —GEORGE CARLIN

The Art of Costars
and Lunatic Directors

I N 1985 I was in Whistler, Canada, filming the movie *Shoot to Kill*. It was a taxing film, physically and mentally.

There I was, the only woman in the cast, 300 feet above a roaring river ravine, in a four-by-four-foot wire cage, precariously dangling from a one-inch twisted metal cable. I had to pull myself and one of my costars across the tremendous gorge all the while repeating my character Sarah's lines, "Just don't look down," as I smiled and assured him that it was "perfectly safe."

After each take, on the other side of the ravine, I would stroll behind this huge rock and bawl my eyes out. I was deathly afraid of heights, especially in the form of wire cages dangling from sky hooks.

My three costars were the legendary actor Sidney Poitier, the handsome Tom Berenger, and the endlessly talented Clancy Brown. The story went something like this: diamond-stealing psycho murdering lunatic (Clancy) kidnaps the beautiful, hauntingly gorgeous girlfriend (Kirstie) of Tom Berenger's character. But Sidney Poitier, FBI man or CIA, I get confused, is on the case to find and rescue said luscious heroine.

The fourth person involved in the film was the wild and wily Roger Spottiswoode. He was a fine director, but he was a bit of a lunatic. When Roger interviewed me for the movie, I told him I was afraid of extreme heights, mainly because there was a scene in the script that required me to walk across a rope bridge above a gorge. I gave him this heads-up before he cast me, so he could evaluate whether or not I was the right actress for the part. He said, "Don't worry, love, I'm not shooting that scene anyway. We can't find a rope bridge in Canada."

I'd never done more running, jumping, hiking, falling, and climbing than I did in this action thriller. Roger, a zany eccentric from England, wanted me to push harder and harder to prove my character was something to "reckon with." On Monday he coaxed Clancy to hit me in the face (it was in the script, so I knew it was coming), but instead of the usual stage hit, Roger wanted Clancy to *really* hit me.

Clancy is the definition of "gentle giant." He has huge muscular hands, is stronger than an ox, and is a hulking six foot four. Clancy has made his career playing killers, monsters, and bad guys in movies such as *Highlander* and *Shawshank Redemption*. But in real life he is a dove. A giant dove, but a dove nonetheless.

Clancy said, "Come on, Roger, I don't wanna hurt her."

"No, no, no, Clancy," Roger quipped back in his fey-sounding British accent. "Of course we don't want you to hurt her—but it must look real—so just give us a good slap, and she will then turn her head away."

I'm by nature a tough chick. I have a brother, and I know how little slaps feel. "Action!" Roger shouted. We said our lines "blah blah blah," and Clancy gave me a little slap. When Roger yelled "Cut," Clancy asked, "Did I hurt you, are you okay?"

"God no, Clancy, I barely felt it," I assured him.

"Now . . . Clancy . . ." Roger continued sounding like Bridget Jones on acid, "that hardly looked like the slap of a dangerous man. Let's go again and give us a good pop!"

The stunt coordinator came over and showed Clancy how to make the "pop" LOOK hard but how to pull the punch so it wouldn't hurt me. Clancy was so nervous, he is such a giant man, and I was all skinny with my silly little face.

Roger yelled, "All right everyone! Rolling!"

"Speed," yelled the camera operator.

"Now Clancy, make it look REAL! Give her a bloody smack, man! ACTION!"

Blah, blah, blah, we each said our lines again and WHACK!

Injuries always feel as if they occur in slow motion. The whack resonated like W-H-A-C-K-K-K-K-k-k-k-k. The stage directions in the script designated that the actors say their lines, then the bad guy slaps my character. Then my defiant character, Sarah, speaks again, spouting some wise smartypants wisdom.

But my defiant character could not spout. Her jaw was dislocated.

Clancy was beside himself freaking out. "Oh god, oh god. I'm so sorry, are you okay? Jesus, did I hurt you?"

Roger was calm, "Oh dear, do we have a bloody medic up here?"

We didn't have a bloody medic up there on top of snow-covered Whistler Mountain. But what we did have was an Inuit hairdresser/makeup artist/acupuncturist.

I couldn't speak or close my mouth, and my jaw was pushed way to the right. I gotta admit I was slightly freaking, too. I needed this star-studded film for my résumé. And of course, I needed my jaw intact.

The Eskimo girl pressed a spot between my shoulder and neck. She pressed it with a mighty force, sorta like a Vulcan death grip—and easy as a tiny dick sliding into a whore, my jaw was back in its correct location. The crew applauded!

Roger merrily proclaimed, "Luckily, we got the shot. Let's move on!"

Every day was a new injury. During a chase scene with Roger yelling on the walkie-talkie in the car, "Faster, Clancy, faster. Harder turn at the intersection Clancy! Crank it!"

Clancy and I braced ourselves for take number 37. We barreled down the alley of a Vancouver ghetto. The car flew over a big bump, which torqued my spine, and then Clancy cranked the car sharply to the left at the intersection. FYI, there are these people in movies called STUNTMEN. There are also the ones known as STUNT DRIVERS. Roger opted for neither, as he wanted it to LOOK REAL. My back wrenched, and I screamed in excruciating pain. I laid there in the back-seat of the STUNT car while Clancy profusely apologized.

Roger opened the car door to see if I was okay. The medic examined me and said, "She probably just threw her back out, but let's get her to the hospital." That was a keen observation that any idiot could have observed, and I'm pretty sure medics on movies are from local high school first-aid classes. Roger replied, "Thank god we got the bloody shot, let's get her to the hospital," whereby he accidentally slammed the car door into my head, jamming my skull into my neck like a turtle.

Henry Kingi, the most gloriously cool-looking stuntman in the history of stuntmen, rushed me to the hospital. Henry Kingi is six foot five, a Native American, and has jet-black hair to his waist. He is a spiritually enlightened human being and has remained a lifelong friend. After being examined, it was recommended I take lots of pain meds. Ugh! I didn't want to go through the next week of filming doped up. I called the production company and asked if there was a good chiroprac-tor in the area.

The production people recommended a particular chiropractor because he utilized a rare form of therapy called Grostic. I won't forget that word as long as I live: "Grostic."

Soon I was lying facedown on the chiropractic table, and Henry

Kingi was standing in front of me four feet away. I commented to the doctor, "You can't crack my neck. I won't let anyone crack my neck."

"That's not how I do it. I use the Grostic technique. I won't even touch you," he proudly proclaimed.

I tilted my eyes up to Henry with a *Really? He's not even going to touch me? What the fuck?* Henry raised his eyebrows.

The chiro started hopping around like he had ants in his pants. I'm not exaggerating. He began hopping and bending and "gathering" something. Gathering and scooping at the air around him. Scooping, gathering the air, and rubbing his hands like people do when they're freezing. Jesus, it was all too much and way too comical and stupid looking. I peered up at Henry again, and we had to divert our eyes lest we fly into hysterical laughter and interrupt the Grostic process.

Well, Dr. Freakshow did this bizarre ritual for about three minutes, and then what occurred was literally inexplicable. He swooped in and pressed his hands down hard, landing one to two inches from my back. If I hadn't been there, I would never have believed this ridiculous story. Thank god Henry was there as my witness.

It felt like a cross between being electrocuted and having a two-by-four smashed into my spine. A shock wave of the most painful pressure smashed into my body, and I threw up when I was hit by the crush that almost rendered me unconscious. This was a violent hurl that was immediate and reminiscent of Linda Blair in *The Exorcist*.

And it was TRUE. He hadn't so much as touched me.

I'm no voodoo witch doctor occult-believing kind of girl. I need explanations. I need analytical reasoning. I need to understand fully how something works.

All I know is that I did get up. I did run, not walk, out of Grostic Central so my back was somehow working properly. But it freaked me out so terribly that I became violently sick, puking my guts out for days, like I'd been possessed by some alien demon. I have no idea what the hell he did to me. I've asked other chiropractors what the hell he did to me, but only one had heard of Grostic, and he merely replied that it was "energy work."

I can testify that I will never again have energy work.

This is how the movie went on, injury after injury. Remember, Sidney Poitier and I hadn't worked directly together up until this point. My character was with the psycho killer, being dragged around the mountains, while he was killing off all the campers I'd taken on a camping trip. They kept falling off cliffs or being stabbed—you know, psycho-murderer kind of stuff.

Meanwhile Sidney and Tom were joined at the hip, just a few days behind us in pursuit of the murderer and trying to ensure I wasn't his next victim. The only reason Clancy didn't kill me was because he needed me to guide him out of the mountains, plus he was holding me for ransom.

My point is, the only people who saw me get whacked, pushed, terrified of heights, or whiplashed were Clancy, the crew, and of course, Rog.

When we completed shooting at Whistler, we segued to an enormous ferryboat. This is where Sidney Poitier, Tom Berenger, and I began working together.

Clancy's character had me at gunpoint aboard the vessel, as his hostage. At one point he had to jump from the ferryboat railing and smash me to the ground. Needless to say I was horrified at my impending doom. I had a stunt double, but Roger had yet to use her. Clancy also needed to "pistol-whip" me, causing Tom to leap in and rescue me. Sidney was sitting behind the camera watching the scene.

Clancy grabbed me by the throat and put the fake gun to my head. Roger explained, "Now, Clancy, when Kirstie struggles to escape, you must take the butt of the gun and pretend to smack it across her face. The gun falls to the floor, you jump on the railing to escape, she grabs the gun so you jump on her and 'smack her across her face' again with your fist, rendering her unconscious."

"QUIET ON THE SET!" yelled the first assistant director.

"ACTION!" screamed Roger.

Clancy grabbed me by the throat—I struggled—I screamed—and Clancy pretended to belt me across the face with the gun. The gun fell to the ground, and I grabbed it. Clancy leapt from the railing, pretending to smash me onto the hard metal decking, and "play" smacked me across my mouth. I ACTED like I was rendered unconscious.

"CUT!! CUT CUT cut cut cut," Roger complained. "Clancy—that looked fake. Just place the butt of the gun in your palm. It will look like the gun is striking her. When you leap on her, go for it, man! Knock her to the ground, grab her face, and act like you belt her!" By this point in the film the stunt coordinator was ready to shoot himself; this is a perfect example of how actors get hurt. Really hurt. I could see the coordinator shaking his head behind the camera. He was whispering to Roger, probably telling him this was dangerous, beckoning him to use my stunt double.

Even the pretend fighting was painful. Being pushed down onto a metal floor, no matter how gently it's done, hurts like a bitch.

"All right everybody, let's go again!" Roger announced.

But Mr. Poitier strolled around from behind the camera, took me by the arm, and said to Roger, "She's done. Bring in her stunt double and one for Clancy. This is ACTING, Mr. Spottiswoode, ACTING."

It was magnificent! I mean, who the hell is going to argue with Sidney Poitier? His intensely powerful voice is enough to quail a Marine.

While Roger reluctantly summoned the stunt doubles, Sidney sat with me, and that's where our friendship began. What an awesome person he is. Everything out of his mouth was riveting. I prompted him to tell me stories about all his movie adventures. From *Guess Who's Coming to Dinner*, to *To Sir, With Love*, *The Defiant Ones*, *Lilies of the Field*, to *In the Heat of the Night*.

He was terribly gracious. I'd ask him what it was like to work with movie greats such as Spencer Tracy and Katharine Hepburn. For days he told me intimate, funny tales of all his experiences. We had lunches and dinners together, and we have kept in touch throughout the years. He is very special to me. But at that moment in time he was my hero. He stuck by me throughout the remainder of the movie. Roger never asked me to do another stunt, nor did he ask my costar Clancy Brown to belt me.

Sidney taught me to stand up for myself on movie sets and to stand up for other actors who are green and being taken advantage of. I guess you could simply say, he taught me, "I'm an actor, not the bionic woman."

Oddly, I ended up adoring our wacky director, Roger. He really was a well-intentioned man; he simply needed a new moviemaking mantra . . . "Stunt doubles"—*namaste.*

> I, with a deeper instinct, choose a man who compels
> my strength, who makes enormous demands on me,
> who does not doubt my courage or my toughness,
> who does not believe me naive or innocent, who
> has the courage to treat me like a woman.
>
> —ANAÏS NIN

The Art of Cheerful Men

F I hadn't walked into the *Cheers* meeting at the Four Seasons with the confidence of Atlas, I

A. wouldn't have gotten the part and,
B. wouldn't have had the opportunity to star in one of the most famous sitcoms in history.

Jimmy Burrows, undisputedly the finest, most talented sitcom director/producer in history, had first seen me as Maggie in *Cat on a Hot Tin Roof* at the Mark Taper Forum in LA some three years prior. He remembered that I was funny, which in itself is funny because *Cat on a Hot Tin Roof* is a drama. But then what all the *Cheers* cast had in common was that all of us were, and are first and foremost, talented dramatic actors. Put any brilliant actor with a sense of what's actually funny in a dramatic piece, but in the wrong place and time, and those will be your comedy geniuses.

I'd just completed *Shoot to Kill*, and I was very cocky when I walked into the *Cheers* luncheon in my skintight Kelly-green leather dress with denim inset details. I'd paid $1,500 for that dress in 1986, so it damn well better have been outstanding. I filled the dress well, was skinny as a stick, and wore Kelly-green stilettos on my feet. My hair was huge and wavy and down to my hips. In my mind I was a cocky film actress who had only done dramas and only done movies, except for a short-lived series and a cruise on *The Love Boat* because I wanted to make sure my new boyfriend, Parker, wasn't cheating on me.

If I could have walked in slow motion toward the *Cheers* table like a cheesy hair commercial, I would have. It felt like I was. I remember these moments in time vividly because usually I walk into a meeting feeling like there's toilet paper on my shoe.

There they all were, all famous and popular, but they were TV people and *I* was a movie star. So was Ted, but I blocked that out . . .

I ordered orecchiette. When it arrived, I commented that it looked like a plate of dick heads. And they do, literally. Whoever invented orecchiette certainly had a circumcised penis because orecchiette is an exact replica of the end of a circumcised dick.

They all laughed, which reinforced my belief that although I had never been hired to do comedy, I certainly had the chops to do it. Ted and I were flirting with each other, and it was clear we had chemistry. I soon got the offer to do the show, and it was one of the best all-time TV offers in history. My plan was to do *Cheers* for one year, then move on to do comedy movies, so I asked for a one-year contract. The standard is a seven-year contract so that actors don't have the advantage of negotiating for more money the following years. But in success, every actor renegotiates anyway and gets more money. I somehow got a one-year contract, probably because I was replacing Shelley Long as the female lead of *Cheers*, not a small act to follow. She is an awesomely gifted comedy actress. The powers that be probably thought I wouldn't be accepted on the show anyway, or some dude in business affairs just screwed up the deal. For whatever reason, much to our surprise, I scored a one-year deal. My plan was in motion and perfect, one year and I'm outta here.

But the first week on *Cheers* it was clear to me that I not only didn't wanna be out of there but that I'd found, at least as an actor, a home.

I wasn't that good in the beginning. My character was designed to be a hard-nosed bitch. Although I can be that in real life, I just wasn't funny on film portraying that. After the second week the writers slyly watched my personal mannerisms, like running into doors, and crying at the drop of a hat over everything happy and some things sad. They saw how in real life I was extremely vulnerable and klutzy. And so Rebecca Howe was shaped. I could see the writers watching me do cigarette tricks, smashing my fingers in the cash register, doing shots of tequila at *Cheers* parties, and dancing, a lot of dancing. These bits would always show up in my character Rebecca Howe's story lines.

The men of *Cheers* are beyond compare and beyond comprehension. It was group love at first sight for me. Each one was unique from the next, but each one was an extraordinary human being, and a genius actor.

If I had written the script myself of how I would be accepted into this group of men, I couldn't have written it more perfectly. It seemed impossible. They'd had a hit show for the previous five years, critically acclaimed and awards for all. *Cheers* was not just a well-written and -acted show; it will stand throughout time as one of the top comedy shows in history.

So here's this girl from Kansas who had done some dramatic movies. A girl who had never done comedy, except for the drama *Cat on a Hot Tin Roof.* And they accepted me with open arms. Come on! They had to have been terribly nervous about the future of *Cheers*, their futures, the futures of their careers and livelihoods. But they never alluded to it or gave me an inkling that they were anything but confident that I would be an asset to their hit show.

It never dawned on me that my presence on *Cheers* would be anything but successful, but I'm sure it dawned on NBC, Paramount, Jimmy Burrows, Glen and Les Charles, and the entire cast. My blissful ignorance came from my undying confidence that I could do anything and would go to the mat for any of these people.

We were a hit, and we soon rose from number three to number one, but the memory I'll carry with me throughout my life is how sweet and supportive and generous they all were with me. The next six years of my life proved to be my glory days that I'd never experienced in high school or college or at any time in my life.

When I tell you that every single day at *Cheers* was like Christmas, I do those days a disservice. I became one of the boys along with Rhea Perlman, who'd been one of the boys on *Cheers* since its inception. I will try to articulate the kind of people I spent six years of my life with, but even today, their amazingness amazes me.

THE BOYS WHO BELLIED UP TO THE BAR

Jimmy

In case you aren't aware of who Jimmy Burrows is, you really should be. Jimmy is the most sought after sitcom director in the world. He is primo on any savvy producer's wish list. He's directed *The Mary Tyler Moore Show*, *Laverne & Shirley*, *The Bob Newhart Show*, *Taxi*, *Cheers* (he and Les and Glen Charles created *Cheers*), *Will & Grace*, *Veronica's Closet*, *Frasier*, *The Big Bang Theory*, and *Mike & Molly*. Phew! That, of course, is not all, but you get the idea. Jimmy came by some of his talent honestly. He is the son of Abe Burrows, the Pulitzer Prize–winning author of such legendary musicals as *Guys and Dolls* and *How to Succeed in Business Without Really Trying*.

You can't not fall in love with Jimmy Burrows. He is genuine, hysterically funny, and an all-round decent, dedicated human being.

His sitcom genius is unparalleled. Jimmy always sets the tone and the pace of the show. He oddly has 100 percent control over his actors without them knowing it. The *Cheers* squad seemed to be an uncontrollable lot of lunatics who never paid attention to anything anyone told them to do, but in reality, that wasn't the case.

Jimmy is what a real director should be. He grants infinite amounts of freedom to his stars, allowing them to be their creative best, all the while holding his invisible reins and getting them to do anything he wants them to do.

I spent six years on *Cheers* and never once saw Jimmy lose it. He had created an atmosphere of lightness and camaraderie long before I came on the scene. I walked into an unruly summer camp. No one was ever on time (no one meaning the actors, especially the boys). I've never seen anything close to it. It seemed strictly unprofessional. Woody might show up an hour late, Kelsey, perhaps three hours. George and John, usually only 20 to 40 minutes late. Rhea was on time, mostly. Ted, yeah, Ted was pretty much on time, but the whack part was that no one cared. Jimmy could have cared less. When I mentioned a few times in the beginning, "Jimmy, no one comes on time," he would just laugh it off.

About four weeks in I made a "late jar." Ten bucks had to go into the jar any time one of us was late. The proceeds would go to some "on time" charity. The jar soon filled up, but never caused anyone to be on time. The guys were all very philanthropic and more than happy to contribute to the charity daily.

By week five I gave up and joined the party. I would show up in the 15-to-45-minutes-late category. Except for once, I never got reprimanded for it. The *only* time Jimmy Burrows got ticked at me for being late was when Rhea and I showed up 45 minutes late from lunch. And that was only because the guest star of the show that week was the chairman of the Joint Chiefs of Staff, Colin Powell!!!

Jimmy is one of the most thoughtful, caring people I've come across. All throughout the show, I was desperate for a baby. Everyone in the cast had kids. I got pregnant while shooting *Look Who's Talking Too*, and everyone, including Jimmy, was elated.

During the shooting of *Cheers* that year I went in for a routine exam with my obstetrician. It resulted in him having to tell me I'd had a spontaneous abortion; the baby had died inside me. I was devastated. Jimmy couldn't have been sweeter and more considerate and consoling to me. All the guys were like that. It helped me heal quickly.

Jimmy is notorious for giving actors comedy bits:

"Hey Woody, pretend like you slam your hand in the cash register."
"Hey Ted, when she kisses you, fall against the door."
"Hey Kirstie, when the Righteous Brothers walk in, fall on your knees, then faint."

Jimmy is in love with his bits. They make him giggle like a lovesick schoolboy. His arms start flailing around. And he sorta bobs up and down, consumed with exhilaration.

Then the actor does the bit, and Jimmy goes into convulsions, laughing. He is by far the best audience a comedy actor will ever have.

If you know what Jimmy's laugh sounds like, you can hear it in every show he directs. When I watch *Will & Grace*, I hear that crazy Jimmy laugh. It's unmistakable and inspires the actors to carry on and know they are funny.

I learned something about the subject of "hire slowly and fire fast" from Jimmy. When guest stars came on the show (the ones hired by the casting director—not celebs, politicians, or sports figures, but just the run-of-the-mill actors who were hired as "guest stars"), they were either funny . . . or gone in a heartbeat. They had one shot in the first run-through to be funny.

The most shocking one was an actress who was hired to play my sister in a few episodes. A model/actress got the highly publicized role. She looked a lot like me, except far prettier. Lots of actresses had tried out for the role, and unfortunately, the one who got the role was publicized in the trade magazines. I'll never forget the fateful day when we had our first run-through and I heard Jimmy utter, "Not funny." I pleaded with him. "Give her another shot. She's a model. Tell her to talk louder. Hell, you can't even hear her."

Jimmy just calmly said, "Not funny, Kirstie. She's just not funny." I can't imagine how embarrassing it must have been for her to be fired and replaced. Marcia Cross eventually was cast as my sister. But, you know what? She wasn't funny. Jimmy is the master of comedy and hastened the inevitable by firing her five minutes in.

That taught me a lot about funny and taking the time to cast properly and not trying to make someone funny. It doesn't exist, nor does it work. Funny, as Jimmy showed me time and time again, is a combination of timing and an innate ability to make people love you, hate you, wanna sex you up, but mostly just laugh.

Jimmy Burrows made me fall in love with being funny. He validated our cast's comedic abilities to the point that we had certainty in our craft. Certainty is the single most valuable quality an actor can have, especially when it's founded in truth. Jimmy gave me a lifelong confidence that I could and should continue to make people laugh.

The Charles Brothers

I don't think in all of my six years on *Cheers* I ever saw Glen or Les Charles alone. Sometimes—most of the time, I must confess—I didn't know Glen from Les. They were just "The Charles Brothers." I tried to make up mnemonics: Glen, glasses; Les, not. Or was it Glen, no glasses, Les, yes?

They were intimidating! The duo happens to be a set of highly intelligent, friendly, yet not giddy men. Glen and Les were the writer/producer cocreators of *Cheers*. When you do a sitcom, you see the director all day every day. The writer/producers are holed up in some windowless room banging out the episodes and punching up the jokes. At the end of a sitcom day, you do a run-through. It's what the audience sees when they watch a sitcom, but no one is in hair or makeup or costumes and the actors are walking around the set holding scripts. Except if your name happens to be Rhea Perlman and you can learn lines via telepathy, so you won't need the script for run-throughs.

There are many writers in a show like *Cheers*. Then there are the network execs and the studio execs. Our network was NBC and our studio was Paramount.

At day's end some assistant director, spelled "g-o-f-e-r," would line up about 30 director's chairs in front of the set. Then all the writer/producers and execs would file in and sit in the chairs and the remaining crew would stand in crowds behind the chairs. All of them had notepads to make notes, even if their job was to get coffee. Glen and Les were always center stage. Glen and Les couldn't have been nicer and more welcoming to me. They were always cordial and conversational. These two Latter-day Saints, Mormon-raised men, were not giddy or ridiculous or loony like our acting troop or like Jimmy.

I was on the show six years and always thought there was a chance that one week the words "Lose the chick with all the long curly hair" would be scribbled on either Glen's or Les's notepad.

I ran around muttering, before I'd say hi to Glen-glasses, Les-not, "Oh, lord, or is it the other way around?"

They flustered me! The stupid thing is they actually look nothing alike. Oh hell, maybe they were identical twins. To me they were like black people are to the KKK: "they all look alike." Of course by this time I could never ask, "What's your name again?" and Rhea had pointed out who was who a bazillion times. To this day I can't figure out why or how I constantly confused them. They were sort of like the mighty and powerful Wizard of Oz to me. They are a team, a pair, a couple. They are one entity, which is about the worst thing you could ever say about anyone.

I loved them. I went to parties and celebrations and funerals and events with them. They wrote thousands of lines I ended up speaking, and I'm eternally grateful to them. I still just wish I could figure out which is which. I guess I can say among hundreds of things, the thing that Glen and Les inspired me most to do was to learn how to differentiate and to wear name tags at parties. I'm so glad I'm not the mother of identical twins. I would have to tattoo my children at birth.

Ted

God, I love Ted!! How he didn't have seizures when I replaced Shelley Long is beyond me. They were the Lunt and Fontanne, the Astaire and Rogers of sitcom world. Beloved by, what, 30 million people a week or more?

God bless Ted Danson for his patience, confidence, and stability during my first episodes. I think Ted had input into me being hired. How much, I never asked. Oh, here's the kicker! I'd *never* done a sitcom! Or a comedy.

Sitcoms are hybrids of plays and television with four cameras whizzing around the stage like bumper cars (without the collisions, usually). I'd only done one play, and movies. No live audience, no having to speak up, or the hardest part: wait for the laughs. You have an entire audience sitting at the edge of the stage. If they think something is funny, they laugh; then you, as an actor, need to hold just long enough for the laugh but not so long that you leave a hole in the entire production. You couldn't mumble, as I'd been accustomed to doing in movies, or speak so quietly as to hear a pin drop. Movie actors can become incredibly self-indulgent. There's no group in front of that camera, no audience reacting to your every move, just *you* in close-up with *one* camera pointed at your face. Motionless. Deafening silence is the atmosphere of a movie when the director yells "Action." No one dares to speak or move or laugh, god forbid, even when you're shooting a comedy—just dead calm. Not a bunch of sugar-pumped yahoos sitting up in the peanut gallery laughing, twitching, squirming, leaving for the restroom, opening the candy the hype-boy throws into their waiting hands. No, no, no, a sitcom is a three-ring circus, and it was all foreign to me!

But Ted, Ted Danson, was a pro! He never let me see him sweat, if he did. I was never party to his possible late-night calls to Jimmy or the Charles Brothers (lying in the same bed, because in my universe they both answer the phone simultaneously), "Will they please, please fire this girl, please!" I would surely have fainted at his feet if he ever so much as hinted that I wasn't funny or talented.

Ted Danson is the most generous actor I've come across in my career. He is so egoless when you're working with him that it seems he must be . . . acting. But he's not. In the comedy world, actors vie for the jokes. They can get snarky and cunning in the ways they go about getting the jokes. The nasty ones will ruin the timing of a joke so that when you say the punch line, it's not funny. The evil ones will cry to the producer or director, "Fuck! she's not funny, give me the joke, I'll make it work." All sorts of shenanigans exist on sets, not just in comedies but in all genres of acting. I'm sure you've heard the term "upstaging." Same thing. It came from the theater, when an actor would move behind the other actors, in which case the others would have to turn their heads to the upstage actor and their backs to the audience. Many actors are selfish and relish the opportunity to upstage other actors, and *Cheers* was Ted's show, for crying out loud. He'd been the star of it for five award-winning years. He never once, for one day, minute, or second acted like

Hi, I'm Ted Danson, handsome, talented, and head-honcho leading man of Cheers.

Ted taught me humility and generosity as an actor. Ted is a true renaissance man. He's gentle. And he also has a very big dick.

One of our weekly games before shooting on show night was to see who could get shots of whom naked in the shower. Woody used a butter knife to unlock the bathroom door while Ted was showering. I manned the camera. George kicked the door open. Woody flung the shower door open. I snapped the photo of naked Ted. I swear to God he was well endowed. I would show you the picture, but my hands were shaky and I decapitated him in the photo.

There was never a nude photo snapped of me, but not for lack of conspiring and attempting. One night while I was showering, Woody came down through the acoustic tiles in the ceiling. But by the time he'd plummeted to the floor and stood up, I'd grabbed a towel.

I secretly think Ted kinda liked us girls giggly and ogling his impressive member—what guy wouldn't?

The thing about the *Cheers* men that was superlative was the way they took care of Rhea and me and Bebe Neuwirth. They were always playful and bawdy, but gentle with us, like they were holding kittens. Ted led the pack, he set the tone of the other men. He could have set it any way he wanted, but chose to be a pro and make it all look easy. Believe me, it's not easy being the lead of any production. All eyes look to the lead to set the pace and the tone. Ted makes it look so fucking easy that I feel he's been overlooked for blockbuster leads in many movies. He is an exquisite actor in both drama and comedy. He has impeccable timing and never pushes jokes or mugs (makes faces) like the rest of us on *Cheers* would do when a joke wouldn't work.

He was swag long before the word was coined, and he dances like a dream. Any actor in Hollywood would be lucky and honored to work with Ted. I know I was. Although Ted and I had countless hilarious encounters, series talks, and six years of shared stories with each other, on and off the *Cheers* set, my happiest professional moment with Ted came in 1990 when he finally won an Emmy for *Cheers* after nine years of nominations! 1990! Halla-fuckin-lujah! Finally, the comedy boy-genius of the 1980s–'90s was validated for making it all just look so simple. Kudos to him for sitting there in the audience for nine long years watching *Cheers* being awarded 28 Emmys, including one to his comedy-novice girl Friday, Rebecca Howe. Now Ted had finally received his just desserts. My heart sang for him, America's hearts sang for him! There was finally justice in TV land.

Kelsey

There are few times in one's life when you run head-on into genius. If you have ever, or should ever, smack into Kelsey Grammer, that's what you've collided with—genius. Kelsey is a dichotomy. He is, was, a bad-boy blend of a very naughty boy and a Rhodes scholar. You will never find a quicker, more articulate wit than Kelsey's, no matter what any of his idiot ex-wives portray him as. He is nothing as he seems or they prattle on about.

Kelsey's intellectual persona is indeed real. He is infinitely talented and ridiculously hilarious. Humor like Kelsey's could only stem from intelligence.

Kelsey's drug and alcohol history is public knowledge. Because I also had drug problems in my past, it gave us a common reality. Not that no one else in the cast ever did any drugs, but Kelsey and I seemed to be the unfortunate ones to make it our life's work for several years. I hadn't done drugs for eight years when I joined the cast of *Cheers*, so my drug past was far behind me. Kelsey's drug and alcohol use was right on top of him.

I made it my unsolicited mission to get him clean. Before he was

My husband whisked me away in a fire truck—this gave a new meaning to a "hot" relationship.

Babies who get married— love that Bob!

Shivers down my spine— ahhh, Jake!

"Funny little good for nothing Nicky" and me at the opera in 1982.

Merrit Butrick and I goofing around on the set of my first movie, *Star Trek II: The Wrath of Khan*.

Tom, Tom, Tom—could you be any hotter? Too bad you were dating my roommate! Hehe

Tom Selleck and I on the set of *Runaway*—right before Gene Simmons murdered me!

Newlyweds on the town in Hollywood!

This is the best present Parker ever gave me—Cinderella. Jeez! He's so f'ing handsome—wow.

"Hormone" (Mark Harmon) and I all dressed up on the set of *The Fresh Prince of Bel-Air*.

Luckiest actress in Hollywood. Hubba hubba.

We came so close . . . and yet so far.

"Oh Woody, I adore you."

David Crosby—love me some David!

McDreamy before he was Dr. McDreamy.

"True" love.

John and I rehearsing
the foxtrot—what? Was
this move part of it?

John and I celebrating in
Vancouver.

We shared everything—
almost.

Who's the most
handsome assistant
in the world? Jimmy,
Jimmy, Jimmy!

Don't all assistants and
their bosses do this?

Dan, Wally, and Chill—
they made "funny" sexy.
Smooch!

Gil and I *not* flirting.

I love my daddy!

At my fave restaurant Joso's in Toronto, filming *It Takes Two* with Steve Guttenberg.

One of my most cherished photos: "Spanky" McFarland all grown up from *The Little Rascals*.

Mother & Son . . .
sun hats.

Hot man—down under—filming *Blonde*.

Fiftieth birthday party. How do people live this long?

Me with my buddy Scott and my newly acquired oil painting of Wallace and Gilbert—LOBSTER!

The last "honest man" and his "now honest" daughter.

"Love Tent" Italian style.

My toy boys jumping for joy.
Photographer: Brian Doben

Mrs. Robinson
takes a time out.
Photographer:
Brian Doben

This is how dancers stand around.
Photographer: Brian Doben

"Love of my life"
turned Bestie Forever.

"True Baby" all grown up.

Connor Cruise—my second son.

Director Robert Allan Ackerman on the beach between takes in *Suddenly*.

Pick one . . . any one. Ahhh, Italians. *Photographer: Troy Plota*

Jonny Boy "Husband #3"?

My favorite designer, Zang Toi—
catwalk interview—*purrr!*

Smokin' Dan Cortese
smoking a Louboutin.

Sorta says it all.

"Jonny" love.

True and Ben Travolta's first
guitar lesson: "priceless."

This is how I rolled for six
weeks: "Club Girl" with
Craig Robinson—"Epic!"

put in jail for a DUI, I went to court to plead his case before the judge to send him to a rehab instead of jail. A group of 20 Mothers Against Drunk Drivers peppered the courtroom. Their goal is to put all DUI drivers in jail. I understood this goal; my own mother was killed by a drunk driver. I differ with MADD in that I don't see 30 days in jail as a solution to drunk driving. Maybe 365 days of jail might do the trick. But since many accumulate double and triple DUIs, not including the hundreds of times they've driven drunk or high without getting caught, I don't see the 10-to-30-day jail stay as a solution.

I pled my case and Kelsey's case, but to no avail. His sentence was not rehab, it was the pokey.

I came to visit him in jail. I must admit, it was sorta star studded. Those in residence included Marlon Brando's son, who had killed Marlon's daughter's lover.

I don't know if I had any influence on Kelsey's sobriety, which he later attained. I guess I don't really care. I'm just glad he's over that monumental hump.

I wish you could all personally know Kelsey. He is such a sweet, insightful person. He is a deep thinker and a genuinely caring person. He is a vulnerable soul and he has lived a very painful and bizarre life, full of losses and strange deaths before he became a star.

Kelsey is as strong as he is fragile. As wild as he is tame. He is a survivor extraordinaire, and I will always be thankful for his vastly different colors. Kelsey makes a Sherwin-Williams paint deck look like a six-color box of Crayolas.

George and John

Lumping George Wendt and John Ratzenberger together does them both a tremendous injustice. However, I, like the rest of America, got accustomed to seeing them sit side by side at the end of the *Cheers* bar.

Although they are night and day from each other, day in day out for six years I chatted with them across the highly varnished bar top, so these are my most vivid memories of the dynamic duo.

The location where John and George perched was the hub of the *Cheers* set. It's where we all hung out, hovering around George and John like flies. Get it? Barflies? Ugh, I digress.

Like his character Cliff, John is a fount of stories and information. Unlike Cliff, among other things, John does not have a Boston accent. George, in my opinion, was the pathos of *Cheers*: the gentle giant who filled the TV with shy intelligence and sweetness. George is exactly like Norm, but with a lot more sex appeal and charisma.

Whether we were sitting on the bar, hanging on the bar, or leaning over the bar, we all hung in that exact location, in front of George and John. If you think it felt warm and cozy when you watched the show, you should have experienced the love when you were in the show, at the bar where everyone not only "knew your name" but wanted to stand and laugh and talk to you for 218 episodes.

When I think of George and John and all of us nestled around them, I have the distinct feeling of being wanted. I have the feeling of well-being a person has when she has found her home, her location in the vast universe. No other men have ever made me feel that safe and wanted.

The night we shot my first episode, while we were all in hair and makeup, John and George gave me a gift. It was a 12-gauge shotgun with a card that read, "If you ever want to leave us, you're going to have to shoot your way outta here."

Can you fathom anything more heartwarming?

I was deeply touched and did what I always do when I'm touched: I cried and fucked up my makeup.

Woody

Woody made me feel like I was in the middle of the scene in *The Wizard of Oz* when Dorothy had to say good-bye to the Lion, the Tin Man, and the Scarecrow.

I had, and have had, a soft spot for Woody Harrelson. Saying good-bye to him the last night of *Cheers* was painful. "And you, I'll miss you most of all," wept Dorothy to the Scarecrow. Woody and I had a very special bond with each other. Come to think of it, Woody called me "Kirst"—perhaps the only man I would let utter that word without me rolling my eyes or slugging him.

Woody felt like half-brother, half-lover to me, although we were neither. Not because he wasn't willing. Woody spent several nights sleeping at my house in the downstairs floral guest room. Once with a girl named Penelope. He was tired of her and didn't want much to do with her, so he came knocking on my door around midnight. "Kirst," he whispered at the door, "can I talk to you?" I threw a robe on and met him in the kitchen. Woody was single, but he would incessantly insist we sleep together, half joking, half serious. He liked to startle me with the suggestion.

"Oh shut the fuck up, Woody, we're not sleeping together!" I would say, half joking, half wishing I wasn't married that night and could bang his brains out.

Woody is a wild child, a flower child, a redneck, and a poet. He is a dichotomy, a walking contradiction. But Woody would laugh that infectious Woody laugh, and we would talk.

He's like my son, True, always giving me too much information. He talked about that Penelope girl who was down the hall sleeping or pouting or whatever she was doing because he had decided he didn't want to have sex with her.

"Woody, why the hell would you bring a girl over here to spend the night in the same bed with you if you didn't want to sleep with her?"

The bigger question was what the hell Woody was doing at my house in the first place. We hadn't gone out earlier that night. He hadn't brought Penelope by to visit us. As I recall, he just showed up to sleep at our Encino estate, twice owned by Al Jolson. He'd done this before alone, but never with a date.

Funny how you never ask, "What are you doing here?" and only give thought to it 20 years after the fact.

When Parker wasn't available, out of town working and such, Woody and I would go to premieres, parties, and other social engagements together. We did this up until not too long ago, even when I was divorced from Parker and Woody was married to Laura and had kids.

It's sorta like this perfect duo in a strange way. I'm happy with Woody just shooting the shit or speaking about the deepest concepts of life. We rarely agree on anything religious, and he has some habits I'd like him to break. I guess I'm the big sister he would occasionally decide he'd like to shag.

Woody is sexy as hell, don't get me wrong, but our relationship never tipped into incest, we were 95 percent siblings.

At *Cheers* parties, Woody and I would dance for hours as he downed endless shooters of tequila. We were whoopers and hollerers. We even shared an office on the Paramount lot for a couple of years. The office consisted of him and his assistant, Laura, whom he ended up marrying, and me with my assistant, Jim. Laura would walk through the white French door that separated our dry-walled offices to lament about the woes of being Woody Harrelson's girlfriend. If I told her once, I told her a thousand times, "Just dump him! He's a player!! He'll never grow up, he doesn't believe in marriage and he'll break your heart."

They've now been together for 20 years. They did get married and as for breaking her heart, you'd have to ask her. But they seem sorta perfect together.

One of my favorite stories about Woody depicts not only the casualness of *Cheers* but our funny relationship. One day at I think around noon, I was driving around Beverly Hills shopping. I was all happy-go-lucky. It was Saturday and I wanted to spend some money. In and out of stores I'd go, relishing my day off shopping.

My car phone rang. It was Woody. "Hey, Kirst, how ya doing?"

"I'm great! I just bought twenty pairs of shoes! How are you?" I asked.

"Um, Kirst, where are you?"

"Beverly Hills, fool!"

"Um, Kirst, um, you wanna come into work today?" he asked in this lazy, laid-back manner.

"Woody, fool, it's Saturday. Why the hell would I come to work?"

"Um, Kirst, um, because it's Friday and we're all waiting for you."

Woody is a cross between Brando, James Dean, and Tommy Lee Jones—a glorious actor, a rare individual, and one of the loves of my life.

• • •

Ted, Kelsey, George, John, Woody. If they could have been my "brother-husbands," I would have married them all.

Sometimes I wonder if men and women really
suit each other. Perhaps they should live
next door and just visit now and then.

—KATHARINE HEPBURN

The Art of Alarm Clocks

OH LORD, my assistant Jim and I had our glory years together. We lived through the last several years of *Cheers*, movies on hiatus from *Cheers*, money rolling in, and wild, raucous, crazy freedom. Jim was a midwestern boy from Detroit who looked like a clone of John-Boy Walton except blonder, bluer-eyed, and sans the birthmark. I have no idea how I met Jim, either he came on board as an intern at Paramount or he applied to me directly. Jim seems to have dropped from outer space, as I can't for the life of me remember where he came from.

Jim and I were a jolly pair, and we were sort of alike in many ways. He and I found most things hilarious, even when other people would have panicked. My favorite Jim moments were when he became tortured by a psycho fan of mine named "Remy."

To let you know just how psycho Remy was, he was in a wheelchair because he'd driven 120 miles an hour into a brick wall—intentionally—"to see what it would feel like."

Remy called Jim many times a day to demand things. I shared an office space with Woody Harrelson on the Paramount lot, a stone's throw from the *Cheers* set. I ran over to the office every break I had to hear the stupid Remy stories from Jim. If I got *really* lucky, Jim would be talking to Remy on the phone when I arrived. Jim always put his hand over the phone and mouthed "Remy" so that I wouldn't speak.

"I know, Remy . . . I know you think you're married to her. Uh, huh, right, but see, Remy, TV people are characters, Rebecca Howe isn't a real person. Okay, okay, stop screaming, Remy, I can't hear you when you yell, uh, huh, no, she won't be coming home soon, oh yes, I do believe you when you say she's speaking directly to you during the shows, yes, many people feel that way, Remy, she's a good actress and playing a CHARACTER. Remy? Remy? Remy? I have to go now. I have to hang up. Uh, huh, yes, I'll let her know she's late for dinner."

Jeez, Jim talked to Remy several times a day over the years. How he was so patient, I'll never understand, but it did provide us with a constant stream of hilarity. Jim would get off the phone and relay all of Remy's hallucinations. Of course we had a private investigator, Gavin de Becker, check him out. Of course Remy had been in and out of institutions, and clearly he'd used a plethora of drugs, but he *was* funny.

"Jim, Jim, get her on the phone Jim! Now! She's my wife, Jim! Do you hear me Jim? Come on Jim!! Put her on the dang phone Jim." Remy's demands always had Jim's name in them. Every single sentence like a bad soap opera. "Jim! I didn't like her hair last night. She's getting too skinny, Jim."

Usually when you have such a psychotic stalker, you *never* speak to them. Jim and I figured Remy would have to roll his wheelchair to my location to murder me, so we would probably see him coming, IF his arms worked. I mean—120 miles an hour into a brick wall?

This was a good example of my relationship with Jim. He wasn't a serious guy, he was like my brother. We fought with each other and did multitudes of sibling stuff, but mostly we laughed at everything and everyone. We were bad and bratty. We spent endless hours together.

When I was filming a movie, Jim traveled with me for months. There was not an ounce of flirtation between us, eeeew, it woulda been like coming on to my real brother. But clearly we were a match made in prankster heaven.

Somehow Jim and I had gotten this chicken alarm clock that was really loud and would yell, "Hey baby wake up, get outta that bed," or something stupid like that. Over and over and over and over until it hit the wall. Jim and I would hide it under each other's bed or in a dresser or in a pillow just to screw with the other one. Endlessly, I tell you! This went on for years! This chicken would show up in Maine, LA, Canada, Wichita. It was so freaking irritating! When I did it to him, it was hilarious. And that's how Jim and I were most alike, in our love of pranks. Most people get tired of pranks and knock it off after a few days. Our pranks lasted years!!

Jim was so handsome and so preppy-looking. But lurking inside was a lunatic.

My kids adored Jim. He was great with them, too. Before True came to us the paparazzi were swarming my house. Hanging on the fences, hiding in the trees, endlessly. Remember, I'd had a miscarriage not long before, and the hospital leaked it to the paps. Anyway, they were on me like black on night.

Jim and I came up with an amazing scheme. I told Jim to tip the paps off that something big was going to happen and that he wanted $75,000 for the exclusive on it. They agreed if "it was big enough." "Oh, it's big enough. Kirstie and Parker are adopting a baby and he arrives next Friday." Ahhh—the eager wolves had blood dripping from their lips. Photos of me have always brought the paps a lot of money, and that's why they're on me nonstop. But $75,000 for a photo in 1992 was big time.

Jim and I giggled nonstop at every "leak/source" call he made to the rags. In the United States, a story does NOT have to be true. There just has to be a source. So basically your sisters, friends, mothers, and aunts could be a source, even if she's never met you. There is no law that the data must be researched or checked out for truth. It's different in the UK. There, the story, legally, must be true and best efforts must be made to prove its truth. That's why in many cases, the same story from the United States will not run in the UK. If you prove somebody in the UK ran a false story, it's grounds for a lawsuit that you WILL win.

In the United States, because a story doesn't have to have a thread of truth, it is very difficult to sue and win. By US law, sources are protected and don't have to be revealed. It's why you rarely see celebs sue. The rag mags are big business making big money. It could cost a celeb into the hundreds of thousands to sue them, and even *if* they win, the apology would end up on the last page of the rag, buried.

Anyway, these roaches had followed me home from the hospital after I expelled my dead baby. They'd snapped shots of me crying on my porch. It *was* payback time!

I made a call to a friend of mine and said, "Can I borrow your baby?"

"Hell, yes!" she said. She had a three-day-old baby boy. Jim cut the deal. On that next Friday I walked out of my Encino mansion and sat in the yard with my "new baby." It was well acted. First Jim and I walked out the door and scoured the area, something I used to do with each exit, spotting the thieves of souls. I sat with "my" baby close to the house. I kept looking around like a robin, looking for a predator. This was perhaps my finest performance to date. Jim was sitting across from me in the grass. He had a camera.

"Do you mind if I shoot a pic with your fake baby?" he asked.

"Why no, Jim, fire away," and those were the shots he sold to the rags for $75,000. After all, the story didn't have to be true, right? It goes both ways, right? It just had to be a source.

Jim handed over the photos, they handed over the money. Jim and I donated it to children's charities. The way I see it, everyone won! When I think of Jim I think of how much work we did in between laughing. Everything made us laugh.

On one occasion, about two years later, Jim was not laughing. I had flown with the kids to Maine after filming a movie in Vancouver. I wasn't willing to fly my cat Trixie in cargo, and the airline wouldn't allow her under my seat. I also wanted my SUV in Maine, as I was going to spend three months there. I asked—hahaha—told Jim to drive Trixie in my SUV to Maine, which was 4,000 miles away from Vancouver. He wasn't a happy camper. I didn't blame him. But I wanted my car and my cat. Jim would give me a nightly update on his cross-country cat trip. I made him put the phone up to Trixie's 16-year-old ears. "Hi Trixie . . . goo goo goo goo goo . . . you're almost home . . . kiss kiss kiss . . . be good for Uncle Jimmy . . . kiss kiss." I'm sure that kind of shit made Jim's blood boil. The duet was halfway across the country when Jim stopped calling. He didn't answer my calls, either. I began to get worried.

Here's what had happened. Jim was cruising along down the highway through a construction zone. A rock popped up, hit the window, and like a bomb blew out the back windshield. Trixie, who wasn't in a kennel, wigged out and jumped out of the car going 70 miles an hour. Trixie was already old by most standards. She was 16. I think that's 340 in cat years. So there 16-year-old Trixie flew—rapidly—into the abyss of a dark, rainy, highway. Jim immediately pulled over. He didn't see Trixie splattered on the pavement as he expected. It was getting late, and wheat fields lined both sides of the highway. The wheat was hip high. The rain was drizzling down. Jim could see a train passing in the distance. The sound was haunting. He called to Trixie but got no response. He couldn't hear her meow, so he began to traverse the wheat fields, calling for Trixie as he sloshed through the muddy ocean of wheat. He kept at it for hours. He sat in the middle of the field and was ready to cry. He was tired. He was freezing.

He had a choice to make. Look for god knows how much longer to probably find a dead cat lying in wet wheat, or to give up, and call me with the tragic news. There are really only two things you can do to make me go berserk. Fuck with my kids. Or fuck with my animals. He chose to keep searching. About two hours later, over by the train tracks, just before night fell, he heard a tiny meow from within the wheat. TRIXIE?? TRIXIE?? TRIXIE!!!!!!!! She was lying there, unable to move. He scooped her up, drove to the nearest town and found a vet. Trixie had a broken pelvis. Luckily it was a clean break. The doctor told Jim that if she could still poop, she would probably live. Jim called me and told me what happened. He showed up with Trixie 10 hours later. I rushed to her, scooped her up, and lay her on the bed I'd made for her. Two days later, she pooped. Ahhh, I could finally sleep!

The morning after her bowel movement I was jolted out of my sweet sleep.

"Hey baby wake up, get outta that bed," screamed the chicken alarm clock hidden beneath my pillow. Touché, Jim, touché.

The great question that has never been answered
and which I have not yet been able to answer,
despite my thirty years of research into the
feminine soul, is "what does a woman want."

—SIGMUND FREUD

The Art of Transcending Love

WITH MY best friend Kelly Preston's blessing, I'll tell you the love story between John Travolta and me. He probably remains the greatest love of my life. This love has spanned over 24 years and has had to go through numerous transformations. With the freedom to articulate, I'll tell you the tale.

Before my pilgrimage to California to pursue Scientology I wasn't aware that I would end up pursuing acting. It was a dream long since buried. At that time I only knew two Scientologists but had heard John was one, too. This was all pre-Internet and social media, so I guess I'd read it in a magazine somewhere. But in the back of my mind I thought, "Well, if I become a Scientologist, who better to marry than John Travolta?" It didn't register that millions of women across the world were thinking the same thing, except for the Scientology part.

People seem to think that all Scientologists know each other, and are besties. Kinda like saying, "Oh, you're a Mormon, are you friends with Mitt Romney?" I supposed there were tens of millions of Scientologists out there, but statistics never scare me. SOMEONE had to marry John Travolta. It might as well be me.

I never thought about the prospect of John again until I was sitting across the room from him, ten years later, in my agent Chris Barrett's living room. By this time I was married to Parker. I was supercocky and confident. I had movies under my belt. I'd worked with film greats and just happened to be starring in the number one TV show in the country. I was wearing jeans, high-heeled gray boots, a thin charcoal-gray cashmere turtleneck sweater, and my favorite jacket, a green-and-gray sort of tweed blazer that I'd picked up at a store called Sax Fifth Off, for $3. He had coal-black dyed hair because he was in the middle of filming a movie. He wore a white shirt, jeans, and boots that looked Italian. The writer/director of the movie, Amy Heckerling, was also in the eclectic living room of my agent. Because I was so full of myself, I wasn't starstruck. I was more concerned as to whether I was willing to spend the majority of my summer hiatus from *Cheers* working on a movie instead of going to Maine for vacation.

The movie being pitched was *Look Who's Talking*, a low-budget $8 million movie about a talking baby. It sounded awfully stupid and at the time was titled *Baby Talk*. But John was attached so I wanted to check it out.

John has an uncanny ability to make anyone seem like they are the only person in existence. He looks directly at you, not only at you, but through you. This is not a gimmick, it's his nature. John bestows authentic interest and genuine attention on whomever he's speaking to. Unlike me, who "works" the room in a meeting. He was calm and sincere, and gave you no choice but to realize you're in the company of something unique and powerful. I felt myself drawn to his irresistible candor.

The director, Amy, was answering my questions. "So is the baby going to talk in a baby voice?"

"No," Amy, a cross between Woody Allen and Amy Winehouse, replied. "The baby will have the voice of an adult famous actor." She went on, "It's the baby's sophisticated train of thought that I'm interested in. People always think babies have 'baby' views of things. I think babies think like we do." She must have had some foresight into the success of Stewie from *Family Guy*, or Seth MacFarlane admired her screenplay and took it up a notch.

John weighed in as to his take on the movie. When he was speaking, I blanked out. All I could see were his voluminous cushy lips moving and his cobalt-blue eyes penetrating my brain. "Blah, blah, blah, blah, blah, blah." He really needn't have gone on, he had me at "blah."

After the meeting he walked me to my car. He admired my $3 jacket, commenting that it reminded him of a jacket worn by a woman he'd been in love with. John had had a long love affair with a beautiful actress named Diana Hyland who was 20 years his senior. "It reminds me of Diana," he said. I had no idea what he was talking about but accepted the compliment. He asked what I thought about *Baby Talk*. I said I wanted to do it but it would have to film when my show went down for hiatus.

I then said, "I always wondered if I'd meet you. I read you were a Scientologist."

He replied, "Yes, I am."

I said, "Me, too."

"Wow, I didn't know that about you," which clearly indicated he didn't know much about me, as I was very outspoken and still am about the subject. "Well, hopefully you can work your scheduling out, I really want you in this movie."

I really want me in this movie, too, I thought as I zoomed out of Chris's driveway in my very bad Baltic blue BMW 633 CSi. It wasn't love at first sight by any means. It was just electric. Electric was not a new sensation for me.

I'd been married for six years when I landed in Vancouver, BC, to shoot *Look Who's Talking*. I was at the hotel unpacking when John called and asked if I wanted to go to this dance place with a couple of his friends for a drink. John and his friends Anson and Linda showed up in a driver-driven van. I hopped in and Anson offered me a shot of tequila. *Why not, we have a driver, hell, who knows, maybe it's legal to drive around drinking Cuervo in Canada.* By the time we got to the club I was tipsy. Other than during my cocaine years, I was a cheap date.

The club turned out to be a country-western knockoff of Gilley's from *Urban Cowboy*, which of course became the subject of conversation. I had a couple more shots of tequila, which is two more than I can handle.

Drunkenly, I started in on him. "Okay, John, for the rest of the night, don't be yourself, be Bud from *Urban Cowboy*, but I'm not going to call you Bud because that would be just too stupid. So imma call you Wayne, yeah, imma call you Wayne."

This began our 24-year passion for doing skits with each other, something that he, Anson, and Linda, his besties, had done for many years prior.

I made him talk only in "Wayne's" voice. If he slipped back into being John I corrected him. We were all drunk, except for Wayne, who never drinks much, and we were very loud. That's when Wayne asked me to dance. I'll never forget it: what Patrick had done for me, dirty-dancing me around the clubs of Charleston and Natchez, Mississippi, Wayne did for me in the two-step.

I instantly felt the electricity go up a thousand volts. He was so smooth, so sexy, so, oh lord in heaven, here I go again! Danger, danger Will Robinson!! "Knock it off," I heard my dad's voice say. "Knock it off!" I heard my dad screaming in my ear. But I didn't want to knock it off, I wanted to take it to the moon.

I felt like the road show version of Debra Winger—no wonder she gave such a stellar performance in *Urban Cowboy*, she had to have fallen for Wayne, er, uh, Texas Bud, er, uh, John.

We danced the night away, and it was love. But was I in love with John or Wayne? Who cared, I was in love with one of 'em.

As filming went along it got worse—or better, depending on your viewpoint. We fell deeper and deeper and deeper in love. As if it weren't messed up enough that I was married, I had to remind myself we were both Scientologists, ugh, half of our religion is about ethical behavior, the quest to take full responsibility for every aspect of our lives, to rise above the status quo and do the right thing, to have integrity and honesty, and to set good examples for people. Well, it all sounded good. And I was—he was—trying like crazy to just keep it friendship, to not step over the line, which mentally we had stepped over the day we danced.

It was becoming a real dilemma, not just a movie crush. We both knew it, and so did my husband because I confessed to him what was happening. Apparently I didn't confess enough because it just kept getting more intense and I just kept beating myself up for being such a shitty Scientologist, which isn't as stupid as it sounds. When a Scientologist gets a divorce or causes trouble on a set, god forbid, the story in the papers is never about the actual offense. I'm pretty convinced that taking a shit must have something to do with my religion, as far as the press is concerned.

But this one was real, for us, and we were both using every ounce of willpower we could muster up to do the right thing.

I tried my very best to "knock it off" and not fuck up my marriage, as I was still completely in love with my husband. We had a relationship that was sweet, rooted in admiration and respect. John also respected my marriage and was very fond of Parker.

It's almost impossible not to fall in love with your costar when you're filming a romantic movie. Can you imagine pretending 16 hours a day that you are in love with someone? And it's your job? Love scenes, fight scenes, makeup scenes, sex scenes. I've heard actors say, "It's just acting. There's a whole crew behind the camera. It's awkward. You have no feelings during love scenes." I wanna punch those actors in the gut for lying. Come on!! That's bullshit! Countless actors end their real-life relationships and run off with their costars. Isn't it a little obvious that within a year of filming, actors get divorces or publicly start dating their new girlfriend, who just happened to have been the costar on their last film? Of course it's our own fault. We chose acting as a profession. But unless the guy or girl lying in bed beside you in that love scene looks like a bulldog, you are going to become titillated!

Most people get office crushes or workplace crushes of one kind or another. But it's not part of the job description to make out by the water cooler.

One of the reasons I became an actress was to act with and make out with handsome costars. It's something I've wanted to do from the time I was three. Who doesn't superimpose themselves in a movie scene with Tom Cruise, Brad Pitt, Ryan Gosling, or Javier Bardem? It's why romantic movies work. You can experience yourself falling in love with the male or female movie stars. Just try making out with Johnny Depp for 12 hours a day and see how you fare.

The average movie takes three months to shoot, and most are on location away from your normal city and your real family. It's actually a recipe for divorce: one cup Ryan, a half-cup Angelina, four tablespoons of sex, and a dash of nightlife. You're fucked. It would take a saint to reject the affections of some of the most charismatic beings walking the planet.

There is an extremely high divorce rate in Hollywood, especially among film actors. It's not surprising. What is surprising is that any of us would get married in the first place, knowing the depth of the love traps. Don't get me wrong, I'm not condoning this shit, just laying out the reality of an actor's life.

Then there is the afterhours routine, usually going to dinner with each other and sometimes going to clubs or parties or premieres. Pretending to be in love 12 to 16 hours a day, then getting off work and going home to . . . each other. Show biz is by no means safe, sane, or secure. It's full of beauty. It's fraught with egos. It's rampant with sex appeal.

Most artists, especially actors, are free-spirited and wild-ass. If they become famous enough, they feel entitled to break all the rules and invent their own. They can usually charm the leaves off the trees. Most are intelligent, intense, funny, and rebellious. Honestly, how I managed to stay married for 14 years without banging any of them is a mystery and a testament to my own willpower. I know myself very well in the arena of sex. I'm not a casual lover, although I've aspired to be one. Sex is the nail that seals the coffin for me. If I wasn't in love with the guy before I had sex with him, I would surely convince myself I was by the time we were basking in the glow, smoking a Kool.

I'm not lying when I tell you the one thing I wish I could change about myself is the ability to have an affair without falling in love. It seems so groovy, so jet-set, so attractive, dangerous, exciting—so Hollywood!

But it's never worked for me. I've also never actually had a sexual affair. I'm the bride, never the bridesmaid. I'm never the date. I meet you, I love you, you love me, and you don't worry about seeing me next Saturday night, hell, you never take me home! From the time I was 16 until I was 50, I had one three-month break of not having a boyfriend or a husband. The only reason for the three-month sabbatical was to get a grip on myself and land a movie. I exiled myself into isolation so that my attention would strictly be on work, not some dude lying next to me who needed to discuss something. My personal belief is that "discussions" wreck relationships. Just shag each other. You'll either have angry sex, crying sex, or some other emotion of sex, but it will be evident what the sentiments are, and unlike a discussion, you get a big bonus at the end, which usually makes you forget what the discussion was about in the first place.

On movie sets you are living the dream, the fantasy. The line of reality versus acting is blurry at best. Your perceptions are clouded, a pseudoreality mixed with a pseudofable. It's sort of like an extended version of the most idiotic show on television, *The Bachelor*. While it's being filmed, it's nearly impossible to sort out the real feelings from the heightened realities of the production.

For John and me, the movie took a backseat to what we were, in fact, experiencing. We are two peas in a pod, volatile, passionate, funny, inventive. We both like to hold court and "outstar" each other. We vie for positioning in a room. We both suck the oxygen from the space.

We had to do a dance in the movie. He is world renowned for his movie dancing. I wasn't, but I still fought like a cat in heat with John and the choreographer to do the dance the way I felt was best. John and I would fight, slap each other, storm out of the rehearsal hall, endless drama. It was way more dramatic than the simplistic romantic comedy we were shooting. Then one of us would call the other at three o'clock in the morning and apologize for being an ass, then explode in mad laughter, you know, the way lovers do after coming to terms with their own stupidity.

One day, sitting in my trailer, we had "the" talk, the talk we had skirted around having for months. He wanted me for his wife. I wanted to marry him. We admitted to each other the truth, as best we could unravel it. There was a clarity there. For once, among all the chaos, there was clarity, right or wrong, good or bad, Scientology or no Scientology. We wanted to spend the rest of our lives together. There was only one thing standing in our way—my pesky husband. The only thing left for me to do was to decide whether I would divorce Parker. Parker and I didn't have children. John wasn't married, so there was no tie for him to break. The decision was clearly left in my hands.

Oh, I left one part out. The movie John had done before *Look Who's Talking*, the one where he had to dye his hair black? It was with Kelly Preston. Kelly was married during that movie, but John and Kelly had become a little smitten with each other. The attraction hadn't moved forward because of that, probably. I'd known Kelly for several years prior to meeting John because we had the same agent, Chris Barrett. The same agent who represented George Clooney. Chris frequently had all of us young up-and-coming actors/clients to his house for barbecues and to swim. I didn't know Kelly well, in fact I can't remember if Kelly and George lived together before or after she was married to some dude named Carl or Kevin or Kenny. Anyway, I knew Kelly and John had formed little crushes on each other. It was all becoming quite incestuous, which is typical of Hollywood. The six degrees of separation, Kevin Bacon theory, is not far off.

It was all quite complex and on the verge of becoming a Rubik's Cube. John and I together decided the best thing to do to make my decision is the thing Scientologists do when they are contemplating divorce or having marital difficulties. It boils down to a confessional, but not one-on-one with a priest, like Catholics do. In this case, Parker and I sat before a Scientology minister taking turns telling what we'd done and what we'd withheld from each other. Oh lord, I wished I was a Christian or a Jew or a Catholic at that sitting. How easy it would have been to say to a priest, "Forgive me, Father, for I have sinned, I've fallen in love with John Travolta." Perhaps he would have sent me on my way with 45,000 Hail Marys, which wouldn't have been spectacularly embarrassing.

But no, in my church you have to confess it to the person you've transgressed against. I mean, you don't *have* to, but it is the objective of the confessional—to fess up to what you've really been up to, to the person who should actually be in the know. It's the respectful thing to do.

Shit, I was squirming like a kid who just stole a Schwinn. The minister says nothing except for two things: "What have you done?" and "What have you withheld." Oh lord, I was first! "Um, let's see, um, what have I done? Let me think . . . um, oh yes, I, uh, danced with John in a sort of, well, a seductive way." Phew! One down.

"Thank you," said the minister. "What have you withheld?" he asked.

"Um, let's see, well that . . . um . . . That I was dancing all sexy and stuff on more than one occasion," I answered sheepishly.

"Thank you," he said, and it went like this for about 30 minutes with me peeling off my indiscretions. I tried not to make eye contact with Parker, but when I would get a glimpse I could see the steam shooting from his ruby-red ears.

Then in true Scientology fashion, the tables were turned. Now it was Parker's turn to answer the two questions. I'd just assumed he had been all Goody Two-shoes while I was loving up Mr. Travolta, and because I knew I was the culprit I hadn't given much thought to what he might have been up to.

Again, only this time addressed to Parker, "What have you done?"

Blah, blah, blah, blah, er, a um, blah, er, um, a blah, blah, my ears perked up, um and blah, blah. Confessionals are confidential, so what he said is of little importance in this story. But I can tell you, he was not up to what I was. His indiscretions were different from mine, but I was so pissed off that I wanted to leap across the desk and strangle him. But then why wouldn't I? So far I'd only confessed the small stuff.

Blah, blah, er, um, I'm so sorry, but blah, blah.

Ah hah! I thought, I'm definitely going to divorce him!

I've never been such a good listener in my life. I clung to every sordid detail as it justified an imminent split.

"What have you withheld?" asked the minister.

"Oh, this ought to be good!" I yelled.

"Kirstie, you're not allowed to comment during Parker's confessional," the minister said.

"Allowed?!" I screamed. "He's my fucking husband. I'll say whatever I want!!" I protested.

"You'll have your turn to comment when we come back around to you," the minister replied.

Oh shit! Back around to me? You mean we keep going back and forth in this "he said, she said" until we actually come clean? Oh, for fuck's sake, this is the meanest, dumbest religion on earth, I thought. I began mentally lining up the order of the next stuff I was going to have to tell, in order of the easiest to the big babonza: "I want a divorce so I can marry Travolta." I became quiet as a church mouse as I tried to contain my overwhelming urge to run next door and sign up at the Lutheran church.

It took us three days, back and forth, back and forth, spewing our guts out to come fully clean of *all* our indiscretions. We had dated two years before we were married and had been married for six, so we'd both racked up all sorts of crazy shit. Most of it was fairly innocuous, but we also both had some doozies.

A funny thing happens to people when they come clean with each other. Along the journey of the confessional, it went from grounds for murder to *I'm gonna kick the fuck outta you when we get outta here,* to *God, I'm so sorry I betrayed you,* to *Oh, so you're not so innocent either, mister,* to *Wow, I respect you for having the balls to tell me that,* to *I sorta remember why I married you, we're both a couple of louses,* to *I'm deeply sorry for hurting you,* to *I sorta love you,* to *What the hell was I thinking? I'm still madly in love with you!*

Not all Scientology confessionals have this end result, and it is not the end purpose. It's a huge achievement for all involved if it ends in rehabilitating a marriage to the point of staying together, but the end result is actually when the two people are in good affinity, reality, and communication with each other so that they can sanely discuss their future, together or apart.

I made my decision at the end of the confessional, and it was to salvage my marriage and continue on with my husband.

I called John and told him. He respected our decision. I'd like to say, as it would make my life seem more righteous and Candy Land–like, that it was the end of yearning for John. It was not. Every incarnation possible occurred over a multitude of years. I was the bee to his honey and vice versa. It was nearly impossible, no matter how much I loved my husband, to not be madly in love with John. If brother-husbands had been an option, I would have opted.

Look Who's Talking became an enormous hit! It made $300 million and was the highest-grossing comedy of all time (at that time). John and I were the talk of the town, even the world. *Cheers* was number one on TV and *Look Who's Talking* was number one at the box office, so of course *Look Who's Talking Too* was imminent. The only way I can keep track of my crazy evolution with John is by viewing the timeline of *Look Who's Talking* 1, 2, and 3, ugh, only in the life of an actress would a love affair be traced via IMDb.

John and I were struggling with our newfound "friendship only" relationship. He could not hold the line of us not being together as a couple. I wasn't great at it either, but on one particular occasion he was the absolute worst!

It was the Christmas after *Look Who's Talking* had been released. We were all being "very ethical" and civil to one another in the same fashion that I'd been civil to one of Parker's costar crushes when I had her to dinner to show Parker I was okay with her now. I made two pork chops for the three of us and drank half a bottle of Château Mouton Rothschild before I set about interrogating her and scoffing at every word out of her mouth.

No, no, we were all good. John, Parker, and I were all very adult about everything. So we invited John to spend the holidays with us at our Encino house. John hadn't pursued Kelly at this point because I think although she had divorced Carl/Kevin/Kenny, she was now engaged to Charlie Sheen. Anyway, all was going swimmingly, we hired a chef and dined like royalty. John and Parker smoked Cuban cigars on the porch as I decorated the house like Macy's windows. Christmas Eve was skits, laughter, and singing Christmas carols around the piano, all very Norman Rockwellish. We actually were doing very well together, all three of us.

Then came Christmas morning, the time for gift giving. I don't quite remember what Parker gave me, but for as long as I live I will recall what my good "friend" John gave me. He gave me a diamond-and-sapphire ring he'd brought from Singapore, a gorgeous dress, a check for $25,000 to keep or give to my favorite charity, a gray roan dressage jumping horse that was being shipped to our ranch in Oregon, and a telephone that had cameras in it. This was pre-computers, iPhones, cell phones, and Skype, but he had found somewhere in his journeys some futuristic contraption that I hooked half of to my house phone, he hooked the other half to his house phone, whereby every day when we spoke we could see each other on tiny screens. The invention was so cutting edge that one had to have a company to hook it all up and monitor the system. If I had been my husband I would have disemboweled John, right there on the spot in Macy's window. If it wasn't clear to Parker then that we all had a lot of work cut out for us, I don't know what could have jogged him into reality.

A good two-year period transpired before John and I got fairly good at our attempts to "just be friends," and even then they were fairly lame attempts. And yet we kept trying to be ethical.

Charlie and Kelly had broken off their engagement. I'm not sure if she returned her enormous bajillion-carat pink diamond. I'm not so sure I would have. John and I were having a conversation during the filming of *Look Who's Talking Too* and he brought up Kelly. I can't deny that although he wasn't mine, and it looked as though he never would be, I wasn't ready to let him go to anyone, let alone someone as gorgeous and remarkable as Kelly. It fueled the jealousy flame like a funeral pyre.

"Well," I said, "she is very pretty," in a weak, half-assed attempt. It's all so occluded for me. I can't remember the sequence precisely, but during the shooting of the movie I got pregnant . . . by Parker; jeez, I wasn't that gonzo. And this sorta changed the whole profile. Instantly I began ignoring John and promoting Kelly. John was in shock because of my abrupt about-face. He was right, me being pregnant was not grounds to ignore him, almost shun him. But when those hormones and those baby dreams start surging through the core of your being, all flirtations go out the window, rightfully so. In my case all communication had flown out the window. The thought of being pregnant and even speaking with John was abhorrent to me. Even being close friends felt tainted. Parker and I were like magnets to each other, and I became consumed with becoming a mother.

John and I later talked, and I apologized for being so cold and heartless. He understood, and we got our first glimpse of what "friendship only" might feel like. And it felt good.

Within the first month of my pregnancy, John had bought me enough maternity clothes to last through ten pregnancies. He was so sweet to me. Of course I wasn't showing yet, but I tried on the maternity clothes daily. It was a truly joyous time for Parker and me and also for John. We were forming a legitimate friendship, all three of us.

I got to know Kelly a little bit, without George or Charlie. I really liked her. And soon John began dating her for real.

I had a miscarriage three months into my pregnancy, so there was a brief time about six months after when I reconsidered divorce and going after John. But by then he was falling in love with Kelly, and I could see that even if I weren't with Parker, that she was the better choice.

Kelly has this beautiful way about her. She is a nourisher. She loves John so thoroughly, and she is the kind of woman who has the patience to handle him. He is a very intense, powerful, headstrong person. So is she, but it never conflicts with John. John and I would have ended up in some sort of *Who's Afraid of Virginia Woolf?* drama, no doubt.

There were other differences between John and me that would have clashed. I'm a farmer. I get up at 6:00 a.m. or earlier and am in bed by 10:00 p.m. John is a vampire. He goes to bed around the time I wake up. He lives for the night. His passion is flying airplanes; I used to be terrified of flying, actually, up until six years ago. We both have nonstop careers, always in motion, always in different parts of the world. I would never be willing to sacrifice my career for a man. I'm a gypsy by nature and get uncomfortable being in one location too long. Someone in a relationship has to be willing to be the one who takes care of the other and make them their priority. Call me old-fashioned, I probably am, but when a woman marries a man as powerful as John, she must be the one who yields to and supports him. I've never seen any woman do it more beautifully than Kelly. It's admirable. And she does this all while being one of the most powerful women I've met.

When I could clearly see this for myself, I urged John to marry her and not let her get away. There were a lot of men pursuing her. She's Kelly Preston, for Christ's sake. He was an idiot to not go in for the kill. I'm not saying he wasn't already intending to do it, but he was moving too slowly, even for me, so she was certainly ready to tell him to take a hike if he wasn't ready to take the lead.

Months passed, and I hadn't spoken to John. Then they called me from Paris. "We're married!!" they screamed.

"Oh, my god, congratulations!" I screamed back.

I was genuinely happy for them, joyous in fact. But regretfully, I was also the teeeeeniest bit envious. I also, hideous as it may seem, had thoughts like, *Well, neither of us has kids, so . . .*

We hung out together from time to time, but mostly went on about our lives. John and Kelly bought a house in Maine on the same island where Parker and I had a house. There were occasional light flirtations between John and me, but they were mostly just dying habits.

Then Parker and I adopted True, and John and Kelly had Jett.

When John and I did *Look Who's Talking Now*, we had our babies on the set. John and I were doing a scene where I was dressed in an elf costume because in the script, he wasn't cutting it as a full-time commercial pilot so I had to take on a part-time job. We were shuckin' and jivin' and doing our John-and-Kirstie thing between takes. Kelly was on the sideline holding Jett and watching.

When we broke for lunch, I was holding True in my arms. She was holding Jett in her arms. We were filming in a department store, and Kelly and I were also looking at some clothes on a rack. We were alone, no John, no Parker. She looked right at me and sweetly said, "Are you flirting with my husband?"

This was my "come to Jesus" moment. Shyly and almost inaudibly I whispered, "Yeahhhh . . . I think I sorta am. I'll knock it off."

She smiled that beautiful smile of hers and said, "Okay, good."

I've been put in my place several times in my life, rightfully so, but this was the sweetest, most gentle ass-whooping I've ever endured. I took it seriously, and it hit home like a ton of bricks falling on my out-of-line head.

I cannot tell you the impact it had on my life. It made me *look* at my marriage. It forced me to inspect why I *was* still married if I was going to fall in love with other men or flirt chronically. She had posed a very important question without actually asking it: *What the hell was wrong with me?*

And also, possibly, *What the hell was wrong with my marriage?*

If I'd come clean, squeaky clean, with my husband, which I always did, what was there about that relationship that was unfulfilling? I stopped looking at me and started looking at us. We were both fine people, individually, but how were we really collectively?

Kelly herself is no saint, believe me, but I didn't need a saint. I needed a friend. And that was the day we became friends.

We raised our kids and did our jobs and stayed married. John and Kelly, Parker and I. In 1997 I decided I wanted a divorce, partially for the right reasons and partially for the wrong ones. John and now Kelly were there for me.

I still knew John a lot better than I knew Kelly. At one point in their marriage, probably around 2003, they went through a little rough patch. That's when I got to really know Kelly. I was put in the position to test my "friendship" with John—my "real" friendship. My decision was to help her. To help them. To do everything in my power to help them build an even stronger marriage. This is when I realized there were no more blurred lines. My destiny was to be his best friend.

Kelly asked me to be her best friend. I'd never been asked that before. It was so sweet—so "Kelly." I accepted!

Wow, what a bonus I got by accepting that proposal. Now I have two best friends. Friends who would go to war for me and vice versa.

Courageous, hilarious, crazy-assed, warm, generous, brave best friends.

We've been through heaven and hell together. The darkest hours and the brightest days imaginable. They have changed my life forever, for the better.

John was the love of my life. Both Kelly and John know the new love of my life is waiting in the wings. And I agree.

Your children are not your children. They are the
sons and daughters of life's longing for itself . . .
You may house their bodies but not their souls,
for their souls dwell in the house of tomorrow,
which you cannot visit, not even in your dreams.

—KAHLIL GIBRAN

The Art of True Love

WAS 39 years old. I'd bought into the Hollywood myth that all those actresses who were older than I were belting out multiple babies by conceiving the old-fashioned way. Guess I learned the hard way—the painful way that if you want to have children, your mid-to-late thirties is the cutoff time to conceive the old-fashioned way, for the most part.

This was the Kansas girl, the babysitting, nannying lover of babies and kids. The girl who wanted four boys. The one with the plans by 33 to have two biological children, then adopt two children.

As I've said before, I got pregnant during *Look Who's Talking Too*. Parker and I were both usually on opposite coasts, but we were used to that. He came to visit in Canada during shooting, and we had sex one night. I remember it well because, call me nuts, but I knew the instant we were finished I was pregnant. It was true. Four weeks into filming my second film about my talking baby, I was pregnant.

Why I hadn't tried to get pregnant during my twenties or early thirties remains a confusion to me. But I was pregnant, and I was ecstatic. So was Parker.

It seemed too good to be true. Thirty-nine years old, the number one TV show on the air, the number one comedy in history at the box office. Mid-filming the next blockbuster and a new baby on the way. I loved my husband madly, and *Cheers* welcomed their actresses to have babies during shooting. Rhea had three children while shooting *Cheers*. They just "write it in" to the story line—wow! I was on top of the world!

All the people who worked for me were people I loved. Jim was my assistant. One of my relatives worked for me at my house, another relative was caretaker at our Oregon ranch, and my other assistant LeeAnn was by my side.

John was so happy, and he would bring maternity clothes and gifts to the set every day.

I craved only two things, caviar and spinach. I was a little nauseated, but not barf-every-morning sick. I was very sleepy, but it was such a blissful sleepy. I was so happy, the world seemed as close to perfect as possible.

When I finished filming *Look Who's Talking Too*, I spent a month in Maine with Parker, dreaming of how our new child would someday run through the grand, turn-of-the-century 22-bedroom house that Mainers refer to as a "cottage." It's funny how you have a kid's entire future planned out for them before they have even hatched. This home was heavenly. Parker and I had owned it for several years and had hundreds of friends and their children run the halls of the cottage that sits on the rocky shores of Islesboro, Maine. But this time, visions of OUR child danced in our heads.

That month went by quickly as I planned the future of my new child. We returned to LA to begin filming *Cheers*. Everyone on the set was ecstatic for me; they all had kids, except for Woody. They were so excited and set about babying me. I was starting to show a tad bit, a little chub around the waistline, which the tabloids immediately picked up on. And thus began my 21-year "fat" taunting by the rag mags.

"Kirstie Alley is getting fat and NBC execs are worried." The NBC execs knew I was pregnant and weren't getting worried. Of course, I didn't spill the beans to the press that I was pregnant; it was too early to go public. After all, I was 39 years old, and "things" can happen in the first trimester. Although they were cruel, I really didn't care much about the articles, as I was soon to be a new mother.

One day a month later, at a routine visit to the obstetrician he looked concerned during a sonogram. "Kirstie, honey, your baby's heartbeat has ceased. The baby is dead," he gently said. I lay there silent, which was odd for me, and tried to take it in.

"What happened, how could this happen? Are you sure?" I pleaded.

"It's called a spontaneous abortion. We'll do tests to see what occurred, but see here on the sonogram, this is your baby and there is no heartbeat." And yes, I could see there on the sonogram there was no heartbeat, and for a moment there I'm sure I had no heartbeat.

Parker was not in LA. He had gone to Oregon because the girlfriend of my relative, the caretaker in Oregon, had died in a car wreck two days prior. He had gone to help my relative and his girlfriend's two teenage daughters with funeral arrangements and such.

I went outside the Beverly Hills doctor's office after being told that my next step was to wait for the child to come out on its own or go into the hospital on Monday for a D&C. I sat on the bus stop bench. I was dazed, alone, and broken. I sat there for a few hours, luckily not accompanied by the paparazzi.

After the baby had not come out on its own, I went into the hospital for a "routine" D&C, although nothing about it felt routine to me. I'd lost my baby and lost the reality of its existence and the dream of its future. Little did I know I was about to lose far more.

Remember my beloved, trusted relatives who were part of my glorious team? Well, it turns out that my house was actually filled with chaos and deceit. My trusted sidekick, a female relative—I'll spare her daughter by not publishing her name—had in fact been embezzling money from me over the years. When confronted, she fled back to Kansas to "sell her things and pay me back." Instead of doing that, she hired an attorney to ensure I would not extradite her to California to press charges. If I had wanted to press charges I would have pressed them weeks prior to her departure to Kansas. But being a die-hard Scientologist, I believe you allow people to repent and make amends. She repented all over the place, sobbing and voicing her deepest apologies and shame for betraying me. I believed it all and yes, yes, I told her, "Go back to Kansas and sell your things, pay me back, and let's get on with the business of being friends . . . family."

She not only hired an attorney and lied about her treatment as my assistant/housekeeper/cousin/friend, but continued to charge money on my credit cards, and demanded I return her TV set and the jewelry she had left behind. Meanwhile her boyfriend, the "animal guy" who also lived at our LA house, admitted doing drugs in the house for quite a while and neglecting the animals while I'd been filming in Canada, resulting in the death of a couple of them.

Meanwhile, back at the ranch in Oregon, Parker found out that my other relative and his now-dead girlfriend (who ran her car off a bridge because she was drunk and high) had been in fact selling crack from our 400-acre Oregon sanctuary. All this bullshit had been right under my nose for at least two years. I'd been so happy and so busy working that it never dawned on me that anything was going on, that anyone, especially my own family, was betraying me.

But there I was, without my baby, without my husband, without my relatives, without a clue how I could sort it all out. So I turned to my *Cheers* family, especially Rhea, Jimmy, and Ted. They were of great help.

I also turned to other women who had had miscarriages, including my sister, who lost a baby two days before her due date.

I stopped feeling sorry for myself and went about the business of sorting my life out. Again! I left relative A in Kansas and sent her the TV. Then I made the choice to cut her from my life. I got a new assistant. I fired the animal guy and hired a new one. I sent relative B to a rehab, after buying him a truck that he would later repay me for. That was 21 years ago. Hopefully he's drug-free, as I definitely haven't seen a penny of the payback. He's actually a good guy, but it seems without much sense of responsibility. I got my life in order. Again!

Then one day on the set of *Cheers*, about six months down the road when all seemed to be going swimmingly and I was trying for another pregnancy, I got some more crushing news. After multiple tests, I learned that I was in early menopause, no longer making eggs. At the tender age of 40, I was no longer fertile.

Oh lord oh lord oh lord! What the fuck?! This was the straw that broke my broken heart in two!

I began sobbing in Rebecca Howe's office on the *Cheers* set. I fell apart. Now, if you've ever seen a sitcom, the rooms only have three walls. The front side of each room is open to the audience who attend the live performance each week.

So there I was, hiding and sobbing in plain sight. It was a rehearsal day, so thank god the audience wasn't there. I was torn apart, I thought I'd seen my darkest months. Jeez! This was really fucked up! I'll never forget Jimmy Burrows that day. He hugged me—and he's not a big hugger—and said, "Oh honey, that sucks. That's so fucked up." That is exactly what you want to hear! No one wants to hear "You'll be fine, you'll be okay, it will pass!" He said the exact right words. It did suck! It was fucked up! I wasn't fine, and I wasn't okay, and it would never pass!

When I cry, I cry hard and loud and as if I'm dying. Then in about five minutes I stop. I get a grip on myself. I know that the only way to survive life is to get hold of yourself and quickly make a new plan. Within an hour I had a new plan. My original plan was to have two children, then adopt two children. By lunchtime I'd decided to reverse it. I'd adopt a child and meanwhile I'll sort out this fertility shit, then I'll have a baby. I thought it was an excellent plan, so I set about adopting a child.

The adoption laws in California were a recipe for disaster. Private adoption did not exist in hippieville (California). In the last six months of the birth mother's pregnancy she was allowed to live with you! Can you imagine a birth mother knowing who you are and living in your house for six months prior to giving birth? All while maintaining the right to *not* give up the baby after she delivers? I do sympathize and respect mothers who opt for adoption instead of abortion, but can you imagine the blackmail position this would put celebrity parents in for the rest of their lives? Especially the period from birth until the final sign-off, which was something like six months? You could just see it: "I need a new car. Hope I don't have to change my mind." "I'll go to the *Enquirer* and tell them you fed me bread and water if you don't give me more money." God! We had heard enough horror adoption stories by the time we started seriously pursuing it. We were terrified and paranoid, apparently rightfully so.

We had places in Oregon and Maine. The adoption laws in Maine were sane. Private adoption was legal, for both sides. We didn't know the mother, and she didn't know us. We took residency in Maine and began spending months at a time there. We got driver's licenses and voted there. We established legal residency in Maine. A friend of a friend of a friend knew this person "Mary." She was very adept at this business of adoption.

Meanwhile, back in California, I was having fertilization work done. I was being tested for everything, and my body was going cuckoo. I would be in full-blown menopause one month, then producing eggs and estrogen the next—without fertility drugs. It felt like my body was a car, and when I hit the gas in neutral it would rev up but never slip into drive. I kept lamenting to my specialist, "I'm forty years old! Tons of women older than I am have kids every day! Twins even!" This was around 1991, and not as much was known about fertility. But my doctor laughed. I could have babies too if I visited the "egg man." What?! Kookookachoo, I am the walrus—what egg man?

"Dr. Sawyer," my doctor said. "He's the egg donor specialist."

I was barely able to utter the words "I can't have children" and certainly not ready to throw in the uterus and admit "I've waited too long," so "Definitely! I want to meet the egg man."

"Kirstie," my ob-gyn said, "Dr. Sawyer is the reason it appears that all these actresses older than you 'easily' get pregnant and, in particular, have twins. But the rate of birth defects, including Down syndrome, is seventy percent higher in women over thirty-seven."

Well, shut my mouth! Why didn't I know this? Why had I assumed I could easily conceive into my forties? And what about those women in the *Star* who live in Bolivia and have babies in their fifties, even sixties? Suddenly the tabloids were my reference materials. Jeez! I was confused more than ever. *Get thee to the egg man.*

I did go see the egg man, and I had lots more tests. I was indeed in full-blown menopause at the young age of 40. It's fairly rare, but it does happen to the unlucky idiots who think they can conceive when they're 48. I knew it was true! My mother had friends who had babies at 48, 49, and even 52. What about THOSE women??? They sure as hell weren't out shopping at the local egg farm. And even my gyno admitted that some women do get pregnant naturally in their forties, occasionally in their early fifties, but never women who have gone into menopause.

I was ready to choke myself out. Had my drug use made me prone to early menopause? Wasn't it odd that three months after I had surgery for my miscarriage I went into menopause, for Christ's sake? Had they screwed up? Had they removed more than the dead baby? Perforated me, implanted me with an alien baby eater—jeez! I was going insane!

The egg man was cool. Without giving names of his celebrity clients, he made it clear that he'd had only two nonceleb clients over age 42 who conceived without egg donors. And they conceived with in vitro. I tried artificial insemination, the turkey baster technique. I shot my ass with hormones until the day of. But it didn't work. This wasn't shocking, since the odds of IUI success are like 10 percent. I was lost. I needed divine intervention. And then, BAM! I remembered something. I remembered all those babies I babysat for from age eight until I was 25. I recalled how I would pretend the babies were mine. The best thing I remembered was how much I loved them. How happy they made me and vice versa. None of them came out of my body, yet I loved them like they were mine.

I also thought about my own mother. We were never close, and yet I came out of her womb.

Of course bodies are genetically created, but I believe souls inhabit those bodies. Souls are not created. I feel they are connected to God but not created by God. I also don't believe that one must love their family because they are blood. It's important to do your best to honor your parents. I think that usually works out fairly well, but what about those parents who beat their children? Molest their children? Mind-fuck their children and so on. What about those parents, brothers, sisters, aunts, uncles, and cousins who are criminal, psychotic, dangerous, unloving, belittling, and heartless—why would anyone have to love them? Perhaps saints still love those idiots because they're family, but I'm not in their category. I actually believe on some level of consciousness, that we can choose our parents, as they can choose us.

Thoughts began to make sense. Concepts began to gel. Love was more powerful than blood.

I could feel him out there. I could perceive him every mile of his plane ride as he was being delivered to us by Mary. When she arrived with him—I already knew him.

We named him William True Parker. William after my grandfather,

Clifford William Alley, and True because I like the combination of different numbered syllables in a name. William (three), True (one), and Parker (two). Instead of names like mine, Kirstie (two), Louise (two), Alley (two). Mixed syllables skip the singsong effect. William has never been used. I love the name William and like the name Will. But Bill, Billy, and Willy sound common. True is the name that stuck. True suits True.

Before my daughter was born, True created the most exhilarating effect to date on my life. There was no break-in period, no adoptive-parent syndrome. It was natural and profound. We had located each other. It became obvious that the spiritual universe is where the real party was going on. He was worth the heartache and the wait.

True was physically perfect, and every inch of him was beautifully formed. He had no hair on his head, but his eyelashes draped down to the middle of his cheeks. When he was sleeping he looked like he was an old-fashioned baby doll. They always made those dolls with exaggerated lashes to make them cuter.

We welcomed him to earth, to Encino, and to his home. We lay for hours as he slept, just looking at him. For the first time in my life, I was still. Calmness is not my forte. The entire noise of living ceased. *This* was my purpose. *This* was my destiny. I'd known it since I was three years old. Through all those years of begging to hold everyone else's babies, I knew my purpose was to be a mother.

You could tell True was funny from day one. You could feel his quirky sense of humor, but above all you could loudly perceive his artistry. It was so evident that he was a musician. *That* was eerie. Parker and I spent the first week alone with True, no visitors. Just us alone with our son. I had the week off from *Cheers*.

The day I went back to *Cheers* I was given a surprise baby shower by all the cast and crew. Even at the shower people must have had a foreshadowing of True's abilities, a perception of who he was, his artistry. Tim Barry gave True his first guitar—he was eight days old and received a Fender Stratocaster! There hadn't been talk, prior to True's arrival, that he "should" be a musician, as I believe children should be whatever they decide to be. But I got amazing gifts at the shower, held upstairs above the *Cheers* stage on the Paramount lot.

But how could Tim have known? I certainly have no musical skills. I can sing a bit, but I play no musical instruments. Parker didn't play instruments, so when I opened that Stratocaster I was pleasantly shocked.

I believe in cause and effect. I believe the physical universe is junior to the spiritual universe. I believe accidents are predisposed by suppressive people fucking with you. I believe the being, the spirit, the élan vital, whatever you wanna call it, is the entity driving life, like the driver in a car. The car can be an Aston Martin, but without a driver, it's just a bad-ass piece of art. I believe we can know things that appear unknowable.

Tim knew True was a musician and by 18 months, so did everyone else.

True is one of those rare musicians who have no ambition to be famous or flashy. He's all about the music. The words, the riffs, the way it makes him feel. Heehee—he's such a sixties child. He's such a "I've been here before people!" kind of guy. If True weren't raised in Scientology, he would have become a Buddhist or Hindu.

True has always smelled like sugar and butter combined. My nickname for him is "Butter." I've never smelled anyone who smells as good as True. Perfectly clean scent of sugar butter and a tiny hint of lemon, and that's his natural scent!

True's best and worst quality is that he will defend the ones he loves to the death. He's courageous. He is a tiger defending someone's honor or reputation. The problem arises when he defends the wrong people. I've had the pleasure of watching him grow into a man who can differentiate the bad guys from the good. This kid was born trusting everyone. When he was young, he was the most gullible child ever born. When True and Lillie got to a certain age they asked me if I breast-fed them. True was around six, Lillie four. I told them no, and explained when children are adopted their mothers don't have milk. They went on, "Well, then what did you feed us, Mama?" I wove a wild tale to make them feel special. To let them know they hadn't missed out on breast milk. I told them that they needed lots of protein because they hadn't gotten breast milk. Special protein.

"We had to feed you the highest-quality protein available. We fed you tiny baby snake heads and fried bat wings."

They were delighted! "For real, Mama, for real?" True asked.

"Yes, for real," I said.

"Well, how did you find them?" he asked as they both sat there clinging to my every word.

"I had to raise them," I continued. "They were very exotic baby snakes. They were the kind you didn't have to kill. They grew multiple heads and the little heads would just fall off like petals when the baby snake was done using them. Then they just grew more heads."

"And the bat wings, Mama? What about the bats?" True inquired.

"Same thing. Remember when Mama went to Italy? Mama was collecting bat wings in a Franciscan monastery. They were blessed—by monks."

"I'm glad we didn't have breast milk, Mama," True said. "I bet that's why we're so strong."

"Yes, baby, that's why you're special." Lillie and True were satisfied. They giggled and made me tell them more about the exotic creatures they'd been reared on. My children never wanted to hear fairy tales. They only wanted to hear stories of all the bad things I'd done in my life. They were especially interested in times I got in trouble, and the impersonations of my mother's rants.

The years passed. True was 13 years old. He was talking to some of my friends in the backyard. One of them was nursing her new baby. "Ya know . . . we weren't raised on breast milk 'cause we're adopted," True said.

"What were you raised on, soy milk, goat's milk?" my friend asked.

"Nope, Mama fed us the finest protein in the world. Snake heads and bat wings." My friend started laughing. "I'm serious, Kate, ask my mom," True said.

Oh lord, what had I done?!

I took True and Lillie inside and told them it was just a tale I'd told them when they were little. They both started laughing hysterically. True asked, "For real, Mama, for real?" Then we all laughed.

True is also one of the sweetest, most patient children I've run across. One time, about a week before he went into the third grade, he needed a haircut. I volunteered. His hair was down to his shoulders and I didn't want him to cut it but he was sick of people saying he looked like a girl. Of course the majority of those people were from Kansas and were rednecks. Any hair longer than a burr looks like girl hair to them. But IF he HAD to get it cut I insisted that I cut it so it didn't get screwed up. He agreed. He'd seen me cut countless friends' hair, so he trusted me. It was true, countless GIRLfriends received haircuts from me. I'd yet to do a short boy haircut. I asked him how short he wanted to go. "Really short, above my ears," he said. I began by lopping off his golden locks. Then I started crying and had to excuse myself. When I came back I began chopping away. I was really getting into it. Snip snip, cut cut . . . it was looking very professional. "There!" I said. "It's done! It looks awesome!" True went in the bathroom to take a look.

"OH MY GOD, I LOOK LIKE FREAKIN' TINKER BELL!!!" he squealed.

I yelled back toward the bathroom, "TRUE!!! IT DOES NOT LOOK LIKE TINKER BELL, IT LOOKS AMAZING!! IT LOOKS *GQ*! GET OUT HERE SO I CAN LOOK AT IT AGAIN!!" When he rounded the corner I burst out laughing. So did he—my lord, he looked exactly like Tinker Bell! We were crying because he looked just like a little fairy. His hair was choppy and poufy with pixie sprigs sticking out around his ears. He looked like he should have been holding a wand. He was so sweet about it. He never got mad. He kept referring to himself as "Tink," and every time he said it we would go into convulsions laughing. I took him to a pro to have the stylist "boy" him up. When we walked out of the salon he had transformed from Tinker Bell to rocker boy.

True's first love was "Pokenhantist."

The sweetest thing my son ever said to me was "Mama—you yook just like Snow White." Apparently we had a Disney thing goin' on all up in there.

I hate, absolutely hate, parents, especially mothers, who prattle on incessantly about their children. I get it. I get that every word they say is precious. I get that everything they learn is of milestone status. I get the loss of their first tooth, their first Christmas, and the first step they take. It is monumental—to *them*.

So I will refrain from telling you every cute thing my son has done, even though every cute thing he's done is far cuter than any boy on earth.

True's arrival marked the beginning of loving a male just because I loved him. Child love, son love, is so simple and pure. So easy, so natural. It is perfect. It is intimate and personal.

I saw True giving Ben Travolta his first guitar lesson a few months back. He was so sweet and patient. Ben loved it. True loved it. And it was a lovely sight to behold.

The only love advice I've given True, who's now 20, is "Your name is True. Don't give some girl cause to shout 'You say your name is *True* but you're a liar! Your name should be False!'"

You just know it's gonna happen—heehee—you just know it.

This guy goes to a psychiatrist and says, "Doc, my brother's crazy. He thinks he's a chicken." The doctor says, "Well, why don't you turn him in?" And the guy says, "I would but I need the eggs."

Well I guess that's pretty much how I feel about relationships. You know they're totally irrational and crazy and absurd but I guess we keep going through it because, uh, most of us need the eggs.

—WOODY ALLEN

The Art of Not Being a Cunt

WOODY ALLEN is an eccentric, peculiar cat. He is also a genius and quite likable.

Since 1977 I envisioned being in a Woody Allen movie. It's not clear if I wanted to be an actress in a Woody Allen movie or just to be Annie Hall. The uniqueness of Woody Allen or one of his movies is actually unique, not for lack of a better word. He's like the Barbra Streisand of moviemaking: one doesn't have to see the album cover to know who's singing.

I know people got all wrapped up in the Soon Yi drama and shunned him for a while, but my first experience with both of them was that they were delightful, eccentrically delightful.

I've never met anyone like Woody Allen. No one comes close. I could never say, "Woody is exactly like so-and-so," since there is *no* so-and-so that he's even remotely like.

My agent called me around 1996-ish. I was dicking around in New York City on my way back from Italy.

"Woody wants to meet with you for his new fall movie."

"Woody Harrelson?" I asked.

"No, fool, Woody Allen," he said in curt agent-speak.

Me: "When?"

Agent: "Tomorrow."

Me: "Where?"

Agent: "New York, fool."

Me: "What's the role?"

Agent: "He doesn't let anyone see the script, we have no idea."

Me: "Fool, then how am I supposed to know if I'm right for it?"

Agent: "Woody thinks you're right enough for it to meet with you. The meeting's tomorrow at two." Click.

Wow! I'm going to be in a Woody Allen movie! I thought.

"Meeting" means meeting. It can result in being hired or just being beckoned into a room to see "if you're still fat." However, I was pretty sure we'd hit it off and he would hire me. I'm fairly eccentric myself, so it seemed like we would click!

I walked into a little outer office and was met by Juliet Taylor, Woody's casting agent. She's his ONLY casting agent. She's the shit.

"I'll take you in [to see Woody], let's go."

We walked into a very large, long room. The draperies were drawn and were sort of a dark asparagus–green. The room was so dimly lit that I could barely see Woody Allen sitting on a long, asparagus-green sofa next to Soon Yi. The room could have been puce for all I know because it was so dark, but it felt asparagus-green.

"Hi," he said.

"Hi," I said back.

"I saw you on *Cheers*," he said with his New York accent. "Cheeas."

"Thank you." I never know what to say when people say that, let alone Woody Allen.

"Thank you for coming in," he said abruptly, and it was clear that the meeting was over.

"Thank you for having me," I said as I got up to leave.

Oh brother, had I blown that meeting or what? And I wasn't even fat!

I smoked 3,000 cigarettes in the limo on the way back to the hotel that was 10 minutes from Woody Allen's asparagus office.

That was my BIG chance to be in a Woody Allen movie, and I blew it! I don't know how or why I blew it, but it really doesn't make any difference because I've clearly blown my only shot of being the next Annie Hall!

I was staying at the Pierre Hotel in room 642, the same room I'd stayed in many times and the only NYC hotel I'd slept in for almost 20 years. They were like family to me at the Pierre. I knew the staff better than I knew most of my relatives.

I pouted and sighed as I stomped past the hotel personnel. When I'm miserable, I appreciate everyone else suffering along with me.

"You okay?" was every hotel worker's reaction.

"Grrr, blah, ger, grrrrr, bla, oooagh" was my response.

I opened my hotel room door and did a 1940s theatrical "slam, turn, throw my back against the door, and slide to the floor" number.

As I sat on the black-and-white parquet marble floor, staring at the ceiling like Joan Crawford, the phone rang.

I crawled, crawled I tell you, into the butler's pantry of the suite.

"Hello," I answered with the angst of a love-lost swan.

Agent: "Woody wants you for the movie. They're sending your sides [parts of a script with your lines in them] over tomorrow."

"OH MY GOD!! What did he say exactly? Tell me everything he said exactly as he said it," I gushed.

"He said, 'I want her for the movie.'"

"He did? Oh my god, he *wants* me for the movie!!!!!"

I hadn't been that exhilarated since I got my first movie. Cloud nine was just a cloud compared to how excited I was!

I took my kids to Serendipity to celebrate! Frozen hot chocolates all around!

Oh my god, I could barely sleep and couldn't stop saying to myself or out loud, "I'm going to be in a Woody Allen movie!!"

Even *I* thought I was cool.

The next day I got the sides. As I began to read over the lines I realized two things. The first was that I was playing Woody Allen's wife in a movie called *Deconstructing Harry*. His wife? My heart was pounding. Annie Hall, Annie Hall, Annie Hall! Here's my Annie Hall role!

The next thing I noticed was that I was playing the role of a psychiatrist. Ugh. Oh no! Jeez, I hate psychiatrists!! Well, to be more accurate, psychiatry! Oh god, what are you doing to me? How ironic! It was like rain on my wedding day, only it was sleet.

I wouldn't mind playing a psychotic psychiatrist or a mind-fucking psychiatrist or a really screwed-up psychiatrist, as I feel this is at least reality. But a straitlaced, role-model shrink? Never!

What was I going to do? My personal integrity was clashing with my exhilaration.

"Hello, Woody?" was my icebreaker after being given his number.

"Yeah."

"I know this is going to sound weird, but I hate psychiatry and shrinks."

"Yeah, so, who doesn't?" was his reply.

I started chuckling. That was fucking funny!

"I just don't want to glorify a shrink. Can I play her wackier than she's written?" This was risky, as Woody is the writer of all his movies. "Can I take drugs and drink while I'm counseling the client?"

"Sure, yeah [beat, beat, beat] as long as it's funny."

OH MY GOD!! I was in! I get to portray a lunatic psychiatrist, but I repeat myself. And still be Mrs. Woody Allen!!!!!! (in the movie).

The first day of filming I got to see the genius of Woody Allen first-hand. He works with the same crew every movie, so they hummed like the engine of an Aston Martin.

My hair was pulled back in an ugly low-slung ponytail. I had no makeup and wore a long skirt and turtleneck. Woody wanted it that way. He wanted me to look like the average uptight Upper East Side shrink. There was lots of chatter. Not about the script. Instead it was baseball chatter. Woody is a huge fan of the sport.

I came to find out that Woody doesn't shoot long days. On many movies the shooting drags on between 14 and 16 hours a day. The average is 12. On *Deconstructing Harry* the average was eight. Woody directs in a precise manner, and he knows what he wants and doesn't waste his time or anyone else's. Maybe because he simply wants to get out early to watch baseball, which is a valid reason in my book. He also shoots his movies in the fall because he likes that hue of autumn. Most movies are insured for rain days. His movies are insured for sun days.

I liked the way he let his actors improvise. Meaning me. He was sort of short with the other ones. The lines were all there to support driving the story line forward, and of course they were distinctly Woody Allen funny. The first day on the set I asked him if I could improvise, and his answer was "If it's funny." No pressure there! There are many things I'm less than confident about. Being funny is not one of them. He also allowed me to bring my own bits to the scenes. I asked for breakaway glasses to throw at him during the scene. The character he was playing was such a misguided asshole. If I had really been married to a guy like that I would have thrown highball glasses at him on a regular basis.

Woody is afraid of bridges and tunnels. How he ever made it to the set avoiding bridges and tunnels in the tristate area is beyond me. I really loved my experience working with Woody, and the hardest part of acting opposite him is not laughing. If you think he's funny when you watch him in a movie, try standing three feet in front of him and not cracking up. He's also weirdly sexy, and I have no idea why. Maybe it's because he's not trying. Maybe it's because smart men are sexy. But I think I just made that up. It sounds good, but are we really looking for smart men? *Oh, Dawn, look at that smart guy standing over by the hydrangeas, he just exudes IQ—let's go hit on him.*

The movie turned out cool. I personally got a lot of notice, which is all that matters. (It's so hard to write things after being on Twitter using smiley faces after every sarcastic comment. I have the urge to do it constantly in this book.)

;)

Deconstructing Harry was chosen to open the Venice Film Festival. I went with an idiot boyfriend who didn't like me getting attention, and it's pretty hard to stroll over the Ponte Vecchio, or its equivalent, with thousands of people cheering and hundreds of lightbulbs flashing, without being noticed. Woody had personally asked me to attend the festival opening to represent *Deconstructing Harry*. The asshole I was with was furious because I had to do so many interviews. And he refused to go to the gala that was thrown for us after the premiere. I was a sheep by then, so I didn't go to the gala, either.

The acting business is actually a bitch. Think about it. You're out of work after every job. You're basically a door-to-door salesman. So when these premieres, these grand opportunities to show off arise, the celebratory thing to do is revel in it. I was trying to revel. I was surrounded by international film stars such as Gerard Depardieu, and I was trying to revel with him. I hate the word I'm about to use but my date was being a cunt. Don't EVER be with a man who wants to diminish your power—EVER. If he doesn't have big enough balls to allow you to shine, he is the wrong man. Oddly enough that's who my character was in *Deconstructing Harry*.

Anyhoo—it was a great privilege to be at the Venice Film Festival, and it was a life-changing honor to perform alongside Woody Allen, Robin Williams, Demi Moore, Judy Davis, Julia Louis-Dreyfus, Richard Benjamin, and Billy Crystal.

After the festival I got a note from Woody. I still have it somewhere. It said something like—I'm paraphrasing here—"Thank you for coming to Venice. You were superb in the movie and thank you for all the publicity you did—although you were a bit of a cunt."

I wanted you to see what real courage is, instead of getting the idea that courage is a man with a gun in his hand. It's when you know you're licked before you begin but you begin anyway and you see it through no matter what. You rarely win, but sometimes you do.

—HARPER LEE, *TO KILL A MOCKINGBIRD*

The Art of Maks

I WAS SUPPOSED to meet him at a club in LA, but he was late, as usual. I had always wanted a tattoo, and I noticed a tattoo parlor to the left of the club. Here was my big chance. I asked the artist and proprietor to write the word "unbroken" freehand on a piece of paper. It was delicate and beautiful. As paparazzi flashed away through the windows, like they did when Britney Spears shaved her head, I suffered the electric pain of "unbroken" on the inside of my left wrist. The thought crossed my mind with each flash, *Am I just as nuts as Brit?* Did I want ink because HE had just started getting some on his rib cage, or was this word being burned into my virgin flesh a representation of newfound freedom? Perhaps it was a little of both.

There have been six categories of men in my life. Relatives, friends, husbands, lovers, mentors, and "guys I really love but am not in love with who are sorta like friends but sorta not who I want to shag sometimes."

Relatives include grandfathers, uncles, fathers, brothers, and sons. Friends are men I could sleep next to in a fancy hotel room without the thought of having sex with them enter my mind. Husbands are men that I want to create a future with, spend the rest of my life with, envisioning children and weddings, houses, money, family, and how am I gonna pretend like I wanna have sex with them for the next 30 years. Lovers are those men whom I don't actually love, the ones I can't see a future with but who are charming and hot and look good after midnight and three cosmos. Mentors are the men who have changed the course of my life in business, education, and spirituality. Men of the sixth kind are strange friendlike creatures that I could not sleep next to in a fancy hotel room without wanting to shag on occasion. These men are maddening, as they really have no specific place in my life, they are just put there, apparently, to haunt me and screw with my mind for the rest of eternity. These men are a category of one . . . this is the category of Maks.

ABC told me you are not allowed to choose your dance partner but you are allowed to say who you won't dance with. Being five foot eight narrowed the field. Most *Dancing with the Stars* male dancers are not tall . . . it was obvious I would not be the partner of Derek Hough, for example. I named what tall guys I would not dance with, leaving but one contender—Maks. It was clear to me after watching a few seasons of the show that Maks was either a raging psychotic or had something under that angry Russian facade that could crack my weary soul. Even after the warnings of a few of his ex-partners, a handful of ex-contestants who had not been his partners, and a couple of ABC execs who blatantly told me "he will destroy you," I chose Maks. The one thing I could predict with this choice was that I would not be bored.

When I first laid eyes on him I had two thoughts. He is much more polite and charismatic in person. The next thought was *Isn't this the exact combo of every psycho I've ever encountered?*

I've observed one distinct trait of charming, psychotic men: they never have "psycho" carved in their foreheads.

My perceptions are my most keen gift and curse.

I instantly perceived his disappointment that he had the task of teaching an overweight middle-aged actress to dance. Sure, he was impressed by my acting pedigree and my slew of awards and sure, he knew he had landed a bona fide "star" to prance around the ballroom with, but I could read his mind: *Why the fuck can't I get some hot bitch like Nicole Scherzinger, who has danced her whole life and makes me look like the hot piece of ass I am, to spin around on the dance floor? What the hell have you saddled me with, ABC? Do you really hate the bad boy of the ballroom this much? And how do you expect me to conquer the mirror ball with a trophy like this? I might as well pack my bags and head back to Ukraine to lick my wounds in the arms of one of my bachelor rejects* Poor, poor Maks.

• • •

After Maks and I LOST the mirror ball, while we were in New York City I threw a dinner one evening for the extended Ukraine clan, to thank them for all the love and joy they had shown me over that five-month period. By then I'd fallen for each one of the members. Jhanna, Eugene, Teddy, Nicole, Val, the other Eugene, Sergey, Alex, Sasha, Lora, and of course Maks . . . Maks announced that night that I was an honorary member of his family. Wow! In Kansas we don't roll that way. We barely acknowledge our own family members as family members. This was foreign to me, like some Russian Corleone ritual, some Ukrainian rite of passage. I was flattered and delighted to be part of a new group of people that I'd grown so fond of, so close to, so quickly.

These Russians are tightly knit, like a 600-thread-count cashmere sweater. Hmmm, and what are my obligations as a family member? Just the normal stuff like birthdays, weddings, bar mitzvahs, sporadic visits when the north wind blew me into town? Or would I be called on for hits and such? Is my new family mob, or just immigrants that look like mob? And does this make Maks my brother, uncle, son? Hmmmm.

You see, I don't presume to know anything about Maks. He is as mysterious to me as he is capricious, rude, thoughtless, and bossy. He is also gentle, childlike, fragile, and sensitive. He is a dancing contradiction.

The one really funny thing about Maks is that he presumes you will always love him no matter how much of an asshole he is. Unfortunately, it's sort of true. That smile is honestly his most valuable weapon—it gets him back into good graces like a black Amex gets an ugly guy into a club. It's truly irresistible to the point where I've trained myself to pretend he's the Cheshire Cat, hopped up on opium, and I'm not allowed to listen to his gibberish.

Maks rarely says he's sorry and he never engages in a conversation that would lead to an apology—the Artful Dodger—he moves in and out of the dialogue like a snake, slithering through a maze. If he touches on anything relevant he recoils and just continues sliding. Finally I give in, and when he says things like "I know you have drawn a line between us," I just laugh. "*I've* drawn a line between us??!! I give up!"

Along with my relationship with Maks, I've inherited his fans. Of course there are the amazing, loyal, sane ones. But then there are the trolls. I've not inherited them as *my* fans—rather I should say as my antifans. They prattle on endlessly to get their vital messages through to Maks's thick skull! "She's older than your mother!" "She's using you!" "She betrayed us! She led us to believe you were in a love affair." "She's perverted!" "If she's going to be at your event, I'm not coming!!" "I'm trying to warn you! She's DANGEROUS!!!!!!" To them I quote the great prophet, Kelly Clarkson: "You don't know a thing about me."

Now this is where Maks and I truly differ. If it were reversed and my fans were attacking him, I would come swooping in like a mighty eagle to devour them, to rip them to bloody shreds. Perhaps this trait comes from having a career that spans 30-some years. I've seen friends, costars, and people I love maligned, lied about, and chewed up by the press. I have zero problem publicly defending them. Suffice it to say if I had destroyed my career by coming to the aid of my comrades, I would still have intervened. Maks needs to learn how to take a stand, publicly. Not do "nothing" when his compadres are being attacked. Which is what he did with me and what I've seen him do with other people he loves. He needs to learn the art of defending his friends. If I were to give Maks one solid bit of advice, as his oracle, it would be to rethink sincerity, courage, loyalty, and generosity. It's the "family" thing to do.

If I were to acknowledge his finest attributes, I would commend him on tenacity, strength, talent, ability, sweetness, perceptiveness, and intelligence. I'd also throw in a nod to humor. I would be remiss not to include the good with the bad, as Maks is a mixed bag of tricks dominated by mostly good traits. But the jury is out on which location he will finally reside in.

It amazed me that I ended up loving Maks so much—"AH HAH!!" the skeptics proclaim. "She DID fall for him!" Duh, wasn't that pretty obvious?? The amazing part is HOW I fell for him and WHY. That part might surprise a lot of people. I did not, as most would think, fall in love with Maks. My definition of the kind of love you "fall in" has future connected to it. Like I fell in love with Parker, Bob, Jake, and a few others, with the intention of marrying them or being with them forever. That's my definition of falling in love with someone.

Maks was not that for me. For as much as I loved him, I always knew there would be no future with him. Strangely, for me, that was not because of the 29-year age difference, although I wasn't keen being dubbed Harold and Maude. I knew it was a moment in time, sort of a porthole punched in the universe that got me to fall for him—as I once told him.

Those moments in life are strange and magical, yet fleeting. They are gone as quickly as they arrive, but the opportunity to have loved Maks for that five-month period of my life was breathtaking. He was like oxygen to me. He woke me up.

I told him everything. He became my confidant. He confided his love problems to me and sought advice about life, women, love, and business. We have talked business for hundreds of hours. We got very close. He was my best audience. He thought I was hysterical, and I thought he was unintentionally hysterical. I'd catch him staring at me in a sort of awe sometimes, not as other men have in my life, but that kind of awe children have when you've shocked or surprised them. I felt Maks yearned for a certain freedom that perhaps he saw in me. I perceive a spiritual lostness and lack of freedom in Maks sometimes, and a struggle for a lightness of being.

We had so much fun together, yelling at each other, trying to get the upper hand and controlling each other, dancing, falling, losing our shoes, almost winning, texting each other crazy fake-love texts that weren't really loverish at all. Freedom was going on there, freedom to communicate freely and wildly, and for me like I've rarely communicated with men before. I could tell him anything. Weirdly, the men I've actually lived with or been married to have been the opposite. They were never my confidants, and I never told them my deepest thoughts, concerns, or passions.

Poor Maks probably to this day has no idea what he truly meant to me. I think that at the end he sorta bought into the publicity view of who we were. We were not that—we were superior to friends and lovers but without the future of people who fall in love.

Before I did *Dancing with the Stars* with Maks there was a part of me that was so broken and so tired of loving men and then fucking it all up that I honestly had zero desire for any kind of relationship. I somehow sorted through my own demons, while dancing with a demon. *Ahhh, Maks.* I certainly never set out to love Maks, and it shocked me that I ended up loving him to the degree that I did.

The thing about love is that it doesn't even exist unless it is continually created, and to continually create something you have to work at it. To this day I have no idea the role Maks will play or not play in my life. I know this: I would like to love him forever. I would like to work hard to keep him happy. I would like to be there for his wedding and the birth of his children.

I say, "would like" because as I said, one never knows for sure where you stand with the Cheshire Cat. The Dark Angel doesn't make it easy for people to love him. He won't agree with what I've written here, but then agreement has never been our forte.

Alas, I hope my stint as a Chmerkovskiy was not a sprint but is a marathon.

I've been holding on to the offer to dance again on *Dancing with the Stars All-Stars* since before Christmas. Oddly, this time around, they gave us "stars" the choice to dance with our original partners or to choose a new partner. That seemed sort of like wife swapping. My first reaction was *Oh hell no!!! I can't go through it again!* You have no idea how physically and mentally grueling that show is. *IT'S A BIG PASS!*, I thought to myself. But I was told by ABC, "There's no hurry, take your time making your decision." Then around February I started giving it some thought, as sly ABC knew I would, by not forcing me to make a decision.

I certainly wouldn't want Maks to dance with me if he had a better chance at winning with someone else. And I certainly didn't want to choose some other pro. How weird would that be? What a mighty slap to Maks's beautiful face and ego.

The months passed, and I still wouldn't and couldn't commit. I would have two projects to shoot in the fall and one book to release within the same time frame as *DWTS*. The offer still not accepted or refused, I began wondering, *If I did it again, could I be better? Have I become a better dancer or just a road show cha-cha-er? Would we have fun as we had the first go-round, or were we jaded about each other?*

Then in May the north wind blew in, and I suddenly got a wild yearning for another voyage down the rabbit hole. Perhaps it was a glitch in the Matrix. Perhaps it was my desire to dance with the Cheshire Cat one last time. Perhaps I'm certifiable. Yeah—that's probably it. So come September, the bad boy of the ballroom and the unbroken actress will throw down, one last time, on the dance floor—or throw up, depending on how mean he is.

> I was nauseous and tingly all over. I was
> either in love or I had smallpox.
>
> —WOODY ALLEN

The Art of Knights on White Horses

'D INVENTED these reading glasses called Looky-Loos. I even have the patent on them! Looky-Loos work like this: they have magnets in the temples, and no, this is not some New Age shit. Looky-Loos are accompanied by a gorgeous, color-coordinated picture frame. On the back of the frame, under the felt, the arm thing that props up the frame is metal. When you're done wearing your readers, you pop 'em on the back of the frame. The magnets connect with the hidden metal and voilà! You know where your glasses are! They aren't lost in your purse, swimming around with the other debris getting scratched. They aren't in a kitchen drawer with the scissors and disposable diapers. They are right there on the back of the frame where you left them! Looky-Loos!!

I really think I need to make a trip to the *Shark Tank* and pitch the idea . . .

I'm aware that this is an uncommon introduction but it's what led me directly to Mr. New Kids on the Block boy bander . . . to my Jonny-Boy.

As I recall, we started talking to each other via Twitter, mostly about the glasses. But our first encounter via Twitter was when Jon boldly defended my religion and fired away at my attackers.

Religion is a hot-button topic. And on social media sites, religion can become explosive. Personally, I've never been harmed by any religion, although I have been harmed by a few people who happened to be members of certain religions. But the harm was not connected to their religious persuasions; they were just dickheads.

Anyway, the important part of the story is that Jon jumped in to defend me, without even knowing me. WOW! That's some admirable stuff right there. It's indicative of the bravery and loyalty that IS Jonathan Knight.

Men are not naturally brave, but when duty calls, the courageous ones rise to the occasion to defend and protect. That's Jon's beauty. He is an honestly good, brave, valiant man. I'm sure he's come under fire for defending me, but the truth is, he's willing to take the bullets.

I took my Looky-Loos to HSN midway through filming my TV show *Kirstie Alley's Big Life*. They gave me a whopping seven minutes to sell them. I was exhausted from flying and filming and agreed to HSN's ungodly hour of 3:00 a.m. My Looky-Loos are both innovative and beautiful, something you would see in a department store for $200 for the combo of glasses and frame. They were also of that quality. And I was selling them for 39 flippin' dollars!!! They sold all right, not great, but all right, and one of the people who bought them was Jon, for his mother. Then he tweeted about the glasses he bought and how much his mom loved them. It was just common chitchat.

The first time I saw Jon in person was when I invited him to be my guest on *DWTS*. He came up behind me in the makeup trailer, flashed his pearly whites, and the rest is history.

We were like peanut butter and jelly, we just belonged together. You can't help but love him. He's sincere and funny as hell and, as I said before, loyal.

Jonathan is the first to tell you his shortcomings. He's much harder on himself than on other people. His self-deprecation makes up most of his comedy genius. He came to most of the *DWTS* shows, and we always went to dinner, then out afterward.

It's impossible to communicate the love I have for Jonny. If one of us weren't gay, we would be married. You choose.

We are almost like twins. We both love gardening and house repairs, interior design, telling stories, lying around in bed watching movies. We're homebodies, basically. Together, we are happy being anywhere and doing nothing.

Here's another thing I love about Jon. When most people come to visit, especially for extended stays, they need to be entertained. They have an agenda—shopping, dining, sightseeing. UGH!! They are high maintenance. I loathe high-maintenance GUESTS!!! GO STAY AT HOTELS!!!!

When Jon came to Italy we were just as content to lie in bed watching movies as we were zooming around the Amalfi coast on a yacht! We left Positano only once, to sail off to Capri. Other than that, we just hung out, eating watermelon. He doesn't care and neither do I, as long as we're together, we're happy. It's REFRESHING!!

We also like to do really dumb stuff, like shoot bottles at cheesy rifle ranges. We both adore animals, all animals. Jon tells a hysterical story about his beloved pony June, being given away to an amusement park when he was at school!

We're both from middle-class families. Jonathan is game for anything, anywhere. This past January 12—my birthday—my kids and I were holed up in Maine during a blizzard. After my kids made breakfast for me and gave me gifts, they said, "Let's go out on the porch and plan our next dance." This was in the beginning of this crazy fiasco I created called "100 Days of Dance." I kid you not, it was a flippin' blizzard, but I went out on the back porch . . . and there stood Jonny, all bundled up, smiling that killer smile he has. "Happy birthday!" he said with his crooked grin. For me he was the damn Christ child. I flew across that porch like a G6 into his now-frozen, outstretched arms!

There's a quality that I've noticed with only three of the men I've been in love with. Our bodies fit together like pieces of a jigsaw, like a hand in a glove (unlike OJ's glove). It's this bizarre physical sensation. I'm one of those girls who sticks her ass out when you hug her, can't get too close, you can't press your junk against this girl, oh no . . . But with these three men it felt like melting into them, just the right height, arm length, temperature, just the right feeling skin, warm, soft, cozy. I melt into Jon every time we hug. That's another thing we have in common. We're not long huggers, and I never pat him like a child.

Maks and Sergey go berserk when I do that to them. Mid-hug, I pat them on their backs like I'm their granny. The reason is, they stay in too long for the hug. I like a nice, solid, warm hug . . . then a release! If you hold me there too long I panic and start patting you. It's my escape route. Jonathan is like that, too. If too much attention is on him, he gets nervous.

There's NOTHING about Jonathan that bugs me. Now *that's* saying something. Even if one of us was gay, I would still marry him. I wouldn't care. That part of life is actually pretty boring to me. It's all hot and heavy for what, a year? Then you get down to the real business of living a life together. I figure on a good day, two hours of sex is about all I could tolerate and to be honest, sex more than three times a week (save for that first 12 months of a fuck frenzy), yep, three times a week for an hour sounds good to me. I get bored so terribly fast, and sex usually doesn't feel like the romance of the relationship anyway.

Jonny wants babies, and that's where our like minds part ways. He'll make a brilliant father. I'm done raising kids.

Jon's manners are impeccable, and manners are very important to me. He'll never let you pay for a thing, even if *you* invited *him*!! Every door is opened. Every kind gesture is thanked. His mama raised him right. He always returns calls immediately or texts or tweets. He puts his coat around you if you're cold. He insists you order first.

One thing you could never guess about Jonny-Boy, among his multitudes of talents, is that he's an awesome cock blocker! It began when Jon and I went to a club in LA called Colony. I'd go there after every *DWTS* show night and dance with black men. Oh, how I love black men! Shockingly, I've never shagged one but the thought of it is exhilarating and I see that in my future! I know all people are supposed to be looked upon as equal, but black men are superior! Exotic! White men are, well, white. Like the difference between a glass of milk and a hot fudge sundae. You can tell the difference between THOSE, can't you?

Getting back on point with the cock blocking. Jonny-Boy is THE best at it. He does it without even pissing the dude off! There I was dancing my brains out with every guy who asked me. This one! That one! I was having a ball! Then a nasty boy wedged himself between me and the guy I was dancing with. You could tell he was a nasty boy because he had "Nasty Boy" written on his hat. The nasty boy was getting carried away with his gyrations. I went there to dance, not fornicate on the dance floor, but apparently Nasty Boy didn't get the memo. I was getting pretty uncomfortable. I had my nervous giggle going on, and my eyes were darting around the room.

In flew Jonny to the rescue! He slipped his arms around my waist and said, "Babe, we gotta get home. I have to work early." Then he flashed that big friendly smile at Nasty Boy. Nasty said, "Oh, sorry ma'am, I didn't know you were married," and backed his nasty ass up. AHH, my hero, Jonny Boy!

Jonny will be in my life until it ends. We've promised each other that we WILL be married in our next lifetime but I'm an optimist—I'm thinkin' next June. :)

> Well-behaved women seldom make history.
>
> —LAUREL THATCHER ULRICH

The Art of Clubbing Men

THE LAST time I was a clubber was . . . well . . . never.

I've spent very little time in clubs. They are pretty ridiculous to me, especially now when all you do is stand in booths and wait for slutty girls with sparklers instead of slutty girls with cocktail trays to zip by and plop $600 bottles of vodka on the table. Club dancing is near extinction, and clubs are more crowded than municipal swimming pools in the sixties. The secondhand weed smoke is nauseating. The reason for no dancing is that there's no room, or well, just enough room to grind on one another in drunken stupors. All the clubbers are chronically texting or tweeting cool things like "We're going in!" or "This place is sick!" which makes me wonder why, if it's *so* sick, they're sitting there tweeting.

I've often wondered how "epic" it would be to "go in" without drugs or alcohol. Is it really the DJ? Does he really mix the sound so differently than the DJ spinning next door? I know; I'm old, I don't get it, 'cause it just seems like the exact same songs played endlessly with different amounts of time before the next one is bled into the last one. And call me old-fashioned, but when I see some exec in a suit or some rapper smoking a blunt, pony up 50 to 100,000 Gs for a tab, it just makes me wonder, *Wouldn't that be better spent on Habitat for Humanity?* And don't the chicks with the glorified Roman candles look identical to one another? And how about those X'd-out go-go girls gyrating on the back of VIP booths? Couldn't they use a hot bath and dancing lessons?

Oh jeez, here I go again sounding old school. It's apparently the clientele that make the clubgoers keep on clubbing. But aren't the only new people you see there the out-of-towners or the not-so-pretty people who couldn't get in the door? The ones you tripped over who were freezing their asses off the night before? The ones who got smarter tonight and paid the doorman $200 to make them seem more beautiful?

Oh sure, the girls are pretty, you know the ones, the underage "models" paid by the club owners to pretend like they aren't hookers. I'm not saying there is *no* value to standing around in a club getting shit-faced. I'm just saying let's not pretend it's because we're hot.

We can't possibly take "hooking up" seriously as proof that we're hot. Maybe at 10:00 p.m., but certainly not at 2:00 a.m. when anyone short of the Elephant Man could get laid. Even then, Elephant Woman would probably be right around the corner putting salve on her sparkler burns, willing to throw down. I'm pretty sure even a corpse could get fucked if it was propped up, wearing a G-string.

I'm not trying to be all "bah, humbug" here, really I'm not. In fact, I gave it all a whirl, a six-week whirl.

Before iPhones and sparkler girls, there were selections of alcohol and dancing was an integral part of the evening. Even then I had little interest. But in the six weeks following *Dancing with the Stars*, it became my life.

My copilot was my assistant Kelly, and our captain was limo driver extraordinaire, Jeffrey. He veered us in and out of more clubs and restaurants in that six weeks than I'd frequented collectively throughout my life.

The night we got runner-up on *DWTS*, we flew on a private G-6 to NYC to appear on *Good Morning America*. I ended up staying in NYC for six weeks.

I felt like a *That Girl* Holly Golightly banshee on the loose.

It was crazy fun. The only bad part, which didn't seem bad at the time, was that I drank too much, which for me means "anything." I almost never drink, maybe a couple of glasses of wine every year. Not because I'm an alchy or a puritan, it's just that I never think about it. But boy, was I drinking in NYC. Every night, I'd say, between one and three drinks with the occasional five-drink night. For me that's like a fifth of vodka every hour.

This was my New York City DAY schedule: up at 7:00 a.m., eat breakfast, dance, and then go to meetings. I was the NYC "It" girl. Broadway, commercials, TV series, book publishing, brands—you name it, I was meeting on it. Appearing on *Letterman, Fallon, The View*, and everything in between. Selling our QVC Organic Liaison line, walking the catwalk for Zang Toi, and shopping . . . lots of shopping for shoes. I collected an estimated 40 pairs of heels, split among Louboutin, Manolo Blahnik, YSL, and Prada.

And clothes, I never buy clothes. I hate clothes shopping. I'll drop five Gs on a sofa but never on a dress. I went wild shopping for my new fitter figure. So meeting and shopping by day, but mostly meeting. Then back to my way-too-expensive hotel by seven, shower, doll up, dress up, and go out to dinner by nine.

By the looks of the press and the gossip, Maks and I were inseparable. It couldn't have been further from the truth. Maks was mostly in the Ukraine doing the show *The Cube*, making appearances, or judging dance contests somewhere. Honestly, I can't remember where he was, but he wasn't in NYC. He popped in and out during that six-week period, mostly out, and when he was there we saw each other.

Anyway, nightly, I was "on the town" and amid "the scene." I'm rarely on the town and never on the scene. I've had a bazillion opportunities to be on the scene in my 30 years as an actress, and I'm not good on the scene. The scene is usually druggie and almost always boozy, and it's exhausting and usually boring. If you are on the scene very much, you will see the exact same people you saw the night before, and before and before—you know, the "scene" people.

Before my six-week post-*DWTS* romp, I would come in and out of NYC for a meeting, premiere, publicity appearance, or to be on *Saturday Night Live*. This six weeks was my longest stint by far, except when I was filming movies. But that was work, this was playtime, so the scene was fresh and spectacular.

My hangs were SL, Abe & Arthurs, 1 Oak, the Greenwich Hotel, the Boom Boom Room, Soho House, Cipriani, Christian Louboutin, and Mr. Chow.

I spent all my time with Kelly, my free-spirited assistant of many years, and my friends Mona, Nicole, and Teddy. But the best part of my six-week romp was my limo driver, Jeffrey. Or "Jeffy," as all us girls like to call him.

Jeffy has long, curly silver hair and always says the word "man." Jeffrey was witness to every backseat make-out session, every onslaught of paparazzi, and, well, everything. Jeffrey was basically my driver from 9:00 a.m. until 2:00 a.m. We were only apart for seven-hour sleep interludes.

Jeffrey owns a limo company called EZ Ryder. He employs many drivers and owns lots of cars, but Jeffrey is the reason that big-name movie and television stars swear by EZ Ryder. Jeffrey is this laid-back ex-stoner guy who looks like he lived fairly hard between the 1960s and the '90s. He is 100 percent trustworthy. He never gossips about any of his famous clientele, even though he must be filled with book-worthy tales.

I had a movie premiere to attend one night. I'd gotten sort of bored with my "every night out on the town" behavior, so I needed to take it up a notch. "I need an Aston Martin," I squealed. "Fuck yeah man! I'll get you one!" he squealed. Jeffrey showed up at eight with this white Aston Martin convertible. I was staying at one of my two favorite NYC hotels, the Greenwich. It's owned by Robert De Niro and is decked to the nines with his father's artwork.

Jeffrey pulled up. "Oh my god!" I yelled. "They leased me an Aston Martin?"

"Fuck no man   they're just loaning it to you, man."

They should give me one, I thought. I've been hyping Aston Martins on Twitter and to friends like I'm their spokesperson. Truth is, I have just always adored them. The first one I drove was in my TV series *Fat Actress* and it was love at first gear.

I looked ravishing, I must say, and Jeffrey was dressed to kill in a cool black suit. As we pulled up to the movie premiere, I said, "Jeffrey, what the hell am I doing? I see premieres all the time! Let's drive!!!" We sailed past the theater with the red carpet, press, photographers, and celebs and he drove and drove and drove, blasting the radio, hair flying in the wind, laughing like teenagers. We just drove!!

Jeffrey's the dude that can sit silent for hours or converse like a long-lost girlfriend. This night he just drove!! I had him pop me by the after-party for the premiere, but even *that* couldn't compete with the drive. So back into the Aston I hopped, and off we went again, this time all over the city, with Jeffrey yelling, "This is freedom, man, this is freedom!!"

There are other things that made Jeffrey the best driver in NYC. He always has tons of violet candies in between the bucket seats in his grand candy basket, filled with every candy you could dream of. And gum, cigarettes, and phone chargers. It feels like Halloween in there!

Jeffrey has another phrase, my favorite phrase: "That's fucked up, man." All of my friends who know Jeffy know this phrase. If I'd leap in the car a little intoxicated and say, "God Jeff, I drank too much," he'd say, "That's fucked up, man." If Mona told Jeffrey, "My ex is breaking my heart!" he'd reply, "That's fucked up, man," and he was always right! It *IS* fucked up to be stood up or drunk or anything else we complained about. In Jeffy's car, whatever's been done to you that you don't like, he will agree, "That's fucked up, man." He doesn't give you his opinions or tell you about what you should do or not do. He just empathizes with your grievance.

He's also hysterically nutty and funny. Everybody loves Jeffrey. He is now so sought-after by Hollywood royalty that I have to call a week before I get to NYC. His other drivers are cool, but its Jeffrey we all want behind the wheel.

He's also like this invisible guardian. One night while I was doing one of the dumber things I did in NYC, making out with a baseball player in the lobby of the Greenwich Hotel, I could peripherally see Jeffrey scouting for the paps. And probably checking to see if I took the guy up to my room and was in danger of ending up on *Snapped* or *48 Hours*. He just sort of invisibly strolled by, but it made me start laughing to see him out of the corner of my eye because I could hear him whisper, "That's fucked up, man."

Almost daily there were pictures of me on the cover of something or other with my latest boy toy. It was so far from reality that I sorta started to get off on it. Younger men have always been into me—ever since I was 16. My brother's 12-year-old friends would fall for me.

But my preference has never been younger men, so when I'd see paparazzi hiding around the corner I began to ham it up a bit. I'd give 'em a look of shock that I'd been caught with my pants down. I'd stand a little closer to the guy or kiss him when I got in the car. I was having so much fun with my fake lovers that their parents were being called by the tabloids!!

Teddy was my "lover" for three weeks. The reporters would ask Teddy's mother, "How do you feel about your son with an older woman?" She would decline to answer. His dad would yell from the background, "I think it's great!"

When Jeffy picked me up in the a.m., he would present me with the latest articles and photos of me with my newest lover. The funniest was this rapper named Shancie whom Lil' Romeo introduced to me in LA during *DWTS*. Shancie and I went dancing at the Colony on a few occasions with Romeo and the rest of the *DWTS* cast.

But this particular story said that Shancie had broken up with me because if he didn't, his mother was kicking him out of living in her basement. Oh lord, I couldn't stop laughing, and neither could Jeffy.

Although affairs with young men sound good in print and in movies or on *Sex and the City*, I can't imagine having a life with a man 20 or 30 years my junior. Jeffrey will testify that I do have more in common with 30-year-old men than with my own age bracket, but I couldn't marry them. I have a theory that men over 45 are mostly dead. They are either way too serious and significant about life or they bore me to death. Oh lord, they become serious about everything. Thirty-something-year-olds are in the prime of their lives creatively. They are planning their futures, and they are awake and vocal about what they want to do. They are usually game for anything, and they have endless energy. They are interesting.

Those six weeks were pretty ridiculous for many reasons, but an uptown girl can't tell all her tales. They were also fulfilling. Everything I did by day turned out productive. I got the Poise account. I got three play offers, two Broadway and one West End London. I got a TV pilot for ABC and landed a book deal with Atria.

Everything I did by night was memorable—and ridiculous and well, sparklery.

I have no regrets. It was splendid because it was unique for me. But I did worry for a moment when after my last night out, after hitting the Boom Boom Room, SL, and 1 Oak, I found myself sitting with Kelly on the fire escape of the Tribeca loft I was staying in, smoking a cigarette (I hadn't smoked in over seven years) and drinking a Beck's as the sun rose over Gotham. I was three sheets to the wind. "Ya know Kelly, I don't know what I've been doing for the last ten years," I slurred, "but I should have been doing this, why don't people live like this every day of their lives?" And somewhere from New Jersey I could hear Jeffrey say, "Because that's fucked up, man."

> There is no time for cut-and-dried
> monotony. There is time for work. And time
> for love. That leaves no other time.

> —COCO CHANEL

The Art of Men
I Have Not Hit On

BURT REYNOLDS taught me how to be good on a talk show. He took me from my Kansas one-word answers to being worthy of watching on TV. I was going to be on Johnny Carson for my first guest appearance. Burt was directing and starring with Parker in a movie in Atlanta called *Stroker Ace*. I think he was married to Loni Anderson at the time, and if not, they were a couple. I mentioned I was going on Carson and was nervous because I was in such awe of Johnny. He sailed right into, "Here's what you do with Carson, well, with any talk show host, but specifically Carson. You walk out there and flirt a little and give him a compliment. Then ALWAYS give him the first joke! After he has the first joke and the first laugh, go crazy, tell funny stories, flirt with him, and find a way to throw in that he's hot. Be yourself amplified. It's a piece of cake, try it."

That next week, I went on the Johnny Carson show. I walked out and said, "UH OH, I didn't realize you were so handsome." Then he blushed and cracked a joke. The audience went wild with laughter. I then told a story about being on the back of a Harley-Davidson and threw in, "I wish it had been you I was straddling." The appearance was a hit! I was "in," so to speak, in the guest-star supercircuit. That advice worked like a charm with Johnny and has with each host since . . . even Ellen and Oprah. After all, it's only good manners to let them have the first laugh and give them the first compliment. It *is* their show. Thanks, Burt.

CARL REINER

is a comedy icon and a renowned actor, film director, producer, writer, and comedian. He has received nine Emmy Awards. I had the pleasure of being directed by Carl in *Sibling Rivalry* alongside Bill Pullman, Scott Bakula, Sam Elliott, and Carrie Fisher. He also directed me in a movie called *Summer School*, starring opposite Mark Harmon (or "Hormone," as I fondly call him). He was a memorable director, and a kind, gentle, funny soul. He's also a very deep man. He asked me questions about my personal philosophy and shared a bit of his own. Carl is brilliantly funny; you will meet no one more quick witted. But the thing Carl taught me that I most remember was how to make a leading man look like a sex symbol.

One day on the set of *Sibling Rivalry* we were chatting along. What pure pleasure it was to just sit and listen to the stories of his life's experiences. We got onto the subject of leading men, and he gave me these pearls of wisdom: "It is up to the leading lady to make the male lead a heartthrob." He continued, "It works the other way around, also, but more so with actors than actresses. If you act like he is *the* most handsome, sexy man alive, he will be. You must look at him adoringly as you would your own lover. In interviews you must talk him up, fawn over him, drool if you have to, but always treat him as though he is the object of your affections. The world will follow your lead. Every woman in the universe will fall as in love with him as they *think* you are."

Boy, now didn't that make sense? I'd wondered growing up why not-so-movie-star-handsome men had been so attractive. Spencer Tracy, Humphrey Bogart, Jimmy Stewart, all nice-looking men, but far from the likes of Clark Gable or James Dean. It was true, those actresses like Bacall and Hepburn had adored those actors so thoroughly on screen, and they themselves were so stunning that it made us fall in love right along with them. (They also adored them offscreen, but those are their stories.)

Thank you, Carl, what an honor to have worked with you twice and listened to your captivating stories and viewpoints on filmmaking. And thank you for showing me how to get the world to fall in love with my leading men. It did us all an enormous service.

JASON WEINBERG

has been my manager/publicist for 20 years. We met back when he was a baby. I was filming a movie in Toronto called *Radiant City*. I had . . . a what? Everybody join in: "a slight crush on my costar," Gil Bellows. One night at my favorite Toronto restaurant, Joso's, Gil and I were joined by this black-haired, dark-eyed dude named Jason. I assumed he was an actor. He looked like a cross between Andy Garcia and Al Pacino. We were chatting away, and when I asked him what films he had done, he started laughing. "No films—I'm a publicist." I couldn't believe it! What a waste of a good mug!

Jason and I hit it off immediately. It evolved into a 20-year relationship that has been nothing less than extraordinary. Jason was this *Whiz Kids* math genius and chess wizard in his hometown of NYC. He is one smart cookie! He is also the best publicist/manager on the planet. Jason always remains patient, calm, and professional. When I'm losing my shit, every other day, he soothes me and makes it all okay. Unlike most publicists, he never gossips or talks about his other clients. I can't tell you how RARE this is.

Our success together has been uncanny. The best part is the friendship we developed. Although I've tried to convince him for 20 years that he's not gay (so that I can marry him), it appears that he might be. He's lived with his partner, Merrit, for ten years and they share twins, my godchildren Harry and Jasper.

Jason prefers remaining behind the scenes, so I won't go on about him, other than to say he now owns a management company called Untitled Entertainment and represents every diva in Hollywood. We prefer to think of ourselves as actresses but if the shoe fits . . . I'm just lucky that I was the first actress in his stable.

PRINCE

I met Prince when I was sitting all alone in the middle of an enormous arena. I'd come to participate in the Special Olympics. The rumors were that Prince was very shy and never approached people, at least according to those in Hollywood.

He walked right up to me. I looked up, and there he was. "Hi, I'm Prince," as if I wouldn't recognize him, "and this is my father."

"Hi, I'm Kirstie," I chimed in.

"I know who you are," he dreamily replied.

Prince and I went on to become sweet friends. He visited me on the set of *Cheers* and on occasion would drop in to my Encino house. I met up with him at Paisley Park when I was filming *Drop Dead Gorgeous* in

Minnesota. We had no trouble communicating with each other, and it was never frivolous conversation. We each spoke of life's most complex mysteries. We talked about religion, business, and families. He is the most interesting person I've met to date. I needn't speak of his talent because it's evident. What you might not know is that he is electric. His being radiates and lights up the room. I mean that literally. He lights up a room like a firefly in a jar.

We've spoken on the phone over the years, and I find him as fascinating as the day he said, "Hi, I'm Prince."

We were an unlikely duo by standard observation, as I am anything but mysteriously captivating, but somehow we clicked, and what a fine click it was.

He asked me to be on one of his albums and in his video. I did. I was. He asked me to present an award to him at some VH1 or MTV event. I did.

All I've ever wanted from him was to simply hear his viewpoints on life. They are unique and funny. He is forever funny.

Prince taught me that I was unique, just by being the only "me" in the universe.

I love him.

MICHAEL WISNER

You probably don't know him, but he saved my life. In the mid-1980s, I got terribly ill. I kept working and filming, but I was so sick that I couldn't walk across a room without becoming winded. My neck was in excruciating pain. My body was weak and frozen. I could lie in an almost scalding bath and only after hours would my body warm up inside. I developed tremors in my hands; sometimes I lost all peripheral vision. After two years of countless doctor's visits, expert opinions, and specialists, I was hopeless. No one knew what it was. They knew what it *wasn't* after hundreds of blood tests, MRIs, X-rays, and such—it wasn't MS, it wasn't ALS, it wasn't cancer, it wasn't leukemia. So after two years the expert consensus was—it wasn't anything. A few suggested I was mentally ill and suggested antidepressants. I let them know I wasn't depressed. I was DESPERATE because I was suffering, and there was no apparent cause!

That would have driven anyone to drugs, but I'd already taken the cocaine train, and I wasn't jiggy with the drugging-up mentally ill route, plus, I could FEEL that it was physical. A friend suggested I go see this Michael guy. He was an expert in toxins. Hell! What did I have to lose? Michael looks like a clone of Robert Redford, so I instantly perked up. He sat me down, luckily, because I couldn't stand very long, and asked me to tell him every symptom. Jeez, by then I could reel them faster than 30 Hail Marys. He looked me square in the eye, "Have you been exposed to termite spray, methyl bromide?"

I didn't know what methyl bromide was but I said yes, I've lived in three houses within the past two years and they were all tented for termites before I moved in.

"Look at this," he said, while handing me a large book. It was some toxicology handbook or something. There, listed under methyl bromide poisoning, was each and every symptom I'd just rattled off. I almost fainted from the effect of finally knowing what had happened.

He recommended I redo the Clear Body, Clear Mind Scientology detox. He also introduced me to Alka-Seltzer Gold. It's like mainlining potassium, and it quelled the tremors and cleared a lot of the pain. He said, "We use this with our 'glasshouse' patients, the ones who are supersensitive to environmental toxins."

I did the detox and drank the Alka-Seltzer Gold, and within four weeks I was up to 80 percent of being my normal self. Within four months everything was perfect.

Michael and I joined forces with several environmental groups and with their help got methyl bromide banned in the United States. Michael went on to help thousands, including many of the first responders of 9/11, ridding their bodies of the poisons that were slowly or swiftly killing them.

I'm eternally grateful for my good friend Michael for discovering what was destroying my body and my happiness. He remains to this day my guardian angel.

WALLACE AND GILBERT

are lobstermen in Maine.

When Parker and I first arrived on the island, we had the pleasure of having them caretake our house and somehow take care of us. You don't meet men like this anymore, even in Maine. They are a dying breed. They taught me what hard work looks like.

Wallace had been the caretaker of famed New York City interior designer Sister Parish. Both Wallace and Gilbert are master carpenters, and they restored our 22-bedroom Maine cottage. They also caught lobsters full-time. Is that how you say it? Caught lobsters? Anyway, suffice it to say they worked their asses off.

They reminded me of Hemingway's *The Old Man and the Sea*. Once I wrote, directed, and starred in an independent film in Maine. I titled it *Babies and Butter*. It still hasn't been cut together, but it was a swell film. My friend Scott from Connecticut played an enormous lobster. I had a costume made in LA, and believe me, it was really authentic. The story line was that something or someone was stealing all the babies and all the butter on the island, and no one could figure out who the culprit was. It turns out this giant lobster had been observing how we Maine socialites were ignoring our children, leaving them to be raised by nannies and such. He was not impressed. So every night he would creep out of the water and kidnap the babies. We finally found them all hidden in the fern patches in the woods. They had huge slices of bread.

Huge, I tell you! And he had given them HUGE bowls of butter and jam to spread on the huge slices of bread. All the babies were laughing and frolicking (in the story that is; we had 10 babies in that shot and when one would start to cry, they would all cry). Anyway, Scott played the lobster, I played the widow who fell in love with him, and Wallace and Gilbert played the mean townspeople who tried to kill him and cook him. There was a wild chase around the island with Wallace and Gilbert riding in the back of a truck with shotguns. Gilbert is a lunatic, so he played the part easily. Wallace is shy and soft spoken. He probably still wants to boil me for forcing him to be in the movie.

Wallace and Gilbert were always there for us. Doing clambakes, bringing me bouquets of flowers, building new fireplaces, taking us on boat rides, and helping us lug our stuff back and forth to Camden. Wallace still works for me at my house in Maine. The other day he brought me an enormous bouquet of peonies and 10 Walla Walla onions. For over 20 years, Wallace and Gilbert have taken care of us and made sure we felt like Maine was our home. They are among my favorite men on the high sea of life.

DAN CORTESE, DARYL "CHILL" MITCHELL, AND WALLACE LANGHAM

I would be remiss if I did not include the hot, endlessly talented, and ridiculously hysterical men from my TV series *Veronica's Closet*—Dan, Chill, and Wally. They were the bad boys who shared my stage for three years. They were the "good" bad boys in my life.

My best memory of their antics was the time that we were all called in for a "sexual harassment" briefing by the attorneys at Warner Bros. A lot of lawsuits were flying around the studios in 1998 and as part of our indoctrination into the rules and regs of sexual harassment violations, we were ordered by our producers to show up and be on our best behavior.

Kathy Najimy had her boobs out. They were still in her bra but her bra was hanging out of her sweater. The boys had their pants unzipped and their asses hanging out and vile things written all over their bodies. I had "fuck you whores" written across my rack in red lipstick.

The Warner Bros. attorneys were not amused. I'm not saying we were almost fired but there were flames coming from the attorneys' eyes. But we were in tears, trying to behave respectfully, which we all flunked with flying colors.

If we had been sued for sexual harassment on our own set, all of us would have been in the poor farm or the pokey. Every comment out of my boys' mouths was of a nasty, perverted, hysterical nature.

But it was all in fun and no charges were filed. Phew!

Anybody can look at a pretty girl and see a pretty girl.
An artist can look at a pretty girl and see the old woman
she will become. A better artist can look at an old woman
and see the pretty girl that she used to be. But a great
artist, a master, and this is what Auguste Rodin was,
can look at an old woman, portray her exactly as she
is . . . and force the viewer to see the pretty girl she used to
be . . . and more than that, he can make anyone with the
sensibility of an armadillo, or even you, see that this
lovely young girl is still alive, not old and ugly at all, but
simply prisoned inside her ruined body. He can make
you feel the quiet endless tragedy that there was never
a girl born who ever grew older than 18 in her heart . . .
no matter what the merciless hours have done to her.

—ROBERT A. HEINLEIN

The Art of Young Lovers

IF THERE'S one detail I must share about dancing, it is this; at one
time or another you will think it's a swell idea to shag your dance
partner.

From various conversations with dancers, I've learned that they invariably swap DNA on a regular basis. Oh true, they call it love and at that moment. I understand the love. Hot-bodied folks pressing their hot selves together simulating the reach and withdrawal of lovers.

Whether it be the tango, the dance of sweat and flirtation, or the aggressive paso doble, the dance of anger and greed, the sexual tension is mighty. A dancer gets a sexual respite while doing the jive. Jives are throwbacks to the 1950s where hops and soda pops were the order of the day. Then there's the salsa, aka dirty Latin dancing. And the waltz, the acceptable dance of repressed puritans. Onward with the rumba, which is a heartbeat from fucking each other right there on the highly polished dance floor. The quick step is the fastest way to the bedroom, since you cover more ground.

There's a reason certain religions outlaw dancing. Dancing is the surest route to copulation since Sodom and Gomorrah. It is the foreplay of kings and sinners and whirling dervishes.

At first I thought it was just Maks. Certainly Maks was the sex god of the ballroom. I'd never experienced the power, the passion of the dance with anyone else, or had I?

Wasn't I two-stepping the night away with John Travolta three hours after I landed in Vancouver to shoot *Look Who's Talking*? Weren't we shooting tequila and wasn't I already beckoning him to not be John but instead stay in character all night as Texas Bud from *Urban Cowboy*? Wasn't I immediately, during the sexiest two-step any two people ever stepped, dreaming of marrying him? Or Bud? Or whoever the guy was gliding me around the floor?

Had I forgotten about dancing with Patrick Swayze nightly on location in *North and South*? Had I blocked out the fact that we made *Dirty Dancing* look like a sock hop?

Yes, I'd forgotten it all because when you are dancing with your partner, he is the only man in your life.

At the end of *Dancing with the Stars*, I wanted to keep dancing. I had contracted a delicious penchant for it. I was addicted to it. Maks was zooming off to the Ukraine to work and bang Ukrainian chicks. He had already promised me early on that I could dance in his studios free for the rest of my life, which he probably thought, at best, would be a couple of months, what with the way I was belting down the hooch. We were at his pretty house in Jersey—I would love to tell you the town so you could all rush over there and get signed photos, but Jeffrey had driven me there and I wasn't paying attention.

He and his family had thrown a swell dinner for me. Lora, Maks's mother, had cooked up a Russian feast. I'm afraid of foreign food, so I was leery. It proved to be excellent, free of wacko stuff like the goat's brains and eyeballs I'd been served at a family's home in Rome.

Maks likes to control the world since he has a hard time controlling his mind, his temper (except while dancing), and the lunatics around him. One of the lunatics at the dinner was a cute Russian boy who looked like one of those Russian dolls from a stacking set.

After a most delicious meal, Maks and his dad, Sasha, needed to go into Maks's well-appointed library, with its vast elephant "trunks up only" collection. Maks had somewhere in time decided to control who my dance partner would be while he was away mending the broken hearts of his kicked-off bachelorettes.

Russians don't ask you to do things. They command you to do things. "Kirstie, dance with Sergey. He was trained by me and he knows my technique. He was raised by me. He was born because of me. He would not exist without me." You get the idea. Jeez, the lengths Maks will go to take credit for his creations—called people.

"Um, excuse me, I'm going to be traveling all over the world in the next several months."

Svengali smiled. "And Sergey will be with you."

The thing about Maks is that you thought YOU were going to ask Sergey to travel and dance with you 10 minutes earlier but somehow it ends up that it was *his* idea.

While Maks and Sasha got down to mob business, Sergey and I danced. He had a hard grip on me and flung me around where he wanted me to go. Teddy Voleynets, another student of Maks's and a member of the Voleynets family, the family partners of Maks's dance studios, had a very light touch, a gentle hold. Sergey, on the other hand, is forceful and constantly takes control of your body, just like his mentor, Maks. Put it this way: if you thought you were turning left and they wanted you to turn right, even bloodied you would end up on the right side of the room. They would actually make good traffic cops.

Sergey is a beautiful dancer. All of Maks's students are beautiful dancers. Perhaps he had to beat the beauty into them, but his product is beautiful dancers.

Sergey seemed like a cocky little snot. He wasn't friendly and warm. When I tell my friends someone is cold or aloof, they always say the same thing, "You're an actress, Kirstie, you're intimidating, they're just shy and nervous around you."

Although there is some truth to the logic, my friends have used it to cover all bases. I'll be freaked out saying, "Oh my god, the caretaker is a freak! I swear to God he's psychotic. I'm truly afraid at this point. He could be a killer!" their reply will be, "Oh Kirstie, you're an actress, you intimidate him, he's just nervous around you." Although there is a grain of truth in their observation, the majority of freaks or assholes I've tagged as such are exactly that.

Sergey was aloof and a little cold, and I assumed he was gay. He holds his body in a very elegant manner. He has a faint, tight smile at times, and let's face it, he wouldn't be the first gay dancer.

I instantly danced fairly well with him. He felt familiar. During my six-week "rage," I danced with Sergey a few times in the studio. Also I danced with Teddy and some other guy. Oh yes, and on a few professional occasions I danced with Maks. But mostly I just went to meetings and clubbed.

The first time Sergey danced with me outside of NYC was when I flew him to Maine. That's when I got to know him. I found him to be hysterically funny and a man of deep thoughts, a complex man with a dark history. It's hard to find a Russian with a light history, I've come to find out. We were not dancing for a competition so his demeanor was more that of a student to client, instead of pro to pro. He was professional and forgiving.

Back I went to NYC, to continue my six-week life as a party girl. On occasion I would see Sergey at a club or at dinner, but there was no dancing. When I departed NYC in July, Sergey went along. Don't ask how or why, but a very odd woman I'd met in NYC went with us. She was about my age but luckily looked 20 years older so that I felt no competition. It's always a good idea to surround yourself with women less attractive than yourself when you're single. I'd learned that trick at age 12.

As odd as she was, she had a riveting story of world travel and seductive love stories. Our first night in Maine, the third of July, we sat on my porch, watched fireworks, and drank red wine—Barbaresco, my favorite. The fireworks were on the evening of the third because it's cheaper to get a crew to set them off the day before the Fourth, or even the day after, which I've witnessed in Islesboro, Maine. Sorta like opening Christmas gifts on New Year's Eve.

It was one of the most enjoyable, relaxed nights of my life. We were all in harmony, but I was jealous of her stories of young lovers. She was Italian, you see, and she had had many lovers under the age of 25. Her youngest being 18—recently.

It felt as if I were living vicariously, amid this modern-day *La Dolce Vita*, and it made me question my own resistance to having younger men. As she spoke I felt puritanical in thought, old fashioned. I wanted to be more like her, to take lovers as a housewife selects chocolates from a Russell Stover box. Choose the one you want and if the taste isn't to your liking, bite into the next. Sergey and I listened for hours to her tales of real "loves" and lovers. She was riveting.

The next morning she ended up in Sergey's bed wearing a pale pink silk nightgown asking, "Does it make you nervous when I lie beside you?"

Oh lord, we were late to ride in the Fourth of July parade. I was scrambling to get dressed when I spotted the princess—no lie, she was an actual Italian royal. "Could you please run to the guest house and wake Sergey?" I frantically asked. "We're late for the parade!" I didn't ask, "Could you run over there in your pale pink silk gown with your breasts near your knees and seduce Sergey before the Fourth of July parade begins?"

This caused a little tension. When we met at the car to go to the parade, of course I didn't know what had occurred. But we still rode in the parade, waving, smiling, and throwing candy like parade riders do. On that Fourth of July, Sergey and I decided to go to the barbecue on the island. We danced with all the firemen, lobstermen, army troops, and WASPs, we danced all throughout the day. Of course during our first dance, our alone time from our princess, he filled me in on her early morning visit. Even after all her stories the night before I was shocked and a little envious that she had the balls to hop into some 23-year-old's bed and proposition him. I couldn't fathom being that sexually free or aggressive. I sorta wanted to fathom it, was flirting with the idea of fathoming it, but I had too much fear to actually do it.

All this affair business sounds great on paper. Novels are filled with it. Movies are riddled with it. What woman over 40 hasn't had a desire to be Mrs. Robinson, for crying out loud? But how did she get the guts to seduce Benjamin? It's movie stuff, I thought. It's Italian stuff, it's European for Christ's sake, but is it American? I'd heard the rumors that Susan Sarandon had a 27-year-old boyfriend and she's three years older than I am, but was it true? Did she really? Or was it like the gossip about me where I lose and regain 60 pounds over a period of four weeks?

But it was enticing. It was titillating to think that an actress of her stature and intellect would have a boyfriend 30 years her junior. But I'm from Kansas! Lord Christ almighty, do women in Kansas take young lovers? None of my friends had. Even when they had boyfriends three years younger than themselves, we thought they were going through a midlife crisis. In Kansas you don't date younger and you don't date racially different. We are borderline rednecks. Okay, we're rednecks and we don't marry or date men much older either because it will look like we're gold diggers. Our range is this: if you are 40, your boyfriend is allowed to be from 40 to 42. That's the way we roll in Kansas.

But it really did get me thinking about the subject, for real.

Back Sergey and I went to NYC on John Travolta's darling Jetson jet, the Eclipse. I clubbed around a few more weeks. Maks returned from Ukraine, and we flirted around at dinners and clubs. All of my meetings had been met, and it was time for me to leave NYC, to get on with my life. I had many charity events in front of me, and Sergey and I had a plan. We would fashion *DWTS* contests with all the high rollers who bank rolled the charities. He would teach them how to do a part-ner dance over a period of two to three days. He would choreograph them and then on show night, the night of the fundraiser, they would compete against each other. Sergey, I, and a local celeb from wherever we were would be the judges. Then as a treat for everyone, Sergey and I would perform an exhibition dance.

Our first stop was Italy, Firenze. All of my Italian friends who live in the United States and many who live in Italy congregated at a gorgeous villa in Tuscany called Villa Casteletti. I wasn't into the drinking and smoking in Italy, I'd left them behind in Gotham.

This area, this place, was extraordinary. I was surrounded with all my best friends and I was in heaven. Italy is my favorite place in the world thus far, and Firenze is my second-most-beloved location in Italy, Positano being the first. It was so much fun, all my friends going to town to get dance costumes, Sergey choreographing away. I ordered the lighting and stage men around to have the show look just so. And with my limited Italian and their limited English, it was mostly a symphony of hand gestures.

Italians never go places without their children. Children were running around wildly in typical Italian fashion. I'd adopted a stray kitten who'd just come to the villa. The food was beyond articulation, the weather was perfection, and show night was an enormous success! We raised 1.7 million euros!

After the competition, after my Italian best friend, Elena, and her husband, Marco, had suspiciously won the competition, we all danced the night away under the luscious Tuscan moon.

There was no crush on Sergey at this time, or "Puppy" as I fondly call him. His dark past had been dragged into my life and my only agenda was to get him out of it. No, there was no romance with Puppy under the Tuscan anything.

I was crushing out on this musician, Pierro. A bit of a musical genius, he was. Handsome, blue eyes, big smile, endlessly talented. Hmmm, he looked even better. Elena said he was perfect for me, and he was split from his wife. He had this gorgeous voice and could play any instrument on the stage. And he was genuinely nice and extremely charismatic. The next time I saw Pierro was in Padova for another fundraiser charity event. You know how girls look around to see if "he" has shown up yet? How they nonchalantly inquire to people they don't really know, "So, is that Pierro guy gonna do the show tonight?" Ho hum, you could care less but just checking for a friend. I heard laughter behind me. It was Pierro and some of my friends. Sergey was off training and choreographing the new talent for the show the next night.

"Bellissima, bellissima!!" he ran to me and hugged me madly. "You look so beautiful, I missed you," he went on in his hopelessly sexy accent. "Oh, hi Pierro," my aloof Kansas girl stated. The musicians walked by and said, "Pierro, sound check" or "Pierro, leave her the fuck alone"—whatever they said, it was directed at Pierro. He kissed my cheek and was off to rehearse.

On a scale of 1 to 10, I was riding at a level 5 in crush world. Maks had been an 8, Sergey was a 0, and Patrick Swayze had been a 10, just to give you an idea how my crushometer works. Oh, and Travolta had been off the charts.

I don't count the men I lived with or married as crushes. They were realities.

But crush world is fun and dangerous and terribly giddy. I just love a genuine crush and a budding 5 for Pierro was a good start.

There had been three weeks between the first big show and this next one in Padova—enough time to get a little excited about seeing Pierro. Also, there was crush number two, helping with the show. He was younger than Pierro, equally talented, but a completely different cat. He worked with Roberto Cavalli. He's actually an artist, quite a good one, in his own right but he was in his late thirties, the "too-young zone." I had him pegged as a level 3 crush, with little hope for a future.

It's astonishing how much flirting you can do with a below-5 crush. When you feel you can take them or leave them, the game is so easy. It's when you crush out at levels 7 to 10 that the thought of not having them in your life turns painful. But this one, crush number two was a breeze to flirt with.

I *did* look amazing in Italy. I need to add that. I was at my all-time thinnest in five years and in the zone of sorta hot. My long blond fake hair was rockin' it. I felt confident in my looks and I'm always at my best mentally and spiritually when I'm in Italy. I guess my ideal scene would be to fall in love with a handsome, smart, funny Italian man and spend the rest of my life in some bad-ass villa high above the Amalfi coast overlooking Positano.

Everyone was crazy for Sergey. He's so good at teaching people to dance and at validating all their right moves. Again the fundraiser was a flaming success. My friend Elena danced like an idiot, and she and Marco were reduced to third place but no one cared. We raised another two million euros and everyone was in a delirium with the success and having the time of their lives—even Pierro's wife, who had gotten back together with him over those three short weeks between fundraisers. I recovered quickly; after all Pierro had only been a level 5 crush.

• • •

When Sergey and I did our exhibition performance that night it was nothing short of a comedy routine. Sergey had choreographed the most divine, sexy waltz for us. We called it the "dirty waltz" because it was no *DWTS* waltz. The story behind it was lovers who just couldn't get enough of each other but sadly couldn't seem to stay together.

A huge lawn lies in the midst of extraordinary gardens just in front of the massive villa outside Padova, nearer Venezia. Because Sergey had the job of training all the dance couples, he had little time for us. He created the dance early in the morning, and we had just one go at it in rehearsal. The other dance couples danced on the stage at the end of the endless lawn. Sergey and I had the lawn lit up with periwinkle-colored lights, the same color that was bleeding across the 16th-century villa. Our dance was a barefoot dance in the grass, covering the entire span of the massive lawn.

Wow, it was a sexy dance. It was dynamic and dramatic and riddled with sexual tension. We'd come together and push apart, as lovers do. We would cling to each other and twirl and Sergey had incorporated ballet into the dirty dance—not for me but for him, thank god, with leaps and bended knee and pirouettes. I'd never danced a dance so intense and emotional. At the end of our rehearsal that morning we were sure we would blow everyone's Italian minds. At the previous event we had danced the same cha-cha that Maks and I had danced on *DWTS*. It became our private joke: "Should we do the road show?" That's what we called the cha-cha to Cee Lo Green's "Forget You (Fuck You)." But this night we were doing our own original rendition of the dirty waltz in front of hundreds of appreciative Venetians.

My dress was a glorious, long, lime-green silk with a train six feet long trailing behind when I walked. It was sexy. I was tan and barefoot. Sergey was tan and buff and wore black jeans and a violet cotton shirt that matched the periwinkle lights projected on the villa. The only difference in that morning rehearsal and that evening's performance was all the dew sparkling underneath the violet lights and the moon.

We began our dance. We first walked along the edges, each on opposing sides of the dew-laden lawn. A very dramatic entrance. Then we ran into each other's arms in a frenzy and met in the middle, 50 feet away from the edges, and fell into a lovers' clutch. I pushed him away, and as I was choreographed to do, ran to the edge of the lawn again, sort of; by this time my dress was drenched with dew. It was soaking wet. The breezy silk felt like water-soaked wool. But I made it to the edge. This was the part where I look over my shoulder at my man doing pirouettes and gallant leaps toward me, to win me back. His pirouettes were sort of goofy-looking, awkward, and his leaps were about six inches off the ground when he burst into my arms and said, "This ground is so fucking wet, I can't get any height." I quickly whispered back, "My dress is so fucking soaked, it feels like a wet blanket." And yet we tried to spin and twirl in an emotional burst that symbolized our lover's frenzy.

Sergey, it seems, was standing on my green silk dress that had now grown at least 24 inches longer all around the hem.

"You're on my dress."

"Pull it the fuck out."

"I can't, you're fucking standing on it."

Sergey being the pro dancer he is, in a flourish of hand and arm, swept down, grabbed my soaking wet dress, and threw it into the air! I swooped my arm under it so that the massive weight of the train was over my left arm. We continued. All this stuff only took about three seconds but seemed an eternity.

Twirling, whirling, running, sliding doors, opening out, dips, twinkling, shadowing, until my dress dropped off of my arm. Again, "Dip, fucking dip," he demanded.

"I can't because you're standing on my fucking dress."

Angrily he whispered, "Dip the fuck anyway. This is the finale. Do a back bend, do something. Fuck!"

So I did a back-bend-sorta thing and threw my inside leg up for the extended toe point, the opposite leg that is supposed to be lifted. But fuck, I at least dipped to the soggy ground with my fake blond hair sopping up the dew and my other leg over his shoulder. As we then walked off, arms around each other in the choreographed "walk off the dance lawn," Sergey was walking all over my dress—again! My straps were hanging to my elbows and we both looked at each other with big, professional, toothy dance grins.

"Fuck you."

"No, fuck you!"

By the next morning Sergey's crush status had risen to a level 2.

Sergey and I took our *DWTS* fundraising format all around Europe and England. We never performed the dirty waltz again. It seemed it was too dangerous to our budding flirtations. We stuck with the road show cha-cha as our exhibition dance.

We were together 24 hours a day, and we got to know each other very well—extremely well. We became each other's confidants and would talk for hours about life, dreams, and goals. We were inseparable.

By the time we hit Paris, Sergey was a stone cold level 6. The danger zone. We had flirted from shore to shore, joking or not, that it would happen "tomorrow."

I can't think of a more free time in my life. There were no rules, no limits. I didn't have to do an ABC pilot until December and the book I was writing wasn't due for seven months. I would have to go to NYC sometime in November to shoot a TV commercial, but that was all in the distance.

Sergey and I were always in separate hotel rooms. In Positano I was in a two-bedroom bungalow, far away from the hotel, whereas he had a room on the ocean side of the hotel itself.

Friends would come and go, Italian friends, American friends, Jonathan Knight, assistants. They would stay in my suite in the second bedroom or in a different room in the hotel. Then before we went to Paris, the night before we left Italy, friends just disappeared and it was Sergey and me alone, together.

Nothing much changed. I wrote, he talked to his ex and future girlfriends on the phone and flirted. I flirted with occasional men but mostly we just hung out together and flirted and laughed about "tomorrow."

We flew away to Paris for our final fundraising dance exhibition. I'd booked us in the Hotel Coste, a trendy, high-class boutique hotel close to Place Vendôme. The last time I'd been there was my last holiday with Black. It's a provocative hotel, sexy and chic. Everyone who works there looks as if they've stepped out of an Armani ad.

The hotel is too cool for anyone, actually, and there is always groovy music, oo-chinka-oo music, club music, Buddha Bar stuff. The hotel has its own soundtrack, for Christ's sake.

Sergey and I had adjoining rooms for the first time on our journey. The rooms are lush with burgundy red walls which would usually repel me, but in the Hotel Coste it works. The rooms feel like a high-class bordello from the 1930s. Romantic, provocative, oozing sexuality.

Sergey and I went to see Jim Morrison's gravesite in the famed Père-Lachaise cemetery. We were dicking around with me walking on a short wall while he was beside me in the street. We were holding hands for the sake of my balance. Snap, snap, snap, we spotted French paparazzi scurrying in and out of the historical tombs and little beautiful houselike things where dead people have rested for centuries. Snap, snap, snap.

We joined friends for lunch and looked at artwork. Snap, snap, snap.

We had dinner hours later with the same friends and I decided to have wine. You know, one of my good ideas. We all drank Merlot and

Mouton Rothschild, then visited the most extraordinary Parisian home I've ever laid eyes on. They were treating Sergey and me like we were a couple. Like we were together as lovers. But don't the French always have a lover or two tucked in their back pocket? We played word games, drank wine, and laughed and flirted, said *au revoir* and then walked to our hotel.

I was thinking, *Is this "tomorrow"? Are we really going to do this?* Of course it would ruin our relationship. He's a friend, he's my dance teacher. He's my children's friend. *Shoo, shoo, off you go, sane realities,* I thought. The entire world thinks I'm a cougar, the most overused word of 2008 to 2012. Was it wrong to take a boy lover? And he isn't a boy; wasn't he simply a 23-year-old man!? I'd been married three years by the time I was 23. I've gone on dates with men much older than me, years ago, when much older than me existed. And what about all my guy friends who've married or dated women 20, 30, 40 years younger? Sure they were all rich and that had to have something to do with the women who fall for older men. Let's face it, it's hard to find a woman who fell for a 30-year-old trash collector. And why the hell can't I be like other people? Why can't I just have affairs or brief encounters and go on about my life? Do I have to fall in love or be in love with a man to shag him? But I do love Sergey in many ways. I'll convince myself—yes! The love is there, well, a certain kind of love. And I should do something daring. I should not remain the born-again virgin I've become over recent times. And he certainly seems willing and able. He'd propositioned me a hundred times . . . or was he kidding? Oh lord, stop this noise!!

Back at the den of iniquity I could feel my conviction waning. Doesn't sleeping with a friend always end badly? And especially a dancer friend who hops on and off his partners like a round of leapfrog? Oh my, oh my, I've got it! I'll order some wine.

"What are you doing over there?" Sergey hollered from his adjoining room.

"I'm ordering wine, you want some?" asked the spider of the fly.

"No, I'm good! But you wanna talk?"

"Um . . . er . . . YES I want to 'talk,' " I hollered to the next room.

The wine was delivered by Kate Moss. There were two glasses. "Want one of these?" I said as he walked into my room and plopped down on my bed.

"Nah, I'm sorta tired, why? You wanna have sex?" he laughed. Gulp. He'd only said this to me 350 times during the course of our dance-a-thon. Gulp. He was just kidding . . . I think. He certainly wasn't paying any attention to me. He was lying on the bed beside me looking at the ceiling and fiddling with his phone.

"Okay, I'll drink them both," I resolved. Gulp, down went the first glass. I was still buzzed from the dinner and party wine. Gulp, down went the second glass. Now I was looped.

Parker used to theorize that when I was drinking, you had a 15-minute window of opportunity to shag me: smack between me laughing hysterically and falling asleep.

After the last glass of wine I began to slur and laugh. "Hmmm, do I want to have sex? Hmmmm, do I? . . . Hahahahahahahahahahaha . . ." I was off and running . . . "Let's see here, hahahahaha," I nervously laughed. He began laughing out of control, a genuine laugh, not a wine-induced laugh like mine.

"What . . . what?" I continued. "Can I ask a serious question?" *Oh, fuck, here we go, now I'm out of control.*

"Yes," he said, with a smile on his little Hummel doll face. "Yes, you may."

"Um, er, eh, am I drunk enough?" slipped out. He began laughing more, having no idea what my babble meant.

"Ohhhhhhh yes . . . I could say you're plenty drunk."

"Okay, here's the real quersssstion," I began, slurring the word "question." "You know how chicks always tell people when they have

277

sex with someone? I mean we alrees tell a girlfriend when we've slept wit sormone."

"Yes," he said.

"Okay, so, Puppy, if we ever had srex, who would you trell?"

Puppy thought about it for a while as I was getting a minibottle of wine out of the cabinet. I really needed it. I uncorked it.

"Hmmm, now, that's an interesting question," he pondered.

In my head all I could think of were my ex-husband's words: *Dude, she was in hysterics and now she's slurring, hurry up and answer the fucking question, you got 10 minutes to bang the broad or she'll be out cold.*

"Yeah, that *is* an interesting question. I think I know the answer."

"Really?" I seductively asked, toying with him as I began to drink my third glass of wine while sitting delicately on the side of my Parisian bed, leaning toward him. "Who? Who would you have to trell, Puppy?" I whispered like a sultry French *chat*.

"Yep, yeah, I'd have to tell my mother. My mom is a huge fan of yours, ya know, and I always tell her who I sleep with."

I was out like a light.

By morning Sergey was demoted to a level 0. So was his mother.

For every stunning, smart, well-coiffed hot woman over 40, there is a bald, paunchy relic in yellow pants making a fool of himself with some 22-year-old waitress. Ladies, I apologize for all of those men who say, "Why buy the cow when you can get the milk for free?" Here's an update for you. Nowadays, 80 percent of women are against marriage. Why? Because women realize it's not worth buying an entire pig just to get a little sausage.

—ANDY ROONEY

Closing Notes

SO THOSE are some of my Men stories. There are, of course, many more, but a girl likes to keep some in the vault for her next exhibition.

For the most part I chose to tell you either the funniest stories I could recall or the ones that were most poignant. To the men I didn't write about: you are not forgotten, but perhaps you might wanna take the funny shit up a notch or create a more interesting story line.

During the course of writing this book I've experienced the agony

and ecstasy of reflecting on a life well lived, and have had several benefi-
cial epiphanies. For one thing, I realized that I've purged all of my mis-
deeds like some self-appointed confessional, the same way I've told my
children all the bad things I've done at bedtime in lieu of fairy tales. My
children never laugh so hard as they do when they learn the stupid shit
I've done. So I hope you enjoyed the shit, too.

Secondly, I realized that there's a lot of crap I *haven't* done, so I'd like
to summarize these "*haven't* done" bad things:

> I haven't cheated on a boyfriend or a husband (meaning having
> sex with anyone else).
> I haven't dated married men.
> I've not broken up anyone else's marriage.
> I've never murdered someone or stabbed anyone in the
> stomach.
> I've never slept with anyone for a job.
> I've never practiced prostitution.
> I've never set a house on fire (intentionally) or been a
> polygamist or rapist.
> I've not done heroin, crack, or crystal meth, and I've never
> robbed a convenience store (intentionally).

It gives me great solace to tell you this, as perhaps it balances out
some of the sins of my past.

The next thing I realized was that women actually have had a profound effect on my life. Perhaps their influences have been more subtle,
and for the most part, sans the high drama of the men in my life, but I
can now clearly see the impact, for better or worse, they've had on my
life.

But the main thing I twigged on throughout the writing of this
book was how terribly lucky and blessed I've been to have been sur-

rounded by some of the most powerful, intelligent, loving men walking the planet.

They have each, in their own unique way, shaped me into who I am. The memories of all of them give me something to reflect upon, to be thankful for, and to laugh about. A few have given me nightmares, but nonetheless, they've given me something to gossip about.

My dudes adorn the galleries of my life as do the fine paintings in the Louvre. Their brushstrokes continue to shape and inspire my own artistry, for there is no greater beauty nor larger canvas than the one we call our life.

So to all you glorious, crazy-assed, motherfucking men who have contributed to my art collection: I thank you and I embrace the opportunities I've experienced by loving you.

Acknowledgments

I want to thank Peggy Crawford for typing my book for me and for laughing at my stories along the way.

I also want to thank my children, True and Lillie, for supporting me writing this book, by not doing any totally idiotic things that would distract me. Now that the book is complete . . . carry on.

Twenty years old and starting our new life in Hermosa Beach.

My favorite agent of all time, Chris Barrett, on the set of
Look Who's Talking 1, 2, or 3—I can't remember everything!

When I really have a crush on a guy, I give them this "sexy" face.

Okay, this is just wrong on so many levels.

Jason and I at the *Cat on a Hot Tin Roof* party; I've always liked 'em young.

Yoo-hoo! Oh, sailor!

Oh, Johnny!

Erick looked better in this dress than I did . . .

True's first guitar!

Romeo-me-oh!

Bradley—we fight for the right to have the best hair.

"Hippie Love."

Gianfranco—Italian friend "sizzle."

On our way to an awards show.

My favorite jive band, the Jive Aces—dig those crazy yellow suits!

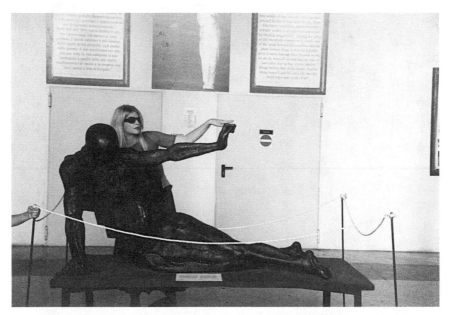

The perfect man—Italian—gorgeous . . . worth a lot of money . . . quiet.

My freaky yoga teacher, Steve—he likes young girls and
Kama Sutra. That's why we're only Good Friends.

Ooh la la—French men!

Stevey, Stevey, Stevey.

LOL—if looks could kill, this producer would be dead.

Caretaker Sam and baby True in Oregon—
and my best dog ever, Lizzie.